tear here

Soccer Rules in a Nutshell

➤ Two 45-minute halves, continuous play, that is, no time outs.

➤ Two teams, each with eleven players.

➤ One player on each team is designated as goalkeeper. Can use hands on ball while in penalty box.

➤ The rest of the team is made up of field players. Can use any part of the body to move the ball except area between shoulders and fingertips.

➤ Object of the game is to move the ball down the field and get it into the other team's goal.

➤ Ball may move in any direction and may be touched an unlimited number of times by any player or team.

➤ Players must keep the ball or two defenders between them and the goal to avoid making an offside violation.

➤ Free kicks are awarded for fouls.

➤ If the ball is sent over the sideline, the other team throws it back in.

➤ If the ball goes over the end line, the other team kicks it back in.

➤ Players are either warned or ejected for any flagrant misconduct or poor sportsmanship.

Kick Fouls

Direct

➤ Kicking

➤ Pushing

➤ Tripping

➤ Jumping at someone

➤ Hitting

➤ Charging (running into someone)

➤ Holding (in the literal sense)

➤ Tackling opponent rather than the ball

➤ Handball

Indirect

➤ Poor conduct

➤ Offside violation

➤ Dangerous kicks (anything near the head)

➤ Obstruction

➤ Goalie interference

➤ Goalie infractions

alpha
books

Card Infractions

Yellow (warning)
- Unsportsmanlike behavior
- Voiced disagreement with the referee
- Persistently disobeying the rules of the game
- Wasting time
- Refusing to stay 10 yards away from free kick
- Moving on or off the field without permission

Red (expulsion without replacement)
- Serious foul
- Violence
- Spitting
- Non-goalie player blocking the goal with hands (also automatic goal for the other team)
- Blocking a player who has a scoring opportunity
- Bad language
- Second yellow card offense

Major League Soccer Teams

- Columbus Crew
- D.C. United
- MetroStars
- Miami Fusion
- New England Revolution
- Tampa Bay Mutiny
- Chicago Fire
- Colorado Rapids
- Dallas Burn
- Kansas City Wizards
- Los Angeles Galaxy
- San Jose Clash

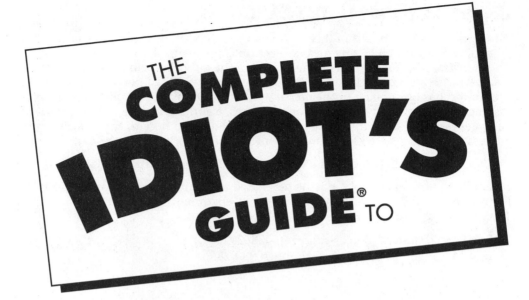

THE COMPLETE IDIOT'S GUIDE® TO

Soccer

by D.W. Crisfield

alpha books

A Division of Macmillan General Reference
A Simon & Schuster Macmillan Company
1633 Broadway, New York, NY 10019-6785

Alpha Development Team

Publisher
Kathy Nebenhaus

Editorial Director
Gary M. Krebs

Managing Editor
Bob Shuman

Marketing Brand Manager
Felice Primeau

Editor
Jessica Faust

Development Editors
Phil Kitchel
Amy Zavatto

Production Team

Development Editor
Matthew X. Kiernan

Production Editor
Linda Seifert

Cover Designer
Mike Freeland

Cartoonist
Jody P. Schaeffer

Illustrator
Stephen Adams

Designer
Glenn Larsen

Indexer
Greg Pearson

Layout/Proofreading
Terri Sheehan

Contents at a Glance

Contents

Foreword

I saw my first soccer game in the fields of my neighborhood. Let me tell you, it only took a quick sprint and the kick of a leather ball in the summer sun to fall in love with this sport!

Over the years, as I became more involved in soccer, I watched the game evolve into an adrenaline-filled chess match among neighborhood kids. I learned that soccer is a creative, intellectual, and passionate sport. But most of all, in its most basic form, it's just plain fun! As I grew older, I became even more immersed in the world's most popular game.

I consider myself fortunate. Soccer has allowed me to see the world: different cultures, different lands, and evolving nations. I have played in front of kings, queens, and prime ministers; small crowds; and hundreds of thousands of screaming fans in packed stadiums. The truth of the matter, though, is that this is a kid's game, and it should be enjoyed as such. It should be, at its core, enjoyment. This sport surely has given me many beautiful memories that I will cherish for the rest of my life.

One of the simplest sports around, soccer is a game of the people. No matter whether you are young or old, you too can enjoy this passionate game, which was created hundreds of years ago. Soccer is both simple and complex. Its simplicity lies in the fact that the game involves a lonely ball and a little bit of playing space; its complexity is shown in how it can inspire the passion of entire populations.

The Complete Idiot's Guide to Soccer establishes a link from the soccer world to you, the reader. From the inception of the soccer, to the fundamentals of the game, to starting your very own game plan, this book helps assist you in your exploration into the sport of soccer.

As you continue your journey through this book, you will find that soccer lives up to its moniker as "the beautiful game." It is a sport that combines strength, speed, agility, strategy, and intellect into one complete package. It has both induced countries to war and brought nations together. *The Complete Idiot's Guide to Soccer* opens the door into the world of soccer and helps you to understand why so many people on this planet refer to it as "the world's game!"

Jeff Agoos

Jeff Agoos, a member of the U.S. National Team program since 1985, is regarded as one of the finest left-footed defenders in American soccer and Major League Soccer. Jeff has appeared for the U.S. National Team 68 times and scored three goals, and has proven to be one of the National Team's most dependable and versatile members during qualifying matches for the 1998 World Cup.

Prior to the 1996 Major League Soccer draft, Jeff was allocated to the D.C. United. He missed the first match of his United career April 19, 1997, with the USA's World Cup qualifier the following day against Mexico in Foxboro. Starting every regular season and playoff game for the United during the 1996 season, Jeff was one of the team's key members as it captured the first MLS Cup and the 1996 U.S. Open Cup. Jeff was a 1996 MLS All Star and Defender of the Year for the United.

Jeff Agoos has garnered many accolades and honors during his brilliant career. He played with the U.S. Under-15, Under-17, and Under-20 teams, and the World University Team, and also starred for the University of Virginia. During his four-year stay in Charlottesville, Jeff scored 17 goals, including five goals his senior season, and was on the NCAA championship team.

Introduction

More people play soccer than any other sport. The game attracts the most fans, creates the fiercest loyalties, and unites countries around the globe once every four years for the planet's most celebrated competition, the World Cup. It's no wonder that you think you might want to learn a little something about the game.

I started playing soccer in high school, late by today's standards. We'd just moved from Massachusetts to New Jersey, which I wasn't pleased about in the first place, and my new school didn't have field hockey. I couldn't believe it. If I wanted to do a fall sport, I was going to be forced to play soccer, and that was only providing that I'd make the team. But I did want to play, so my father, a former college soccer player, showed me a few basic skills, and then I drilled and drilled myself all summer, dreading those fast-approaching tryouts in September.

Turns out, I had nothing to fear. Girls' soccer in 1978 wasn't much to speak of. There were few youth leagues—and none where I was—and Title IX had just started to work its magic, giving girls more sports opportunities. I made the team, was a starting player that first year, and was high scorer and captain by my senior year. College started out equally well. But then I began to notice a change. Each year, the team became stronger and the new crop of first year players were looking a lot more talented than us veterans. Soccer was suddenly shaking up the country, and I was getting all the aftershocks.

I managed to hang in there, went on to play for the New York State Women's Soccer League, and ended up where I am now, coaching from the sidelines and loving every minute of it. Who ever thought that I'd be so grateful for that Massachusetts to New Jersey move?

These days, parents put their children in soccer programs as early as three-years-old. Many towns have youth leagues that start with kindergarten, and if you want to start the sport new as a high schooler, the way I did, you have virtually no chance of making the team. You'll be competing with players who have 10 years under their belts. Everyone is jumping on the soccer bandwagon, and you should, too.

Why Soccer?

The sport is appealing in many ways, but perhaps most for its simplicity. All you need is a ball, an open area, and some makeshift goals, and you can start up a game. Towns can build both youth and adult programs rather cheaply, and little kids and newcomers to the sport can grasp the basic concept of the game without a lot of instruction.

At the same time, soccer at higher levels is incredibly challenging. The fancy footwork that you'll see the pros demonstrate can blow you away. It takes years of hard work and dedication to master the skills, so the game has the ability to sustain an athlete's interest at every stage.

In addition to the flood of youth soccer programs that are overrunning this country, adult leagues have sprung up all over, catering to both the experienced and novice players. Where athletes used to find their only competition in the slow-paced, keg-oriented games of a slow-pitch softball league, they're now finding the action-packed excitement of soccer. Adults are no longer willing to accept slowing down as part of aging. Fitness has gripped the country, and soccer meets all the requirements.

But even if you're not going to be a player yourself, it's in your best interest to become familiar with the sport. If you're a parent or plan to be one, there's a good chance your children will be playing soccer. And if you're just a sports fan, you're going to want to be knowledgeable about the world's top sport. The game has captured the attention of every other country in the world and is rapidly picking up speed in this country.

This book is here to help. Rules and regulations, skills and drills, training and coaching tips are covered. Whether you're player, parent, fan, or coach, there's something in here for you.

I've played many, many sports over the years, and I can say without hesitation that soccer is my favorite. I hope that my enthusiasm for the sport comes through in the pages of this book and grabs you.

Inside This Book

The first part of this book is for those who basically just want to know everything there is to know about the game, except for how you actually play it. In other words, the first part is about the history of the game, including the World Cup, the rules, the equipment, the playing field, the positions, and the programs out there for players—from youth leagues to the major leagues.

But if you're planning to actually play the game, you have to move on to the second and third parts. Here all the skills, from passing and dribbling to shooting, heading, and goalkeeping, are covered, plus the strategy and formations involved in more advanced soccer.

If you're going to get serious about the game, or if you're just old and out of shape, you'll have to delve into the fourth part, which covers basic training, from stretching to conditioning to strength building. You'll also find a chapter on common soccer injuries and ways to treat them. These injuries will happen if you ignore the first three chapters in this part.

Finally, the book winds up with two parts for the grown-ups, one on parenting a soccer player and one on coaching your child's team, with all the joys, responsibilities, and hassles that you'll find with each.

Extras Just For You

As you read through the book, you'll also notice some boxes full of extra tidbits:

Coach's Corner

Sometimes a helpful tip can make all the difference when you're trying to learn something. Take a look in these boxes when you think you need a little clarification.

Heads Up

There are some pitfalls to avoid in all aspects of the sport. These boxes serve up a few warnings.

Learning the Lingo

While soccer catch phrases haven't exactly invaded our language, there are still a number of words you're going to have to be familiar with if you want to understand the sport. Use these boxes and the glossary to stay on top.

Bet You Didn't Know

These are little nuggets that give you something extra, which you might not necessarily need but still might enjoy.

The Thrill of the Drill

Sometimes an exercise will help you learn even more. I've thrown in a few here and there to enhance the education process.

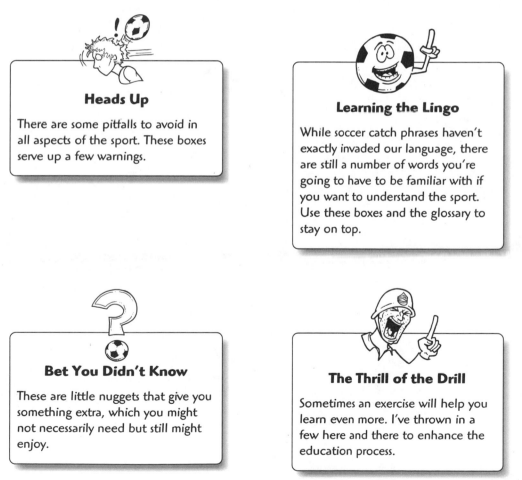

Acknowledgments

I'd like to thank a number of people who went out of their way to help me put this book together: Jim Barlow, for his technical editing; Carrie Wickenden, my MLS contact and former soccer player who still knows her stuff; Jeff Standish, semipro soccer player and very accommodating houseguest; Ollie Browne, a good neighbor and good goalkeeper; Marcy Dolan, my support on the right side of everything; Bob Mulroy and Doug Myers for their infinite knowledge of trivial things; Gary Krebs, Matthew X. Kiernan, and Linda Seifert at Macmillan for their editing skills; and, as always, JAC, JDC, and CBC.

Special Thanks to the Technical Reviewer

The Complete Idiot's Guide to Soccer was reviewed by an expert who double-checked the accuracy of what you learn here, to help us ensure that this book gives you everything you need to know about soccer. Special Thanks are extended to Jim Barlow.

Dedication

And finally, I'd like to dedicate this book to the Blue Crabs, the White Wolves, the Bluegrass Ghosts, and other great teams to come.

Part 1

Soccer:
The World Sensation

It's hard for anyone to fully comprehend the stranglehold that soccer has on the international sports world. If you know next to nothing about the sport, though, it's virtually impossible. The goal in Part 1 of this book is to educate both new and old fans in the nuances of the world's most popular sport.

The background is laid out in Chapter 1. The history of soccer and its development in this country are chronicled, along with the reasons we call the game soccer rather than football. You'll also learn about the World Cup and two efforts that the United States has made to make professional soccer the fifth biggest sport in the country.

Chapters 2 and 3 move you onto the playing field, giving you an overview of all the field markings, the equipment, and clothing you'll need to play the sport, plus detailed descriptions of the rules and the positions on the field.

Finally, this part wraps up with a chapter describing the opportunities that are available for all the different levels and ages of soccer players.

Chapter 1

In the Beginning There Was Football

In This Chapter

➤ The history behind the game of soccer

➤ The ins and outs of the World Cup

➤ The sport's growth in America

➤ Professional soccer in the United States

Soccer. The world's most popular sport. It combines grace, skill, finesse, and pure athleticism into an exciting, fast-paced game where an intricate web of passing can be woven together to produce one spectacular goal. And every four years the world's best teams meet to play in the world's most closely followed sports contest: The World Cup.

But how can all this be true, you ask? You always pictured soccer as a low-profile sport, slow cooking on the back burner with volleyball, lacrosse, and jai alai. Well, not any longer. The United States has turned up the heat and is joining the rest of the world in recognizing soccer as one of the most exhilarating and challenging sports ever invented.

The Theory of Evolution

But just how was soccer invented? Who gets the credit (and oh for the royalties!) for this fabulous sport? Unfortunately for the heirs of that very creative person, the answer remains elusive.

In all probability, the sport evolved in a number of different places, each with its own rules but following the basic concept of moving a round object toward a goal, using only the foot. In fact, those round objects were actually pretty incredible. Look at the list!

➤ Pig bladder

➤ Coconuts and oranges

➤ Animal skins stuffed with grass

➤ Caribou skins stuffed with caribou hair

➤ Skulls (my favorite)

Although historians think it's likely that even cavemen played some form of soccer, the award goes to China for the earliest mention of a game similar to soccer. The Chinese had a game called *tsu chu* that was played as part of a birthday celebration for an emperor in 2500 B.C. There are continued references to tsu chu throughout Chinese history as well.

In medieval England, the sport was extremely popular. So popular in fact, that it distracted young soldiers from their military training and several kings tried to ban it. (They didn't succeed.) The game played in England was similar to the ones being played by the Native Americans throughout North America during this same time. One group named it *pasuckuakohowog*.

The rules of this game, and the others like it, were quite varied. It largely depended on who had gathered to be part of the game. If only a few people were playing, then the area was small. If entire villages showed up to play, then the teams and the playing area were enormous. Frequently goals were at least a mile apart and there's evidence that they were as far as 10 miles apart.

Finally, in the 1800s, the game started to look similar to what we have now. The teams got smaller and so did the boundaries. Matches were more formal and were being played at colleges. Because it was spreading worldwide and there were still disagreements over the exact rules, FIFA (which is pronounced *feefah,* by the way), the Federation Internationale de Football Association, was created. FIFA is still running the show today, and the sport is unparalleled worldwide in its popularity.

Learning the Lingo

In Alaska, the Eskimos played this same crazy game, but they played it on ice! They called it *aqsaqtuk.*

It's cheap, easy to learn, and yet challenging no matter what the level. At soccer's pinnacle, you'll find the world's best conditioned, most highly skilled athletes. At its lowest levels, you'll find enthusiastic toddlers moving the ball inches yet thrilling themselves and their parents. The game appeals to everyone at all degrees of ability. A great soccer coach, Manfred Schellscheidt, would say it this way: In the beginning, on day 1, it's just you and the ball. At the highest level, you actually become the game.

The United States: The Last Holdout

But let's say you lived in the United States in the first half of the century. There's a good chance that if you did, you knew little about soccer. For decades, the United States bucked the trend in the rest of the world, maybe noticing soccer, acknowledging soccer, even allowing some of its children to play soccer, but never embracing soccer. After all, it was played in the fall, competing with that Other Football. (By contrast, soccer has always been a popular sport in Canada.)

In the early sixties, however, the sport started inching upward in popularity. The World Cup and the North American Soccer League (NASL) were early promoters. By the eighties, many towns were finding that youth soccer was an inexpensive and fun way to keep kids out of trouble. Interest in soccer began to climb.

A decade later, youth soccer was everywhere. Two national organizations sprung up to guide communities in establishing programs. They are the Youth Soccer Association (YSA) and the American Youth Soccer Organization (AYSO). Both groups essentially have the same goals: to provide a fun, safe environment where both boys and girls can learn to love soccer.

Soccer is still an underdog in the U.S., but its popularity is no longer inching; it's exploding. After hosting a World Cup and finally supporting a professional league, it looks as if United States soccer is here to stay. In fact, according to statistics gathered by Major League Soccer (MLS), currently 65 million people in the United States have their finger in the soccer pie.

Bet You Didn't Know

According to *Newsweek*, Even robots are taking up the sport of soccer. There is an annual Robot Football World Cup in which teams of robots are programmed to play against each other and score goals. Its intent is to provide another venue for robotic research, but what do want to bet that it's mostly just for fun?

The World Cup: Soccer's Ultimate Goal

When the World Cup was first televised in the United States in 1966, it prompted the first wave of soccer interest. When the United States hosted the World Cup in 1994, that interest turned into soccer mania. This is no surprise. The World Cup really is spectacular.

Soccer is the only sport that is so widespread that a competitive international tournament is a possibility. And the fact that it only happens once every four years allows the excitement to build to a frenzied level.

Getting There

It would be a little overwhelming to have every single country in the world involved in the World Cup, so most teams get eliminated before the tournament even begins.

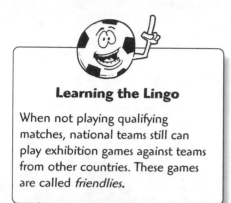

Learning the Lingo

When not playing qualifying matches, national teams still can play exhibition games against teams from other countries. These games are called *friendlies*.

FIFA divides the teams up geographically and puts them into 10 *divisions*. For several years before the World Cup is played, the countries play qualifying matches against the teams in their division. In 1998, 170 teams competed in over 600 matches in hopes of qualifying.

When the qualifying matches are done, the top three teams from each division have qualified for the World Cup, making 30 qualifying teams. These teams join the team from the host country (France in 1998) and the defending World Cup champions (Brazil in 1998) to make up a total of 32 teams in the tournament.

Once they've qualified, the teams wait for their seeding. Teams are broken down into eight groups of four for the first round of the tournament. The groups are assigned letters A–H. The top seven teams are spread out over the different groups, so they don't play each other in the first round, and the host country gets its own group, too, so it is less likely to get eliminated too early.

Here are the qualifying teams and their groups for the 1998 World Cup:

Group A	Brazil	Scotland	Morocco	Norway
Group B	Italy	Chile	Cameroon	Austria
Group C	France	South Africa	Saudi Arabia	Denmark
Group D	Spain	Nigeria	Paraguay	Bulgaria
Group E	Netherlands	Belgium	Korea Republic	Mexico
Group F	Germany	USA	Yugoslavia	Iran
Group G	Romania	Colombia	England	Tunisia
Group H	Argentina	Japan	Jamaica	Croatia

The word on the street was that the United States had a pretty unlucky draw.

Qualifying teams find out whom they are going to play about six months before the Cup. From this point on, they are not allowed to play these three other teams until the actual tournament. Teams do, however, usually try to schedule matches with other countries who have playing styles similar to those they will see in their World Cup assignments.

Team Roster

Countries usually don't finalize their team roster until a couple of months before the World Cup. Usually most of the players they use during the qualifying games will also be the players who make it onto the national team, but coaches like to play it safe and wait until the last minute to make the final decisions. They never know when a player might get injured or slip into a decline, and they can't always predict who is going to have a breakout year.

Steve Sampson, the former coach of the 1998 United States team, adopted an unusual formation for his team, one that was heavy on midfielders and light on forwards. If this hadn't worked for some reason, he would have had to add more forwards to his roster.

A player qualifies for the U.S. team if he is a United States citizen, but he doesn't have to be born here. In fact, quite a few of the players on the 1998 team were born in another country. One player, David Regis, became a citizen (passed the test!) just weeks before the cup began.

Let the Games Begin

The World Cup begins in June and play lasts about a month. Sixty-four games are played. The first round of the tournament is played round robin style. The four teams in each group all play each other. The two teams in each group who have the best record after these games advance to the next round.

The next round is single elimination for the remaining 16 teams. The winner of Group A plays against the runner-up of Group B. The winner of Group B plays the runner-up of Group A. The winner of Group C plays the runner-up of Group D, and so on. The single elimination play brings the teams down to eight by the end of this round.

Play then continues in the single elimination format through the quarterfinals, semifinals, and finals. At the end of the tournament, only one team is the world champion.

The World Cup began in 1930 and has been played every four years except during World War II. Here are the winners of those 16 matches:

1930: Uruguay	1970: Brazil
1934: Italy	1974: West Germany
1938: Italy	1978: Argentina
1950: Uruguay	1982: Italy
1954: West Germany	1986: Argentina
1958: Brazil	1990: Germany
1962: Brazil	1994: Brazil
1966: England	1998: France

The U.S. Soccer Federation has their eye on 2010 as the year that the United States will finally bring home the Cup. Skeptics abound.

Don't Forget the Women

It took a while, but finally FIFA recognized that women were jumping onto the soccer bandwagon as well. As their ranks increased, the possibility of a Women's World Cup grew into reality. In 1991, China hosted the first one with 12 teams participating. The United States' women showed they were a world-class force (unlike their male country-men, so far), and became the first winners of the Women's World Cup.

Four years later, in 1995, the event was in Sweden, with Norway emerging as the victor. The United States hosts the tournament in 1999 and this time the ranks have swelled to 16 teams.

Can a women's professional league be far behind?

The Life and Death of the NASL

World Cup excitement is catching. No one is more aware of that fact than the founders of the United States first Division I professional league, the North American Soccer League (NASL).

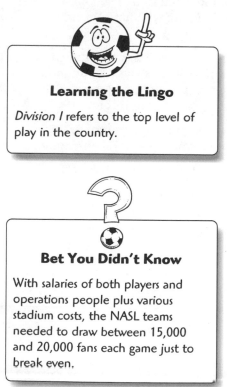

Learning the Lingo

Division I refers to the top level of play in the country.

Bet You Didn't Know

With salaries of both players and operations people plus various stadium costs, the NASL teams needed to draw between 15,000 and 20,000 fans each game just to break even.

1966 was a World Cup year, and for the first time ever it was televised in the United States. What a hit! The ratings far exceeded everyone's expectations, and ideas began to bubble in the soccer community. Perhaps the U.S. would support professional soccer after all.

Two groups quickly hopped on the bandwagon and formed professional soccer leagues. One was the National Professional Soccer League (NPSL) and the other was the United Soccer Association (USA), which was sponsored by FIFA. Neither one was a success.

Fortunately, each league had its head on straight and knew when to cut its losses. They quickly pooled their resources and a year later merged to form the 17 team North American Soccer League. It still was a financial disaster. In 1969, they saw their teams plummet from 17 to 5, with an average of about 3,000 fans attending each game.

Things looked bleak for the next five years, but in the mid-seventies, the numbers started to rise. Then the New York Cosmos took matters into their own hands. Spending $4.5 million, they signed the world-renowned Brazilian soccer phenomenon known as Pele. The U.S. sat up and took notice.

Suddenly soccer was hot. In 1980, the league had expanded to 24 teams and the average attendance around the country was hovering around 15,000, although numbers were inflated by the success in the large markets. The Cosmos, for example, were drawing an average of 30,000 to 40,000 and occasionally as many as 70,000 fans to their games.

Many other teams started to sign international stars. The quality of the play improved, but these new stars demanded prohibitive salaries. Teams in less profitable markets couldn't keep up and were forced to fold or move.

Unfortunately, by continually moving their franchises, these teams weren't able to build a loyal group of fans. And the overwhelming numbers of international players made the sport seem far away from a national pastime.

Bet You Didn't Know

On October 1, 1977, the Cosmos played an exhibition game against Pele's old team from Brazil, the Santos. Pele played for both sides and then bid farewell to the sport. A record-setting 77,000 people turned out to say goodbye.

By 1984, the league had dropped to nine teams. In the championship game that year, the Chicago Sting defeated the Toronto Blizzard in the NASL's last game ever.

Here's a list of the teams in 1980. The seven teams with the asterisks are the only ones who were still around—going by the same name in the same market—in 1984.

- ➤ Dallas Tornado
- ➤ California Surf
- ➤ Rochester Lancers
- ➤ Ft. Lauderdale Strikers
- ➤ New York Cosmos*
- ➤ Toronto Blizzard*
- ➤ San Diego Sockers*
- ➤ Minnesota Kicks
- ➤ Los Angeles Aztecs
- ➤ San Jose Earthquakes
- ➤ Seattle Sounders
- ➤ Vancouver Whitecaps*

- ➤ Washington Diplomats
- ➤ Chicago Sting*
- ➤ Edmonton Drillers
- ➤ Portland Timbers
- ➤ Tulsa Roughnecks*
- ➤ Tampa Bay Rowdies*
- ➤ Atlanta Chiefs
- ➤ Detroit Express
- ➤ Houston Hurricanes
- ➤ Memphis Rogues
- ➤ New England Tea Men
- ➤ Philadelphia Fury

Many people feel that the NASL failed because it expanded too quickly. The fans were there, but there weren't quite enough of them to support 24 teams. Others feel that the international flavor of the league was a problem. Or it could have just been ahead of its time.

The NASL and the Pele years were not for naught, however. A generation of young people had a taste of professional soccer and grew up excited about the sport.

Let's Give That Pro Stuff Another Try

In 1982, the United States put in a bid to host the 1986 World Cup, but they lost out to Mexico. When they tried for the 1994 Cup, they promised the formation of another professional league. This time, they got the bid.

So, to fulfill a promise to FIFA, Major League Soccer (MLS) was born. The founders of MLS were well aware of the failures of the NASL and wanted to avoid repeating them at all costs. Chapter 4 gets into the league in much greater detail, but to describe the outcome in a nutshell: so far so good.

With television time and sports cards that go along with most professional sports, young players are given a taste of some soccer role models. Having sports heroes to follow can make a huge difference in a young child's devotion to a sport. Given that the interest in soccer among young children is high already, the professional league just may make it this time.

What's in a Name?

It's hard to have a chapter detailing the origins and development of soccer without explaining the origins and development of the name *soccer*, which, as you may have noticed, is somewhat unique to the U.S. and Canada.

The game we call soccer is known as football throughout most of the world. The reason why it's not football here is fairly obvious. Another sport (one that barely uses the foot, by the way) was popular here long before soccer and already had dibs on the "football" name.

But who picked the term *soccer*? Where did that come from? Believe it or not, it actually came from abroad, not North America. When FIFA established the official rules of the game, people started referring to the sport as *association football*, to indicate that they were playing the sport by FIFA rules. That, in turn, was shortened to *assoc*, less of a mouthful, and that evolved into the term *soccer*. However, because the FIFA rules soon became widely accepted, there was no longer any need to describe which football you were playing. Football was now the same football worldwide.

Except in the United States and Canada (and Australia, which has Australian rules football), where it remained soccer.

The Least You Need to Know

➤ Soccer has been around since prehistoric times.

➤ The United States got off to a slow start as a soccer nation, but the sport's popularity is growing exponentially.

➤ The World Cup is an international competition that determines the best soccer team in the world.

➤ Two professional leagues have tried to make a go of it in the United States. One, the NASL, didn't make it. The second, MLS, is still giving it a go.

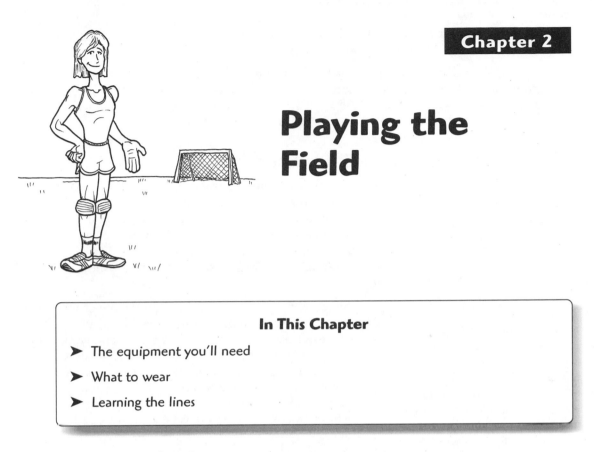

Chapter 2

Playing the Field

In This Chapter

➤ The equipment you'll need

➤ What to wear

➤ Learning the lines

Soccer is simple, right? Kick the ball into the goal the most times and you win. Yes, that is the very essence of the game. But, as you may have guessed from the size of this book, there is a whole lot more you're going to have to learn if you want to enjoy the nuances of the game and take it to more advanced levels. There are rules to be learned, skills to be mastered, strategies to be employed, and roles to be played.

But we'll get to them later. Before you can get into any rules and regulations, not to mention skills and strategy, you have to get to know the lay of the land: the equipment, the clothing, and the playing field. This is not unique to the game of soccer. It's true of most anything. You wouldn't, for example, expect to compose a violin concerto without first learning what a violin is. Soccer is no exception.

Gearing Up

Soccer isn't supposed to be one of those lifetime sports such as tennis or golf, but it sure seems like it is because it begins so early. You can have soccer players who are still in diapers. Many towns have leagues for kids as young as three, and a lot of the national programs start their camps at age three, too. And if you start by buying doll-size cleats and tiny soccer balls at that age, you will realize that by the time your child has reached adulthood, you've spent a fortune.

Even though soccer's reputation is that of a simple sport, played in the poorest of countries by barefoot children, kicking an old ball across the field, that's not reality in the United States. This simple sport can actually become quite complicated when you start discovering the equipment and clothing you're going to need.

That's the Way the Ball Bounces

The first and by far most important piece of equipment you need is the ball. Without a ball, you have no game. You can make do without goals or a regulation size field or—horrors!— without the right clothing, but you can't play the game without a proper ball. You can't even substitute another type of ball, such as a tennis ball or a basketball, because the game would be drastically altered.

Heads Up

Just in case you think that perhaps you might not need your own soccer ball, let me set you straight. Yes, officially the game is played with one ball for 22 players. However, you'll find that nearly every organized soccer program would like to have 22 balls for 22 players. You'll get the pressure to buy one. Besides, it might be nice to have one around for practice.

The soccer ball is a spherical ball (unlike the other type of football) made up of 32 leather panels, which are sewn together. Twelve of the panels are pentagonal and the other 20 are hexagonal—a little tidbit to know just in case you want to sew your own. The professional version of the soccer ball—referred to by people in the know as a size 5 soccer ball—is between 27 and 28 inches in diameter and weighs between 14 and 16 ounces.

Some clever ball manufacturer commissioned a study to show that kicking a regulation-sized soccer ball—the size 5—put stress on small children's knees. So the smaller ball—size 4—was created. And then, because soccer starts at such a young age, the size 3 was added for even smaller players. So keep an eye on your bank account. Unless you are starting at the size 5 level, you have several versions of the soccer ball to go through before you can rest easy with just your most basic piece of equipment.

Setting Goals

The only other significant piece of soccer equipment is the goal. Two of them, in fact. One at each end of the field. In the formal rules of the game, these goals are huge pieces of equipment, made of wood or metal, with a net spreading out on the back. The goals must be anchored into the ground.

The goals are 24 feet long and 8 feet high, which if you think about it is a considerably larger opening than almost any other sport that uses goals, such as ice hockey, field hockey, or lacrosse.

Obviously a goal this large would be virtually impossible to defend for players who have not reached their full height. Even then, many players wouldn't have a prayer of covering the top foot or so. So for youth leagues, at least during the early years, a smaller version of the goal is used, either something portable and smaller or perhaps merely cones. Pick-up games might use sweatshirts or two appropriately distanced trees for goals.

The disadvantage of using cones or shirts as goal markers is that the goals then must all be scored with balls that are rolling along the ground. It's too hard to determine whether a ball in the air was actually through the goal "zone" or if it sailed over the cone, which would not be a goal. But that's a relatively painless adjustment to make given the advantages that these goals offer. That is, of course, that they cost next to nothing and can be found anywhere.

Flag on the Play

Rounding out the equipment and marking the corners of the field are *corner flags*. These flags, which are no more than five feet in height, are placed at each corner of the field to help the referee determine whether the ball went out over the end line or over the sideline.

Just to illustrate the point, if the ref is standing in the middle of the field and all he has is a line of lime on the ground as a reference, he's going to have a hard time figuring out exactly where the ball went out. If there's a flag in the corner, however, he can watch to see if the ball blocks part of the flag pole as it rolled out. If it did, then it went over the end line. If it didn't, then it went out on the side. As trivial as this may seem, where the ball goes out determines the method used to inbound the ball. So, while many teams neglect the flags when they're setting up their field, it's really much better to have them if you want precise refereeing.

Dressing the Part

There are roughly three reasons that an item of clothing is introduced to a sport:

1. Enhancing performance
2. Preventing injury
3. Distinguishing the teams from each other

Because soccer is not much of a contact sport, the need for injury protection is low. And because the feet do most of the work, the rest of the body can be pretty much ignored. So the clothing needs, like the equipment needs, are few for this game. Just five measly "S" words to remember: shirt, shorts, socks, shoes, and shin guards.

Feet First

The most critical piece of soccer-wear is a pair of cleats. One of the sad facts of the game is that occasionally it will be played in the rain (and even snow in some places) and often it will be played on wet grass. Anyone who has ever tried to change direction on wet grass will recognize the importance of a good grip.

The cleats are rubber-bottomed—versus the metal spikes that you might find in baseball—and they can make a huge difference in a player's ability to get a good grip on a grassy surface. Not only will the improved traction help a player run faster, but it will also help prevent injury. A soccer player is constantly moving side to side or forward and backward, frequently changing direction on the run. If a foot slips out on wet grass during one of these reversals, you can say hello to a pulled muscle. The groin muscle, the hip flexor, the quad muscle, and the hamstring are all vulnerable to this type of unintentional motion, and cleats really cut down on the problem.

So cleats fit the clothing requirement in both arenas. They enhance performance and they prevent injury. And you know what they say: If the shoe fits . . . .

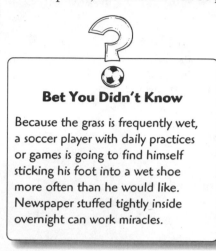

Bet You Didn't Know

Because the grass is frequently wet, a soccer player with daily practices or games is going to find himself sticking his foot into a wet shoe more often than he would like. Newspaper stuffed tightly inside overnight can work miracles.

Learning the Lingo

If you refer to your soccer shoes as *cleats* when you're over in Ireland, they might not know what you're talking about. They prefer *studs*.

An Ounce of Protection

The only other item of soccer "clothing" is a pair of shin guards. In this case, it's protection all the way. The shins hardly play much of a role in the performance arena, but it is important to protect them.

Shin guards are hard, curved pieces of plastic that cover your shin in a variety of ways, depending on which type of shin guard you choose. Socks must cover shin guards.

There are a number of different kinds of shin guards, and (going from cheapest to most expensive) they either

➤ Slide into your sock, relying on sock pressure to hold them in place

➤ Attach to your shin with a Velcro strap

➤ Are sewn into a sock

➤ Are personally molded to fit your shin and remain in place because of the perfect fit

Most programs, even at the youngest levels, require shin guards, but even if your program doesn't, you should get them. The basic ones are not expensive, costing just a few dollars, and they do perform a valuable service by protecting a very vulnerable area from bruises and possible fractures.

Clothes to You

As I've noted, clothing in sports tries to serve a purpose. Because the feet are really the main players in soccer, the clothes that the rest of the body wears are relatively unimportant. Essentially, as long as a player is wearing a shirt and a pair of shorts, she's in uniform.

Some shirts are short-sleeved. Others are long. Some have a neck with a collar while others have a typical T-shirt neck. Some have numbers on the front, some have them on the back, and some have no numbers at all. Most soccer shorts are nylon, but not all. Almost everything is loose fitting. The main criteria is that there is freedom to move.

Soccer socks are really the only part of the uniform that are consistent from team to team. These extra-long socks are pulled all the way up to the knee, so they cover the shin guard. The top of the sock is folded down.

Heads Up

Some players like to wear two pairs of socks, depending on the type of shin guard they use. If you think this is something that you want to do, then you need to remember to wear two pairs when you're buying cleats. The last thing you want to do is find out an hour before game time that your cleats are too small.

Although there are many different types of uniforms, every player on one team will wear the same uniform, or at least the same shirt (except for the goalkeeper—more on that later). Teams at the high-school level and above have two sets of uniforms, one in white and one in a color. The league usually determines whether it's the home team or the visiting team that wears white. This is to prevent confusion if two teams happen to have the same color.

Goalie Gear

Goalies are the exception. As always. Because they are the only players on the field who can use their hands, the refs need to be able to distinguish them from the other players. Therefore, they get to wear a special goalie shirt.

The only requirement for this shirt is that it be of a different color than the shirts of the field players (on both teams), but goalie shirts are usually a whole lot more elaborate. Many goalie shirts have wild patterns on them. There are two good reasons for this. The first is that an opposing team is unlikely to have a psychedelic team uniform, so the odds of matching them are low. But more importantly, a wild shirt is going to naturally attract the eyes of any shooters on the other team. The goalie is hoping and praying that this will subconsciously direct them to kick it right at him.

Most goalie shirts are also long-sleeved, primarily because this allows the shirt to have padding in the elbow area. With all the diving that a goalie does, the more padding the better.

And while we're on the subject of padding, there are special goalie shorts that have padding along the sides (again for the diving). These shorts also are longer than the shorts of the field players so the padding can go down farther and the skin can be protected.

Almost all goalies wear gloves on their hands these days. There are a variety of gloves out there, and most of them vastly improve the goalie's grip on the ball. The simplest might have a rubber insert sewn onto the palm, but you can buy some that are so advanced that you wet them before you play to create a practically supernatural grip on the ball.

Some goalkeepers like to have a small bag with them. In it they can put a small towel (or perhaps some water for those fancy gloves). They keep this bag back in the net and then when the team is at the other end of the field, they can use the towel to wipe off any sweat that might be dripping in their eyes.

Coach's Corner

Another method that goalkeepers can use to keep the sweat out of their eyes is to put Vaseline on their eyebrows. The Vaseline redirects the sweat down the side, which keeps the goalkeeper's vision clear.

The a goalie's feet are outfitted the same as any other player on the field. Goalies wear cleats and soccer socks. Many also like to wear shin guards as well.

Pushing the Boundaries

Soccer is played on a grassy—you hope—rectangle that runs anywhere from 100 to 130 yards long and is between 50 and 100 yards wide. The length always has to be longer than the width. For international matches, the length has to be between 100 meters and 110 meters (which is about 110–120 yards) and the width has to be between 64 and 75 meters (70–80 yards).

These are the official dimensions. But flexibility is the name of the game, and many youth leagues and recreation departments end up creating smaller fields to accommodate a large number of teams and the smaller size of the players. And pick-up games are played in very creative places. The fact that the dimensions are not set in stone contributes to the popularity of the sport around the world. It can be played almost anywhere.

The Line Up

The markings on the official field are a little more complex than the field itself, but like the sport, they're easy to pick up and are clearly illustrated in this figure. Just in case you're curious, each line should be no more than five inches wide, which is the same width as the crossbar on the goal.

The powers that be that created the various terms for the markings on a soccer field were not very creative. They were, however, practical. The lines designating the boundaries on the side of the field are appropriately called the *sidelines* (although they are sometimes referred to as *touchlines*), and the lines at the end of the field are called the *end lines*. In each corner of the field is a small one-yard arc called, not surprisingly, the *corner arc*.

A line referred to as the *center line* divides the field in half widthwise. There it bisects a 20 yard diameter circle called the *center circle*. In the center of this circle, and in the exact center of the field is the *center spot*, which is often marked as an X.

In front of the goal is the area called the *goal area*. This is twenty yards long and six yards deep. The goal itself is only eight yards long, so this goal area is considerably larger than the goal. It is sometimes referred to as *the six*, because it extends six yards to the left and right of the goal and six yards out into the field.

Surrounding the goal area is the *penalty area*. This is 44 yards long and 18 yards deep. For the same reasons that the goal area is called the six, the penalty area is often referred to as *the 18*.

Learning the Lingo

The end lines are also sometimes referred to as *goal lines*, because the goals sit on these lines and the ball must cross the line to be considered a goal. Of course, this would only be true if it crossed the part of the line that was between the goal posts.

The Thrill of the Drill

Soccer players have to be in good shape, so what could be better to get them familiar with the field than to have them run it. Have them run to the six, then run back to the end line, then run to the 18 and back to the end line, and finally to the center line and back to the end line. Of course, if you really want them in good shape, just add more of the markings to the run.

Soccer field markings.

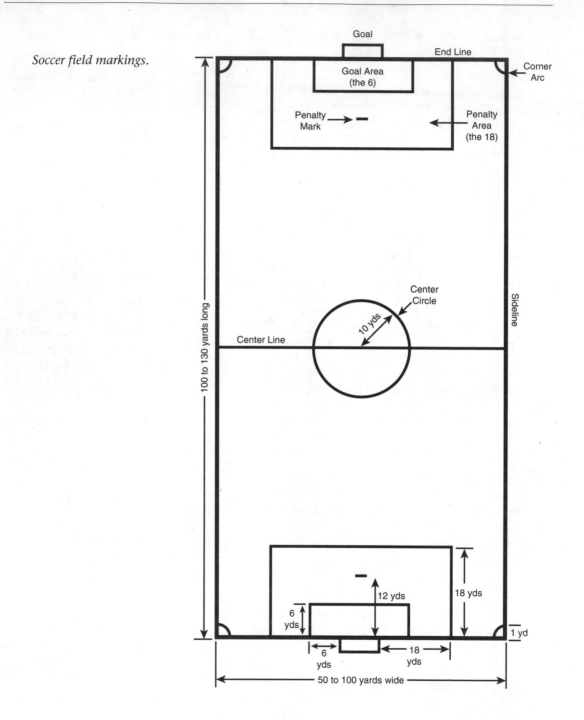

A hash mark, called the *penalty mark*, is 12 yards out from the goal and centered in the penalty area. And finally an arc, called the *penalty arc*, curves out from the top of the penalty box. If this arc were to be completed into a perfect circle, it would have the penalty mark as its center and be 20 yards in diameter, like the center circle. But it doesn't.

The Least You Need to Know

➤ Soccer is played with a ball, some goals, and when available, corner flags.

➤ Unless you're a goalkeeper, cleats and shin guards are really the only crucial items of clothing that you'll need.

➤ The markings on the field are simple, aptly named, and small in number, thereby making them quite easy to understand.

Chapter 3

The Roles and the Rules

In This Chapter

➤ The object of the game

➤ Who plays what where

➤ Kickoffs, restarts, throw-ins, and any other rule you might want

➤ Offsides made easy

For those of you who skipped the history lesson in Chapter 1, the origins of soccer are a little fuzzy. Many variations were played all over the world. And just as fiefdoms changed shape and new laws were enacted with each new king (including the ones that banned soccer), variability plagued the sport until 1848, when the first rules were finally written down.

The sport quickly spread worldwide, but the rules still varied depending on which country was playing. You could hardly have 27 people on a side in Brazil going up against 7 on a side in Italy, so 1913 saw the birth of the Federation Internationale de Football Association (FIFA), soccer's governing body.

Given the fact that FIFA still is the authority over the rules that dominate the world of soccer today, FIFA rules are the ones that you are going to learn in this chapter.

The Object of the Game

When you get right down to the bottom line, soccer is no different from any other sport. The object of the game is to win.

The difference is in the nitty-gritty stuff. The way to win in soccer is to have your team score more goals than the opposing team in the allotted amount of time. The way to score a goal is to project the ball completely over the goal line, between the goal posts, and under the crossbar. In other words, put it in the goal.

The official allotted amount of time is 90 minutes, broken into two 45 minute halves, with a halftime of no more than 15 minutes. This game length is nearly universal and used at almost all levels in North America and globally, although youth leagues may shorten it.

Time is continuous, stopping only for extended delays in the game, such as injuries, substitutions, deliberate wasting of time, or a penalty kick. Whether to stop the clock and extend the time is at the sole discretion of the referee.

Role Playing

Soccer is played with two teams of 11 players each. A team may play with fewer players, but it may not have less than seven or it must forfeit.

Although the rule book doesn't mention any position (except goalie), and technically all 11 players can be in one position (except goalie), most teams divide their players up into roughly four categories:

1. Forwards
2. Midfielders (also called halfbacks)
3. Defenders (also called fullbacks)
4. Goalkeeper

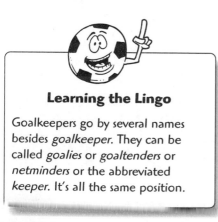

Learning the Lingo

Goalkeepers go by several names besides *goalkeeper*. They can be called *goalies* or *goaltenders* or *netminders* or the abbreviated *keeper*. It's all the same position.

Each of these positions has a job to do and an area of the field to cover, but as far as the rules are concerned, if you're not a goalie, you can go wherever you want to. Your coach, on the other hand, may have something to say about that. This figure shows a typical team lineup.

And while forwards are generally considered the offensive players and defenders the defensive players, all players on the team should consider themselves attackers when their team has the ball and defenders when the other team has it.

The goalies are another story altogether. In essence, one player on each team is designated the *goalkeeper* and he has a totally different set of rules, including when he's

Standard soccer positions.

Forward Forward Forward
Midfielder
Midfielder Midfielder
Fullback
Fullback Fullback
Fullback
Goalie

allowed to use his hands and when he's not, which is his main distinction. Aside from the "hand" issue, you can also always tell who the goalkeeper is because he'll be wearing a different color shirt.

The goalkeeper primarily stays within the goal area marked off with the 18-yard line, because once he moves out of it, fancy shirt or no, he's relegated to a foot player like everyone else. The rest of the rules and regulations governing the goalkeeper's behavior are covered in Chapter 10.

The Game Plan

The game begins with a coin toss. The winner of the toss kicks off. The other team gets to choose which side it wants to defend first. After halftime, the teams switch goals and the team, which didn't kickoff in the first half kicks off for the second half.

Choosing which side to start on can work to your advantage, so often it is better to lose the coin toss.

1. Sun
2. Wind
3. Field conditions

Let's start with the sun. It's hard to play with the sun in your eyes. Many high school and college games are played in the late afternoon and by the end of the game, the sun can be really low. You're probably going to want to choose to face the sun in the first half when it's not quite so low. Of course, if you're playing an early Saturday morning game, then you would want to reverse that strategy.

Heads Up

Be advised that the rule about the coin toss is brand new. It used to be that the team who won the coin toss was able to choose which role it wanted (either to kick off first or choose the goal to defend). As of 1998, there's no choice.

And then there's the wind. The wind is not nearly as predictable as the sun. You might start off with an incredibly strong wind in one direction and by the end of the game it's a light breeze going sideways. So the strategy with the wind is to grab it when you can get it. If the wind is clearly favoring one end, get it at your backs as soon as possible.

Finally, you want to consider the field conditions, specifically mud. If there's a small mud puddle in front of one goal, what do you think is going to happen to it by the end of the game? It's going to be a big mud puddle. And would you like your goalie wading through a small one or a big one? I think the answer's obvious.

There may be other factors as well: a hill near one end that influences corner kicks, more grass on one end of the field, and so on. Take all of these factors into consideration. You might have the sun and the wind competing against each other, and you're going to have to decide which is the greater liability. The coin toss is probably not going to make or break a game, but you might as well try to get every advantage you can.

And from the coin toss, let the game begin.

The Kick-Off

The game begins with a kickoff. The ball is placed in the center of the field. Several of the players from the team that won the toss line up on the center line. When the whistle blows, it is the job of one player to move the ball forward. She then may not touch it again until someone else (her team or the opponents) has touched it.

The opponents will have lined up on their side of the center line, but outside the center circle. They may not move until the ball is moved.

Kickoffs are also used at the start of the second half and after a goal is scored.

Heads Up

Players should be aware that even though a whistle has stopped the ball, they do not need to wait for a whistle to restart the ball (unless a substitution has been made). In fact, the faster they can put the ball back in play, the more likely they will be to catch the defense off guard.

Having a Ball

Once the ball is in play, it is moved up and down the field using any part of the body except for the area from the shoulders down to the fingertips. The ball may go in any direction and may be touched any number of times by the same player.

Play continues until the ball goes into the goal, the ball goes out of bounds, or a player commits a foul. The referee will then blow the whistle and play will stop. Play restarts in a number of different ways, which you will discover if you keep reading.

If a foul is committed but a referee feels that the fouled team would be better served by letting play continue, then he may choose not to blow the whistle.

Throw-Ins

If play has stopped because the ball went out of bounds over one of the sidelines, then it's put back into play by a throw-in. This is the only time a field player is allowed to use his hands. Frankly, it seems somewhat inconsistent with the game of soccer not to continue with the foot theme for this particular inbounding ritual, but the mighty FIFA has spoken.

You can tell that the throw-in was devised by people who did most of their work with their feet because it truly is the most awkward throwing procedure known to man. Pay close attention:

1. You must use two hands.
2. Your hands must be used equally, so there is no spin on the ball.
3. The ball must go fully over your head.
4. Some part of both feet must remain on the ground at all times.

I challenge you to do this gracefully.

The ball is thrown in at the point at which it went out. A goalkeeper may not catch a throw-in from her own teammate. No one is offsides on a throw-in. And no one may score a goal by throwing it directly in to the goal.

Getting Your Kicks

For various reasons, play is going to be stopped. And once it's stopped, it has to start again. Unless the ball goes over the touch line, it's going to start again with a kick. Soccer has six different types of kicks (not including the kickoff) that might be used to restart the game:

➤ Direct kicks

➤ Indirect kicks

➤ Corner kicks

➤ Goal kicks

➤ Drop kicks

➤ Penalty kicks

See the figure for the various locations of kicks. The strategies of each of these kicks will be discussed in Chapter 12, but here are the basic reasons, rules, and restrictions for each one.

Direct Kicks

A *direct kick* is awarded to a team after a foul has been committed by the opposing team. The direct kick fouls include:

➤ Kicking

➤ Pushing

➤ Tripping

➤ Jumping at someone

➤ Hitting

➤ Charing (running at someone)

➤ Holding (in the literal sense)

➤ Tackling opponent rather than the ball

➤ Handball

A direct kick is taken where the offense occurred (unless it occurs by the defending team in the penalty box), and it's essentially a free kick for the fouled team that may go anywhere it pleases, including into the goal. The defending team must stand 10 yards away and may not move closer until the ball moves.

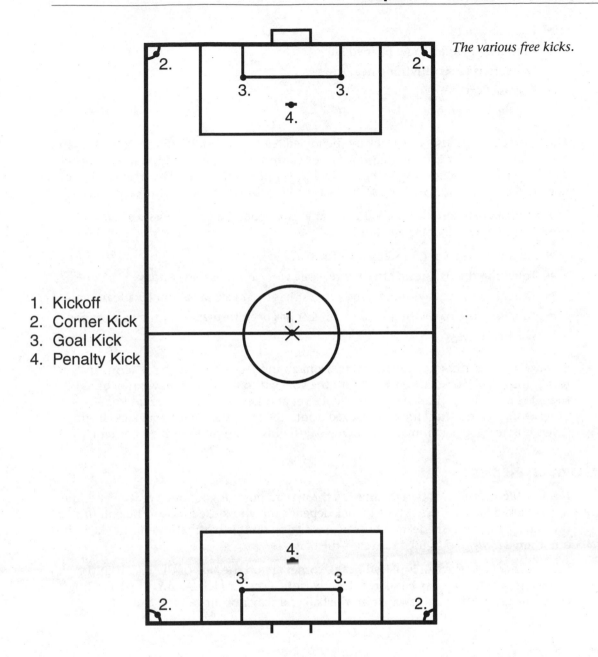

The various free kicks.

1. Kickoff
2. Corner Kick
3. Goal Kick
4. Penalty Kick

Indirect Kicks

The *indirect kick* is awarded to the fouled team for more minor infractions. It is also taken at the spot where the offense occurred. The indirect kick infractions include:

➤ Poor conduct

➤ An offsides violation (explained later)

➤ Dangerous kicks (anything near the head)

➤ Obstruction

➤ Goalie interference

The indirect kick is also a free kick by the fouled team. It is similar to the direct kick in every way except for the fact that it may not go into the goal until it has been touched by two players (in other words, the original kicker plus one more). The referee will put her hand up for an indirect foul so the players know which type of offence was called.

Indirect kicks may also be awarded to an attacking team if a goalie makes a rules infraction. These infractions include:

➤ Taking more than four steps with the ball

➤ Touching the ball again after the release before another player does

➤ Touching the ball with the hands after it has been kicked to him by a teammate

➤ Touching the ball with the hands after it has been thrown to him by a teammate

➤ Wasting time

Because a goal cannot be scored directly from an indirect kick (hence the term "indirect"), if the ball does happen to go into the goal without another player touching it, then it is considered the same as if it went over another section of the end line. In other words, if the attacking team kicked it into the goal, then it's a goal kick. If the defending team kicked it into their own goal (highly unusual) then it's a corner kick.

Corner Kicks

If the ball goes out over the sideline, it's thrown in, but if it goes out over the end line, it gets kicked back in. What type of kick depends on who kicked it over the end line. If the defending team (the team whose goal is sitting on this particular end line) kicks it out, then a *corner kick* is used to restart the ball.

For a corner kick, the ball is placed in the corner arc on the side of the goal that the ball went out. A goal may be scored directly from a corner kick. Again, the defending team must stand 10 yards away from the ball and may not move until the ball has moved.

Goal Kicks

If, on the other hand, the attacking team sends the ball over the end line, then it's a *goal kick*. In this case, the ball is placed anywhere on the six yard line, although most players place it on the corner of the box to get it as far away from the goal as possible.

The kick must leave the penalty box (the 18-yard line) before anyone else can touch it. If someone on the same team as the goal kicker touches it, an indirect kick is awarded to the other team. If someone on the attacking team touches it, the kick is retaken. If the ball never makes it out of the 18, the kick is retaken.

Drop Kicks

Occasionally the referee needs to stop the play for an unusual circumstance, such as an injury or a dog or small child running onto the field. If the referee needs to stop the play, the game is restarted with something called a *drop kick*.

For the drop kick, the referee drops the ball between two opposing players (the coach may choose whoever she wants), and the players may go after it the instant it hits the ground.

Coach's Corner

Because any player on a team can be chosen to do the drop kick, you want to make sure that the player you choose has two qualities: she needs to have quick reflexes and she needs to be fearless. You don't want to lose a good chance for a possession by putting a timid person in a drop kick battle.

The referee may also use a drop kick if he was unable to make the call about who kicked it out of bounds. Most referees make the call however, rather than using the drop kick, even if they are not sure.

Penalty Kicks

Penalty kicks are the créme de la créme of free kick awards. If someone commits a "direct kick" violation within the penalty box (the 18-yard line box), then the other team is awarded a *penalty kick*.

To take a penalty kick, place the ball on the penalty mark, the hash mark that is 12 yards out in front of the goal. It's just you and the other team's goalie now. The rest of both teams must remain outside the penalty box (and behind the penalty circle) until the ball is kicked.

Foul Play

When a player commits a foul, such as those listed under the direct and indirect kick sections earlier in this chapter, it is usually an error. The referee blows the whistle, indicates what type of kick should be taken and play resumes. However, if a player repeatedly makes the same foul or perhaps fouls in an especially offensive way, then the referee takes disciplinary action.

This action takes the form of rectangular plastic red or yellow cards. They're about the size of playing cards, but a whole lot less fun.

The referee takes the appropriate card out of her pocket and holds it up for the offending player, all other players, and any other officials to see. The referee also makes a note of who the offending player was. What follows depends on whether the card was yellow or red.

Yellow Cards

Yellow cards are warning cards. They are for less serious infractions and do not result in any sort of removal from the game. They are given for:

➤ Unsportsmanlike behavior

➤ A voiced disagreement with the referee

➤ Persistently disobeying the rules of the game

➤ Wasting time

➤ Refusing to stay 10 yards away from free kick

➤ Moving on or off the field without permission

As you can see, some yellow card infractions could just be unintentional errors in judgement.

Red Cards

The red cards, on the other hand, are usually for intentional or exceptionally harsh or dangerous acts. These include:

➤ A serious foul

➤ Violence

➤ Spitting

➤ Non-goalie player blocking the goal with hands (also an automatic goal for the other team)

➤ Blocking a player who has a scoring opportunity

➤ Bad language

➤ Repeat yellow card offenses

When a player is given a red card, he is immediately ejected from the game and his team is not allowed to replace him.

The Awful Offsides Situation

There's no proof, but I wouldn't be surprised if the offsides rule was invented just to make soccer seem a little complicated. Before they added offsides, people probably said, "Soccer? That's so easy. A three-year-old can grasp it." But add the offsides rule, and all of a sudden it's a challenge, something to be mastered, a game with a rule much too complicated for a preschooler to grasp, not to mention someone capable of higher reasoning. However, enlightenment is just a few paragraphs away.

Let's start with the actual rule itself:

> Offsides: A violation where an offensive player, without the ball, has less than two opposing players between himself and the end line.

And now let's pick this rule apart.

➤ "A violation": This means it is against the rules, the whistle blows, and the other team gets the ball.

➤ "an offensive player": This could mean someone with a foul mouth or someone who hasn't showered in a while, but it doesn't. An offensive player is just someone who is on the team that has the ball. They are heading toward the goal and on the attacking half of the field. In fact, if the team doesn't have the ball, offsides is one thing the players don't have to worry about.

➤ "without the ball": This is where the rule starts to trip up people. The player with the ball is like the defense. He can be anywhere he wants to be. He doesn't have to worry about keeping a defensive player between him and the end line, primarily because it would really be absurd. Can you imagine a player, breaking away from the defense, heading toward the open goal, and suddenly being forced to hang back to wait for the defense to get in his way? But say you're on the offensive and don't have the ball. What now? You must have

➤ "two or more opposing players between [your]self and the endline". Let's start with that number "two." Why two you ask? Why isn't one enough? Aren't the rules giving an unfair advantage to the defense? Not really. Two really is only one because the goalie almost always is one of the two. So essentially, just try to keep one player or the ball between you and the goal if you don't have the ball. The figures that follow show different scenarios.

That's essentially it. Still confused? Sometimes it's easier to understand a rule when you try to imagine why it was created in the first place.

Picture this. With 11 players on a team, one could certainly be spared to be a goalhanger. This player could just stand by the opponent's goal waiting for a ball to get kicked over or through the defense. Then it's just a matter of a little one on one

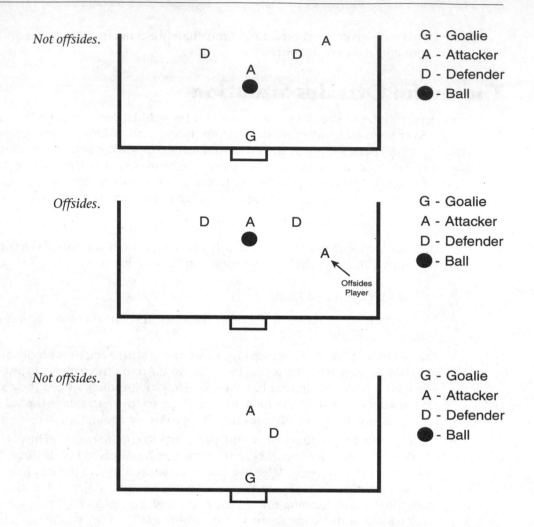

Not offsides.

G - Goalie
A - Attacker
D - Defender
● - Ball

Offsides.

Offsides
Player

G - Goalie
A - Attacker
D - Defender
● - Ball

Not offsides.

G - Goalie
A - Attacker
D - Defender
● - Ball

with the goalkeeper. The game would lose its need for controlled passing, crafty cuts, and creative dribbling. But add the offsides rule, and defensive players can push their opponents all the way back to the center of the field. It's going to be a lot harder and a lot more fun for the players and spectators to move that ball to the goal. Nobody will just boot the ball downfield because the big kick over the defense now just bounces right into the hands of the waiting goalie.

You're now thinking: I understand the offsides rule! *Why did I ever think it was complicated?* The truth is that at this point you *almost* understand the offsides rule. This simple definition left out a key subtlety that you can see in this figure.

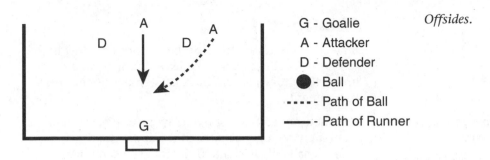

G - Goalie
A - Attacker
D - Defender
● - Ball
----- Path of Ball
—— - Path of Runner

Offsides.

Technically, you do not have to be actually in contact with the ball as long as you are running toward it and the goal. For instance, if a player on the wing passes the ball forward into the center of the field, and his teammate flies past the stunned defense to get it, he won't be offsides. Although he does not technically "have" the ball, he is running onto it, which counts. Another way to look at it is that if a player doesn't have two defense men between him and the goal, he better have the ball between him and the goal.

If the rule still seems unfairly complicated, just keep reminding yourself that it makes the game more interesting. It really does. I promise.

Tie Ball Game

A tie is like kissing your sister, or so the saying goes. Most people want to win, and soccer players are no exception. Unfortunately, soccer is a rather low-scoring game, which considerably heightens the odds of a tie. The good news is that there are a number of tie-breaking options in place depending on the policies of the league in which you're playing.

Double Overtime

The popular option in high school and college is the double overtime policy. Two overtime periods of equal time are played with the teams following the same kickoff pattern they followed in the game. Ten or fifteen minutes is the usual length.

Sudden Death

This is similar to the double overtime set-up, but if one team scores, the game is instantly over.

Frequently the sudden death overtime and the double overtime are combined. First, teams might play two 10-minute overtimes and then if nothing has changed, they might play two more 5-minute overtimes with the sudden death policy in place.

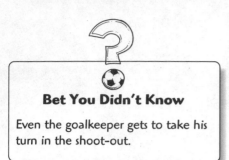

Shootout

If all else fails, a shootout can be performed. Most high school and college teams just leave the score at a tie unless it's a tournament, but occasionally there is that tournament.

The shootout consists of five players from each team alternately taking a penalty shot against the other team's goalie. If, after all 10 shots have been taken, one team has scored more than another, then that team has won the game. If the teams are still tied, then the five remaining players on each team take their shots.

Teams must use the 11 players that were on the field at the end of the game, but they may use them in any order.

The MLS Shootout

Sad to say, but TV ratings rule professional sports. Major League Soccer is no exception. The networks decreed that they didn't want the MLS games extending longer than the allotted time, so overtime and sudden death policies weren't really an option. Instead, MLS went to the shootout, borrowing this version from the old NASL. In this shootout, the shooter begins on the 35-yard line and has five seconds to dribble in and take the shot. The rest of the shootout rules are pretty similar to FIFA rules. The MLS shootout is explained in greater detail in the next chapter where MLS and its policies are discussed.

Call in the Subs

Soccer is a tiring game. The field is big, the game is long, and the direction of the ball changes constantly. Players have to be in fantastic shape. With this in mind, you'd think the substitution rules would be pretty lax. Not so.

In official FIFA matches, only three subs are allowed the entire game. The names of these subs must be given to the referee at the start of the game, and no one who is not on that list may go into play. And once a player has come out of the game, he may no longer go back in.

A player coming in as a sub must wait until play has stopped and he must inform the referee of the substitution before coming on. Even then, he must wait until the player he's going in for is entirely off the field and the ref has given the signal that he's allowed to come on to it.

In college matches, the rules are a bit more relaxed. Any number of subs may be played, but a player is only allowed to enter the game once in the first half and twice in the second half. Starting the game is considered entering the game. So, for example, if a player starts the game and is subbed for after 10 minutes, she may not go back into the game until the second half.

In high school and youth leagues, there is usually unlimited substitution, although players must wait for play to stop and must still get the attention of the referee before coming onto the field.

The Least You Need to Know

➤ The object of the game is to score more goals than your opponent.

➤ Players may move the ball in any direction, use any part of their body that isn't between the shoulders and fingertips, and may touch the ball an unlimited number of times.

➤ The goalkeeper is the only player allowed to touch the ball with his hands.

➤ When the whistle blows because a player has fouled or the ball goes out of bounds, it is restarted by a variety of kicks and throws.

Chapter 4

Soccer from Bottom to Top

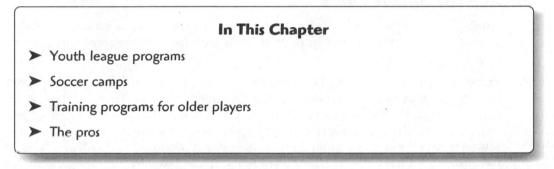

In This Chapter

➤ Youth league programs

➤ Soccer camps

➤ Training programs for older players

➤ The pros

You know the history. You know the rules. You even know how to dress the part. But where in the world can you play? The simple answer is everywhere.

Nearly every country on nearly every continent has a soccer program or a pick-up game going on somewhere, and the United States is no exception. But you need specifics, I know. There's a soccer program out there for everyone: all ages and all abilities. You just need to know what exactly you're looking for and where to look.

Youth Soccer

A few decades ago, preteen children had only limited options from which to choose if they wanted to play organized sports. Most kids instead played pick-up games in a vacant lot, a backyard, or a driveway.

That's hardly the case today. Whether it's because many kids have two working parents or because there's an increased awareness of stranger danger, kids lead very scheduled lives. Even if one child finds himself with time on his hands, the likelihood that he could find four or five others for a pick-up game is pretty slim.

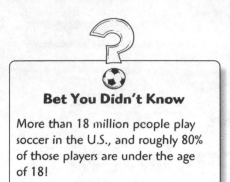

To meet the demands of this new lifestyle, youth programs have sprung up around the country. Soccer has been the sport that's leading the way. Because the rules are so simple and rudimentary skills can be mastered by even the youngest of kids, it's the ideal first sport for many.

Programs range from half-hour soccer playtime for three-year-olds to sleepaway camp for teenagers to Olympic training teams, with everything else in between. And while America's support for soccer hasn't reached the level of fanaticism that is found in other countries (including Canada), the United States has more children involved in organized soccer than any other country in the world. It's just a matter of time before those kids grow up into adult fans.

Soccer for Small Ones

Finding a soccer program for the youngest child can be as easy as walking to the nearest YMCA or YWCA. Nearly all these organizations will have some sort of soccer class for a variety of ages.

Private clinics are also run by local and national groups. These groups employ coaches, college players, recent grads, and other adults skilled in soccer. They rent field space from towns and charge a reasonable fee to entertain and teach your children. The programs often include hour slots during school hours for the preschool set, after school instruction for older kids, and summer day camps, with either half-day or all-day programs. Flyers in the mail or word of mouth will usually help you find these programs if any exist in your area.

Coach's Corner

You'd be surprised how much soccer a three or four year old is going to take away from a clinic. The kids play games like Red Rover, Tag, and Red Light, Green Light, modified to be played with a soccer ball, and they have a great time. This leaves them with a positive feeling about the sport—and they've also learned how to manipulate the ball with their feet.

Many towns have recreation departments that sponsor town soccer leagues. Children are organized into teams and play a series of games throughout the fall and spring against other teams made up of children their own age. Call your local recreation department to see if it runs anything like this.

AYSO

The American Youth Soccer Organization (AYSO) began in 1964 in California and has since spread to nearly every state in the country and as far away as Russia. It offers programs for kids from ages 4 to 18, and now has about 700,000 players.

You can reach AYSO at the following address:

> AYSO
> 5403 West 138th Street
> Hawthorne, CA 90250
> Phone: (310) 643–6455
> Fax: (310) 643–5310

The AYSO philosophy is that everyone plays, no matter what their skill level may be. There are no tryouts, and good sportsmanship and balanced teams are emphasized. Nearly all the coaches and referees are volunteers.

AYSO has two other programs that supplement its youth program. One is called the *V.I.P. Program* for kids with special needs, and the other is *Team Up*, for disadvantaged communities. In the Team Up program, AYSO helps find field space and provides the equipment and uniforms as needed.

USYSA

The largest youth soccer organization is the United States Youth Soccer Association (USYSA). This group is the youth division of U.S. Soccer, and it has over 2,500,000 participants, with representatives in every state. It began in 1974, with 100,000 registrants its first year, and is an effort to provide a positive soccer experience for the youngest players while at the same time identifying and guiding the top players toward the Olympic and national teams.

You can reach USYSA at the following address:

> USYSA
> 899 Presidential Drive, Suite 117
> Richardson, TX 75081
> Phone: (972) 235–4499
> Fax: (972) 235–4480

The USYSA age range is from ages 5 to 19, and there are two types of programs in which players can get involved. On the purely recreational side, there are town leagues that offer noncompetitive soccer and small-sided games. Until players have reached the age of ten, no more than eight players are allowed on a side.

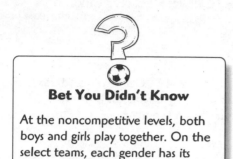

Bet You Didn't Know

At the noncompetitive levels, both boys and girls play together. On the select teams, each gender has its own team and tournaments.

For the more advanced player, there are the select programs. In this case, the player tries out for the traveling team in his or her hometown. The team then plays games against other towns, moving on to play in the State Cup. If the team wins there, it plays for the Regional Cup (there are four regions in the U.S.), and if it wins that, it tries for the National Cup.

USYSA also runs an Olympic development program to identify and train the top players. Players who think they have potential try out first at either the district or the state level and those who make it move on to the regional and national levels.

Camps

Camps are another way that kids can get involved with soccer. Camps, like youth programs, also are widespread and varied. There are day camps and sleep away camps, camps for fun, and camps for serious training. Ask the coach or director of whatever program you're involved with for a recommendation. If you're not involved in any previous soccer program, camp is probably not the place to start. Even the half-day camps can be a little overwhelming for someone who's never played. And what a shame it would be to sign up for a week's worth of camp and find out it's not for you.

If you're playing at an advanced level, then choosing the right camp could be crucial in your development. Ask your coach for recommendations or call MLS or U.S. Soccer to find out about their camps. Major League Soccer runs more than 1,000 camps for kids age 5–18. Many universities also run camps during the summer.

Major League Soccer (MLS) can be reached at:

> 110 East 42nd St., 10th floor
> New York, NY 10017
> Phone: (212)450–1200
> Fax: (212) 450–1300

In an effort to get top prospects some good training, U.S. Soccer is also developing some soccer camps for top high school players.

U.S. Soccer can be reached at:

> 1801–1811 S. Prairie Ave.
> Chicago, IL 60616
> Phone: (312) 808–1300
> Fax: (312) 808 9566

These camps are run by the country's top coaches and provide an intense summerlong workout. Teams are also formed to tour Europe and South America and play against youth clubs.

The Teen Years Dilemma

The teen years are the age where soccer seems to lose momentum in the United States. Because youth programs are so widespread, many players can participate, and the U.S. can claim that they have more youth soccer players than anyone else in the world. But by the time these players reach junior high and high school, they drop out.

There are a number of reasons for this. The teams are fewer, so securing a position on a team, whether a USYSA traveling team or a high school team, is naturally more competitive. The players who don't make these select teams frequently are discouraged enough to drop the sport altogether, even if there is a rec league available to them.

Burnout is also a problem at this age. Kids in the United States have been playing organized soccer for such a long time that it no longer holds as much interest. In most other countries, the youngest kids only can play soccer pick-up style, so they're still excited by the organized team aspect when they reach the teen years.

Also working against soccer at this age are the tremendous options available. At young ages, kids are exposed to soccer, baseball, karate, football, tennis, music, dance, art, and so on. When classes or clinics are one hour a week, they can dabble, but by the time they reach the teen years, they are forced to focus their interests. The hobbies at this age take more time, and if they feel they want to excel at something, they realize they can't do everything.

It's different in other countries. Children don't have as many youth leagues, but they have a lot more time to play pick-up soccer and then later many more club opportunities at the teen level, so for them, the teen years are when organized soccer usually picks up. They start training as professionals, maybe even getting selected for a professional team if they're good.

In the United States, many players don't even think about a pro career until college age, and even then, most choose to finish college before embarking on a professional career. While this may be a wise personal decision, it hurts United States soccer because skilled teens are often undertrained until they get to college, wasting precious training time.

There are many programs that U.S. Soccer and MLS are working to get into place to better train young players. More than anything else, however,

Bet You Didn't Know

Pele, the world famous Brazilian soccer player, began his professional career at age 15. His successor, a young (also one-named) Brazilian player named Ronaldo is only 20 and is already considered the greatest player in the game.

young players need to start thinking of soccer as a career possibility. Young soccer hopefuls in Canada and other countries are saying they want to be soccer players when they grow up. Americans are still saying we want to be basketball or football or baseball players. With MLS in place, however, maybe a real career in soccer will soon catch the kids' attention.

College Soccer and Project-40

One of the problems that faces soccer and young soccer players is the NCAA rules that govern participation in college sports. As it stands now, any player who gets paid to play a sport is ineligible to play on a college team. This might not seem like a big deal, but many of the top players have their college tuition paid for through soccer scholarships. If they're not playing, the college is not paying.

Learning the Lingo

Division II is also known as *A-league*, which is a step down from the pros or Division I.

Enter *Project-40*. This is a program that is being run jointly between MLS and U.S. Soccer, and directly targets college-age players. The program is called Project-40 because it arranges at least 40 games per year for 40 developing players. In addition, these players get intensive training from top coaches. In essence, it's turning these players pro rather than having them play college soccer.

The players earn the minimum MLS salary. Because they are considered pros by the NCAA and will therefore lose whatever scholarships the school might have offered, the U.S. Soccer Federation promises them a five-year tuition scholarship if their stint as a pro doesn't work out.

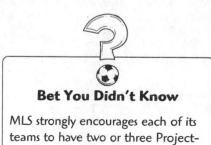

Bet You Didn't Know

MLS strongly encourages each of its teams to have two or three Project-40 players on its roster.

The Project-40 players get to train with the major league teams and occasionally play for them as well. The bulk of the Project-40 games, however, come from Division II soccer, where the Project-40 players have their own team called Pro-40 Select. The players train with the MLS team Monday through Thursday and then play for the Pro-40 Select team on the weekends.

Adult Leagues

For adults, the options aren't quite as plentiful, but they are still out there. At the highly competitive level, there is the Division II soccer called the United System of Independent Soccer Leagues (USISL). Its address is

USISL
14497 North Dale Mabry Highway, Suite 211
Tampa, FL 33618-2047
Phone: (813) 963–3909
Fax: (813) 963–3807

This league consists of organized teams that serve somewhat as a farm league for the pros. There is no direct affiliation with the pros, but many players start here first and then move up.

On a more recreational level are the town leagues. Check with your local recreation department to see what's available. You can also contact the U.S. Amateur Soccer Association at:

USASA
7800 River Rd.
North Bergen, NJ 07047
Phone: (201) 861–6221
Fax: (201) 861–6341

Town leagues are competitive soccer clubs for players age 19 and over. There is a division for Over 30 players as well. They play locally and compete for state, regional, and national titles.

Canadians can contact the:

Canadian Soccer Association
237 Metcalfe St.
Ottawa, Ontario K2P 1RS
Phone: (613) 237–7678
Fax: (613) 237–1516

MLS—The Top of the Heap

When the United States agreed to host the 1994 World Cup, it also agreed to form a professional soccer league in the U.S. After a disastrous end to the shaky NASL, no one was sure that a professional league could actually make a go of it. But on December 17, 1993, the chairman of World Cup USA and soon-to-be founder of Major League Soccer, Alan I. Rothenberg, made the announcement: United States professional soccer was back!

There was lots to be done. The league needed solid investors who were willing to stick with the program during its early lean years, it needed corporate sponsors, and it needed to avoid the pitfalls of the NASL.

Site Seeing

For the talent on the MLS teams to be good enough to compete on an international level, which also means that they're good enough to put on a top-notch show for the fans, it couldn't spread the best players too thinly across the teams. Therefore, there couldn't be too many teams. Ten was the number it chose.

Next it had to choose sites for the 10 teams. Small markets, such as Columbus, Ohio, had the advantage of not having professional teams in other sports competing for the fans' attention. But small markets also meant fewer fans to begin with and would be less profitable.

Large markets meant large numbers of fans but, as is the case with New York City and its two football, two hockey, two baseball, and one basketball teams (not to mention nearby New Jersey's basketball and hockey teams), fans might already be saturated with sports teams.

Twenty-nine cities attended the bidder's conference. Twenty-two sent in formal bids. Ten were chosen.

Money Talks

Now the MSL also had another factor to consider. Some sites were naturally going to earn more money than others. Would this give them an unfair advantage when it came time to hire players? It came up with a plan.

MLS was going to be one company, not a string of linked franchises. This meant that each team would have an *operator* rather than an *owner*. Instead of owning the team outright, these operators would each own a share in the MLS company. Therefore, profits would go into one big pot to be split equally among all the shareholders. The player contracts would also be owned by the MLS company rather than the individual teams.

Lining Up the Rosters

There was no question that soccer had progressed further in the international arena than it had in the United States, so the majority of the top players were likely to be foreign. While the foreign players were important because of their ability, MLS didn't want them to overwhelm what was supposed to be a United States league. With that in mind, team rosters were limited to five international players each.

MLS also wanted to make sure that local loyalties were maintained, and it did its best to keep players near their hometowns. The MLS determined that active rosters should be kept at 20 players.

On January 3, 1995, a full year ahead of the start of the inaugural season, MLS signed its first player. He was Tab Ramos, a star of the U.S. National team. He was assigned to the MetroStars.

Six months later, the league signed its first international player: Jorge Campos, superstar Mexican goalie. He went to the Los Angeles Galaxy.

Team Work

Currently there are 12 teams playing for MLS, divided into two conferences, Eastern and Western.

Eastern Conference Teams

Columbus Crew

D.C. United

Miami Fusion

New England Revolution

MetroStars (NY/NJ)

Tampa Bay Mutiny

Western Conference Teams

Chicago Fire

Colorado Rapids

Dallas Burn

Kansas City Wizards

Los Angeles Galaxy

San Jose Clash

The Miami Fusion and the Chicago Fire were added in 1998. The league anticipates expanding to 16 teams by 2003, as long as it can do it without diluting the quality of play. Seattle, Charlotte, Cincinnati, Pittsburgh, San Diego, Houston, Portland, and Atlanta have all put in bids to be one of those four teams.

Game Time

It was now time to play. The league began its inaugural season on April 6, 1996 when the San Jose Clash played the D.C. United. With the score tied at 0–0 and two minutes left to go in the game, the Clash's Eric Wynalda scored the first goal in MLS history, giving the Clash the league's first victory.

That year went on to be a great success, with attendance records exceeding all predictions, averaging over 16,000 fans at each game. The following season was a success as well.

Bet You Didn't Know

In 1996, the first MLS Cup went to D.C. United as it beat the Los Angeles Galaxy 3–2. In 1997, D.C. United put on a repeat performance, winning the cup for the second time while beating the Colorado Rapids 2–1.

The year culminates with the MLS Cup, the championship tournament that determines the best team in the league. Teams are awarded points throughout the year, getting three points for a regulation win and one point for a shootout win. The teams with the most points meet in the playoffs and from there, the top two teams go on to the MLS Cup game.

MLS follows FIFA rules and regulations in all its games, except when there's a tie game at the end of regulation time. Because MLS hasn't established the fan base of other sports, television stations aren't quite as willing to let the sport run into its regularly scheduled programs. And because ties at the end of regulation time are fairly common in this game, there was a good chance that this would happen. MLS came up with a plan. With the exception of Cup play, MLS has eliminated overtime and invented its own version of the shootout.

The MLS Shootout

Just as with FIFA, five players from each team have a chance to go one-on-one with the goalie. However, instead of taking a penalty kick for a shootout, MLS players start with the ball on the 35-yard line (these special shootout marks are added to an MLS field). The goalie begins on the goal line. Both the shooter and the goalie may move off their starting points, but the shooter has five seconds in which to dribble forward and take the shot. The rest of the shootout is the same as FIFA rules.

Major League Soccer is the country's best hope for improving the level of play for U.S. soccer. It provides career opportunities, training at a young age, and heroes and superstars to inspire a love of soccer in the young fans.

The Least You Need to Know

➤ Youth league programs are abundant and widespread.

➤ Efforts are being made to train top players at a younger age.

➤ Major League Soccer has fixed the mistakes of its predecessor, the NASL, and plans to be around a long time.

Part 2
Getting Your Kicks

It's one thing to know the rules, but what if you really want to get out on the field and kick that ball? Nearly every other sport you've played has involved eye-hand coordination in some way and now you're suddenly faced with the daunting task of learning eye-foot coordination.

Not to worry. All the skills are neatly laid out and described in ways that are easy for everyone to understand. Chapters 5 and 6 cover passing and its partner, receiving. Chapter 7 deals with dribbling, Chapter 8 handles heading, and Chapter 9 is all about shooting.

This part ends with a chapter for goalkeepers, that rare breed that wants to take responsibility for defending the gigantic gaping hole they call the goal.

Chapter 5

Pass It On

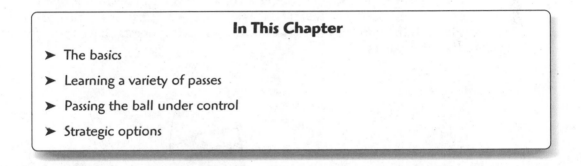

In This Chapter

➤ The basics

➤ Learning a variety of passes

➤ Passing the ball under control

➤ Strategic options

Instep pass, lofted pass, chip pass, back pass, one-touch pass, pass off, pass on, pass out, pass muster, pass judgment, pass the buck, pass the time, pass the hat, and pass away. So many passes, so much to learn.

In truth, while the pass is the backbone of the game of soccer, it is nonetheless a very simple concept. One teammate, in possession of the ball, propels it across the field to another teammate. That's all there is to it … unless, of course, you feel you need more than just a mere definition.

Thanks, I Think I'll Pass

The pass is a vital part of any soccer game, because it's virtually impossible for one player to take the ball from one end of the field to the other and score a goal without help from another teammate. There are a number of ways to execute this successfully, depending on what situation you find yourself in. For instance, any soccer player worth his cleats knows that when passing to a teammate 30 yards down field an instep pass is far preferable than a flick with the outside of the foot. But before you can learn the different types of passes, you need to be familiar with the basic passing fundamentals that all passes have in common:

➤ Your pass should have a destination more defined than just "downfield toward the goal."

➤ Don't pass the ball to a heavily guarded teammate, even if she's the "best player," unless there are no other options.

➤ Passes should be crisp. Even a short pass needs to get to your teammate quickly or it's likely to be intercepted.

➤ Look at the ball when you make contact. The best footwork in the world won't make a difference if you end up missing the ball.

Your Foot Is a Hockey Stick

The most basic pass uses the entire side of the foot, heel to toe, whether it is the inside or the outside of the foot. It sounds complicated, but as you can see in this figure, it looks like the simple, basic pass that it is. This side of the foot pass is the first pass to learn because it is the most accurate. The downside is that it doesn't have the power of many of the other passes.

The inside-of-the-foot pass.

Planting Time

Before you make a pass of any kind you need to take a step toward the ball. This step—or hop if you're on the run—is called the *plant*. Your planting foot is your nonkicking foot, so if you're planning to kick the ball with your right foot, then you use your left foot for the plant. By taking this step, you shift your weight from your back (kicking) foot to your front (planting) foot. And because this happens practically at the same time that you're kicking the ball, the momentum from this weight shift gets transferred to the ball. But enough of the physics lesson.

For this first pass, the planting foot should land right next to the ball (although you want to allow some breathing room of about two or three inches), and it should point in the direction that you want the pass to go, as you can see in this figure. So, if you're running forward and you want to pass to the side, point that planting foot to the side, even if it makes your run a little awkward. You'll have plenty of time to correct that after you get rid of the ball.

Learning the Lingo

The *plant* is the initial step you take before you pass or shoot the ball. It's taken with the nonkicking foot and provides the momentum and weight shift you need to put some oomph into your kick.

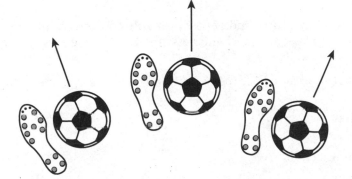

Placement of the planting foot.

Get Into the Swing of Things

When you plant your foot, your body ends up almost directly over the ball. All your weight is on that plant foot because the other foot is now off the ground ready to swing through the ball. The best way to think of performing this leg swing is to picture your foot as a hockey stick. Flex your ankle to make your leg and foot form an L. Keep the ankle locked and swing the leg the way you'd swing a hockey stick to hit a puck. Your want your knee to be slightly bent for comfort's sake, but you really don't have any motion in that joint. All the swing should come from the hips.

The accuracy in this pass comes from the fact that so much of the foot is touching the ball that it's highly likely that it's going to be propelled in the direction you want it to go. While this pass has a high degree of success, you still want to make sure you contact the ball in the center to get the most power. Topping the ball will turn it into a little dribbling pass, and getting too far underneath it will pop up the ball in the air a little with backspin, also reducing the distance it will travel.

Finally, make sure that you *follow through*, which means that you don't stop your foot on impact, but instead you swing it all the way forward. If you have trouble grasping this concept, just picture what your leg swing would do if there were no ball at all. It would swing in a nice symmetrical arc. Or picture a baseball player making his swing. He doesn't stop his swing at the moment of contact at the plate; he brings the bat all the way around. This is what you need to do when you make the pass. Swing all the way through, ignoring the fact that your foot hits something (the ball) at the bottom of the arc.

Learning the Lingo

The *follow through* is a basic motion in many sports—a golf swing, a baseball swing, a tennis swing, a soccer kick—which involves continuing the forward motion of the power producer (in this case, a leg) after the point of contact.

An Outside Chance

Up to this point, the description of this kind of pass primarily concerns using the inside of the foot. But you can keep the mechanics essentially the same and hit the ball with the outside of the foot as well:

1. Plant your nonkicking foot alongside the ball (although this time it should be at least a foot away)
2. Flex your kicking foot
3. Swing from hip
4. Contact the ball in the center
5. Follow through

The outside-of-the-foot pass is used less frequently primarily because it doesn't have the power that the inside-of-the-foot pass has. Not to get too heavily into the physics again, but this pass only has the power from the leg rather than the weight shift of the entire body. You can see in this figure how it's really a sideways pass. The advantage to this pass is that it often takes the defense by surprise, both because it isn't that popular and because the mechanics of the pass mean that you're kicking it off to your side rather than in front where the defender is likely to be.

Sometimes players use the outside of their feet to just nudge the ball to a nearby teammate. It's a flick of the ankle rather than an entire leg motion. In fact, you can almost consider it just an extension of dribbling (which you'll read about in Chapter 7), but because you are handing the ball off, it's still technically a pass.

The outside-of-the-foot pass.

Using the Shoelaces

But let's say you want to kick the ball down field. That short accurate pass you just learned isn't going to help you much. You need to use the *instep pass*. Webster's defines the instep as "the arched middle portion of the foot in front of the ankle" but an easier way to grasp this is to say "kick it on the shoelaces." This pass is essential for any good soccer player. You can get a lot of power behind the foot, because you're using both the knee and hip joint now, plus the instep pass is more versatile. It can be used for short distances, too.

Hop to It

Again, you're going to want to plant your nonkicking foot, but this time, it's definitely going to be a hop rather than a step. You really want to get that momentum going. Also, your planting foot will still be pointed in the direction you want the ball to go, but you're going to place it a little farther away from the ball—about four or five inches—than you would for an inside-of-the-foot pass. And just like before, when you hop on that foot, you want your weight to shift forward and you want your body—and specifically your knee—over that ball. This will ensure that your pass stays on the ground.

The Thrill of the Drill

A great game to play to work on passing skills is one called "Six in a Row." It's a game for two teams, with at least three or four players on each side. In this game there are no goals. Players instead get a point each time they make six consecutive passes to each other without the other team touching the ball. Obviously, the number of passes can be reduced or increased, depending on the skill of the players.

Make the Connection

Now it's kicking time. For this one, you want your toes pointed and your foot extended, the exact opposite of the previous pass. The contact point is your shoelace, because this is by far the most rigid part of your foot and you don't want anything to take the power away from the swing of the hip and the snap of the knee. Timing is important in this kick, because you're both swinging and snapping, but fortunately it's a very natural movement, and it doesn't take long to pick it up. The tough part, really, is focusing on using the shoelace area and not the toes.

Connect the ball in the center. Again, you don't want to top the ball or get underneath it, thereby reducing your power. The instep pass presents another little centering problem, however, and that's side-to-side centering. Because you're not using the wide side of the foot, there's a larger margin for error. If you don't hit the ball square in the center, it's likely to get a spin one way or the other, which usually means that it's going to curve away from your target. Of course, there are times when you might want this spin, so keep it in mind.

Up, Up, and Away

Even though it's harder for a player to receive a ball that is flying through the air rather than rolling along the ground, sometimes you're going to want to lift that pass into the air. If you have a teammate down the line and a defender between the two of you, you might want to lift the ball over the defender's head. A free kick—either a goal kick, a corner kick, or a direct kick—is another time that you might want to loft the ball, because the defenders usually have time to set up, which means they're standing in front of your teammates. The lofted pass is a handy one to know. There are a couple of ways to do it, depending on the length of the pass.

Booting a Long One

Essentially, the *lofted pass* is the instep pass with a twist, and the twist comes almost entirely from the planting foot. As with the regular instep pass, you're going to take a hop before you kick the ball. In this instance—presuming you want this to be a long, lofted ball, which is usually the case—make the hop a big one so you really get your body swinging. Some people like to approach the ball at an angle.

When you plant your foot, you want it considerably farther away from the ball, about eight to twelve inches, although still off to the side, which you can see in this figure.

The planting foot for a lofted pass.

The weight of your body is on that planting foot, as always, but more on the heel of the foot rather than the toes, forcing you to lean back. Because you're leaning back and because the plant has kept your body away from the ball, you are not leaning over the ball on this pass. Do not let your knee get over that ball. When you contact the ball, try to hit on the underneath side of the ball. If you're doing everything else properly, this won't even be an issue. That's where your foot will naturally go.

The Chip

Occasionally you're going to want to get the ball in the air but keep the pass short. You're going to want to use something called the *chip*. If soccer were a fast-food restaurant, it would be known as the Instep/Lofted Pass Combo. Like the instep pass, you're going to plant the foot up nearer the ball and have your body weight forward over the ball. Like the lofted pass, you're going to contact the ball underneath the center line, which will give the ball its lift. This I/LP Combo, however, takes all the power off the pass, because of the awkward motion it requires. Therefore, the pass is a short loopy one.

Out of the Air

An ideal passing situation gives you plenty of time to control the ball, set it up in the position you'd like it to be in, and then execute the pass. But life rarely presents you with ideal situations, and soccer is no exception. Sometimes you're going to have to pass that ball on the fly, literally. There are basically three ways to do this: the volley, the half-volley, or the head pass.

The Volley

The volley is a pass that is initiated while the ball is still in the air. As it comes toward you, you point your toe, contact the ball with your instep, and send it off to another teammate. The volley is far more popular as a shooting option than a passing option, but it can be valuable if you're in a tight situation.

There are a few keys to performing the volley correctly:

➤ Bring your knee up as the ball approaches.

➤ Point your toes toward the ground.

➤ Contact the ball with your instep *only*. On this pass, hitting the ball with your toes will cost you accuracy and hitting it with the side of your foot will cost you power.

➤ Follow through in the direction you want the ball to go.

Heads Up!

While it's good to use the volley to make a quick pass, you have to make sure the airborne ball is low enough to do the pass safely. In soccer, you're not supposed to have your foot in the air at someone else's head level; you'll be called for "dangerous kicks." So if the ball is high, do a head pass, not a volley.

The Half-Volley

Another pass, called the *half-volley* or *drop kick* is similar to the volley because it's a ball kicked out of the air, but it's not quite a volley because the ball is kicked the instant it bounces off the ground. This next figure shows the difference between the two.

You should probably make sure that you are competent and comfortable with the volley before even attempting to try the half-volley, because the mechanics are so similar. With the half-volley you must concentrate on the timing, and the mechanics should be automatic or you'll end up with way too much to think about in the split second you're going to have to make the pass.

Primarily, you want to have your knee up and your toes down, just as in the volley. The kicking is with the instep. The instant the ball hits the ground, you move your foot in for contact. You want to catch it about an inch or two off the ground. The beauty of the half-volley is that it really allows you to fully extend your foot, pointing the toes all the way down, without catching it on the ground. You can really get a powerful pass this way. A good way to practice this pass is to hold the ball in your hands and then drop it. Try to kick it just as it bounces off the ground.

And without a doubt, the half-volley is a kick you're going to have to practice a lot. It's a tough one for a couple of reasons. First, you don't have the ball under control, so your pass might not be as accurate as you'd like. And secondly, if your timing is just the slightest bit off, that ball is going to be bouncing off your shins rather than your

The volley and . . .

. . . the half-volley.

59

instep, and believe me, the shin is no instep. Instead of a hard bullet of a pass to your teammate, that ball is going bounce off in the wrong direction only to die about 10 feet away.

Heading Your Way

If the ball is really high up in the air, you're better off sticking your forehead in front of the it for a pass rather than waiting for the ball to come down and risking the chance that a defender might get in the way and steal the ball. Of course, *heading* the ball is more than merely having your forehead in the right place at the right time, but the mechanics of heading the ball are discussed in Chapter 9. I felt that a quick mention of the pass in this chapter was important, however, because many players forget that it's in an option. Use this to your advantage. If you include the head pass in your repertoire, you'll be able to steal the ball away countless times as opponents wait for the ball to drop.

Coach's Corner

After you've learned about all the different passes, you need to practice them. Your brain might understand the concept, but it needs to teach the motion to the muscles. The best way to practice is with a partner, but if no one is in sight, don't despair. A wall is a great passing aid. It never misses, and it never gets bored.

Control Freak

Just knowing the types of passes isn't enough. There's more to the execution of a pass than just knowing where the feet are supposed to go. Control is the name of the game, because that's the only way you can make sure that the ball is going to get to your teammate.

Target Practice

The first step, of course, is finding that teammate. You might have executed a perfect pass—planting foot in the right spot, good snap at the knee, connecting in the center of the ball—but if you didn't send it to a teammate, all of it is wasted. You should always be trying to look up, see more and take in the information the game is giving. Remember, the definition of a pass is a ball going purposefully from one teammate to another, not a random kick downfield that you hope will be picked up by a teammate. Good odds it won't be.

Before you make a pass, look up and see who is available to receive the ball, and don't limit your vision to those players in your immediate surroundings. Chances are that they'll be more heavily guarded than those farther away. If you can loft the ball, the receiver can be even far afield.

This is not to say that your first choice should be the long ball, however; it's just an option you shouldn't forget. The pass you want to make should be the one that gives you the best chance of creating a goal. Often, this is a long one; remember, the first pass after a change of possession puts more defenders out of the play than any other, so a short pass can help the defense set up. The short pass is more desirable because the long ball is often not as accurate and is also more vulnerable to interception. Frequently a series of short accurate passes can get the ball to the goal more efficiently than the long bomb, even if it takes a while. So, if you do have a teammate open nearby, go for it.

Learning the Lingo

Lofting the ball means kicking it so it rises into the air.

Time to Settle

If you're dribbling the ball before you make your pass, you've already gotten it under control for the most part. It's on the ground, and it's only a few feet out in front of you. If, however, you're receiving a pass and you plan to get rid of it with another pass right away, your best bet is to bring the ball under control first, often referred to as *settling* the ball. If you stop the ball first, or get it on the ground from out of the air, and then kick it, you're going to have a much more accurate pass. You should consider this when you receive the ball without hard pressure from the defense. It only takes a second and can make a dramatic improvement in your pass.

One-touch Passing

Unfortunately, more often than not, the defense is putting the pressure on and you're not going to have the time to settle the ball. This is when you use the one-touch pass. It's exactly what it says it is. With one touch of your foot, you redirect the ball. This method of passing is less accurate than settling the ball. With one-touch passing you must take into account both the velocity and the spin of the pass that's coming at you when you connect to send the ball away from you. In pressure situations sometimes it's more important to get rid of the ball than make sure it's absolutely accurate.

That's not to say that accuracy isn't possible. If you use the inside of your foot for a one-touch pass, you're connecting with quite a bit of the ball, reducing the chances for some unplanned spin. Also, try not to boot the ball on a one-touch pass. A softer touch will provide more control, while a harder kick will pick up on the force of the ball coming in and really go flying downfield. You'll end up with a game that looks more like pinball than soccer. The word "redirect" in the previous paragraph perfectly describes what you want a one-touch pass to do. Your foot just gives the ball a nudge in a new direction.

Say No to the Toe

You may have noticed that in all the various types of kicks there is not one mention of using the toe of your cleats to contact the ball. When you use the toe, you have no control. If the ball isn't kicked in the exact center, it's going to have spin on it. Generally, spin in a pass is undesirable. The toe is a tiny point on your shoe. The odds of having a tiny point connect with the exact center are pretty slim. It is better to use the entire side of the shoe or the whole instep.

Many young or inexperienced players find that they can get more power using the toe rather than the other methods, largely because the inside-of-the-foot kick doesn't produce power and you really have to have mastered the instep kick before you can get power from it. Unfortunately, if you get into the habit of kicking with the toe, your game will be hurt as you move on to more advanced levels of play where accuracy becomes important. Work hard to learn to pass with the instep and avoid the toe kick when you are learning, even if your power suffers a bit at first.

Placement Is Everything

Good passes are only part of the equation. The game of soccer involves a whole lot more than just physical ability, and the mental game is especially apparent when it comes to pass performance. The strategic aspects of passing really must come with experience, but there are a few standard concepts that even the most novice of players can learn and use.

Coach's Corner

Give the ball to your teammates when they need it, not when you feel like getting rid of it.

Lead Your Teammate

When you're passing the ball to your teammate, you have to make sure you pass the ball to where she will be, not where she is now. Remember those dreaded word problems from math class? "If a train is traveling at 40 miles per hour and heading west, what time will it pass the hobo currently eating his baked bean lunch 67 miles away who plans to make easterly progress two minutes after ...." Even the brainiest cringed when they appeared. Well, it's not as bad as that, but you do have to do some (nonmathematical) calculations when you're passing to a moving target.

Learning the Lingo

When you lead your teammate with the ball, you pass it out in front of where she actually is, so that she doesn't have to break her stride or stop to get it.

If your teammate is sprinting toward the goal, your pass should be sent out in front of her, so she won't have to slow her sprint down (or stop or go in reverse). It's going to take experience to perfect just how far ahead of her you're going to want to pass. In general, the farther away she is, the more you should angle your pass, because it will take the ball longer to get to her, which means she's sprinting forward for a longer period of time. The closer she is, the more you can pass directly to her. Look at this figure for a clearer explanation.

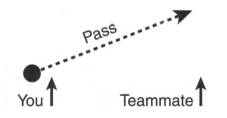

Leading your teammate.

Put It in Reverse

There is one occasion where you won't really be leading your teammate, and that's with a *backward pass*. Most everyone likes to think of themselves as forward thinkers, but in soccer sometimes you have to think backward. There's no rule that says the ball has to go in the direction of the goal all the time. It's much better strategy to send the ball in reverse, back to a half back or fullback who might be wide open, than to push it forward into a wall of defensive players. If you're being pressured, you're going to have enough trouble trying to protect the ball, without having to search for an open teammate. If you pass back, the player behind you might have lots of time to take a look around and then make the perfect pass toward the goal.

Coming Through

Another popular pass is called the *through pass*, which is used down in front of the goal. Because of the offsides rule, a player cannot be waiting behind the defense for a pass to come to him. But he can, however, hover next to the defense waiting for someone to pass a ball through the defensive players and toward the goal. When this happens, the hoverer runs forward to the ball, gains possession (in the best of all possible worlds), and shoots.

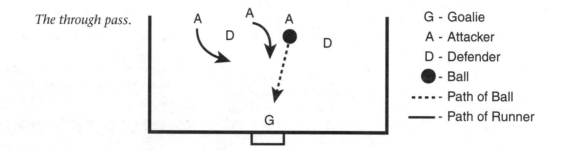

The through pass.

G - Goalie
A - Attacker
D - Defender
● - Ball
----- - Path of Ball
—— - Path of Runner

The through pass has to have a light touch, because your teammate is going to have to reach the ball before the goalie does. A hard through pass might as well be considered a shot on goal. Obviously, the farther you are away from the goal, the harder it can be.

Give and Go

The final basic passing strategy is one of the most effective. It's called the *give-and-go pass*. It's usually done with rather short passes in an effort to evade a defender. One player passes the ball to another and then sprints forward around the defender and receives the ball again out in front. The motion is shown in this figure.

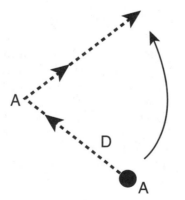

The give-and-go pass.

If you're the one to initiate the give and go, you need to communicate this to your teammate by yelling "Give and go!" While many experienced players look for this option automatically, newer players may not think of it.

If you're the receiver of the first pass and you hear your teammate shout "Give and go!" don't hesitate. Timing is a big part of this pass and presuming that the defender isn't deaf, she'll be reacting, too. With this in mind, the give-and-go pass is almost always done with a one-touch pass. It should also be done with the inside of the foot to make sure it's accurate. You don't need a long, strong pass, so this is your best option.

Learning the Lingo

Some teams also call the give-and-go pass a *wall pass* (because it's like bouncing the ball off a wall and getting it back again) or a *1–2 pass* (because it's a two-step pass). While these aren't quite as obvious a description of the pass, "Wall!" or "1–2" is a lot less cumbersome to shout than "Give and go!" when you're trying to communicate with your teammate.

The Least You Need to Know

➤ There are many passing options for a soccer player, including the inside of the foot, the outside of the foot, the instep pass, the chip, the volley, the half-volley, and the head pass.

➤ Control is the name of the game, both before the pass and during it.

➤ Passing can go in any direction: forward, backward, and sideways, and it's often strategically beneficial to change the direction.

➤ Practice your passes through games or repetition with a wall or partner, so you can execute them well during a game.

Chapter 6

It Takes Two

In This Chapter

➤ The various parts of the body used to trap the ball

➤ How to get yourself into position to receive the ball

➤ The importance of communication

In football, there are people who are actually called receivers, whose main job it is to be the recipient of the pass from the passer, usually the quarterback. But even if the receiver misses the ball, he is called a receiver. He is even called a receiver if someone else gets the ball.

Soccer is a much more logical sport. In soccer, anyone can be a receiver at any time during a game. A pass goes from Player A to Player B. Player B is automatically the receiver. And when Player B sends it back to Player A, then Player A becomes the receiver. Notice that in soccer, you actually "receive" the ball.

But the question becomes, then, just how does one go about receiving a soccer ball? The physical skills are simple to learn. The strategy is a bit more involved.

Caught in a Trap

Receiving the ball in soccer is also called *trapping* the ball. This is largely because you are using some part of your body to contain a loose, roaming ball and get it under control in the small area in front of you. There are many ways to trap a soccer ball, depending on how the ball is approaching your body.

Playing Footsie

The first and most preferable way to trap the ball is with your foot, largely because you're used to using your foot for the rest of the game, so it's the most natural and comfortable part of the body to use for receiving the ball. Also, if the ball is rolling along the ground, it's the *only* method you can use to receive the ball short of lying on the ground to get another part of your body involved.

If the ball is on the ground, the trap is simple. You lift your foot about four inches off the ground, with the inside of the foot facing the approaching ball. You want your toes up and your ankle locked in that position. The ball's midpoint, or slightly higher, is your target.

Coach's Corner

When you make contact with the ball, hitting it right near the middle is quite important. You don't want to hold your foot too low or the ball will bounce up and possibly even go over your foot, and you don't want it up too high, because the ball might sneak under your foot.

Learning the Lingo

The term *give* is defined in the dictionary as "the capacity or tendency to yield to a force." When you're receiving the ball, that's exactly what you want to happen. Your foot (or whatever part of the body is involved) is going to yield to the force of the ball. In most cases that means that the ball is pushing the foot backward slightly.

The minute the ball comes into contact with your foot, drop that foot back immediately, *giving* a little to take the speed out of the ball. If you're having trouble dropping the foot back at the right moment, you can try thinking of it in a different way. As the ball approaches, let your muscles in that leg go limp. The ball hits your foot and pushes it back, because you aren't using your muscles to resist. The presence of your foot, however, is enough to stop the ball.

If the ball is coming out of the air, it's a little harder to get your feet involved. There are so many other body parts that come first. But if the ball has a sharp arc, and you know it's going to be heading on its downward path, then you can try to trap it out of the air with your foot.

Picture yourself as a baseball player with a mitt on your foot. You want to "catch" the ball, giving once again when the contact is made. There are two parts of the foot you can use:

1. The inside of the foot
2. The toes

If you use the inside of your foot, keep your ankle stiff, hold your foot about six to eight inches off the ground, let the ball hit it, and then immediately drop your foot down to the ground. You can also just pull your foot away.

If you choose to use your toes, instead, point them down. The last thing you want is a ball hitting the hard pointy part of your shoe and bouncing off. Pointing your toes will, however, leave your instep open, which is also a hard area that might cause a ball to ricochet. Avoid that, too. You want to "catch" the ball on the top of your shoe where the toes are. Then, drop your foot to the ground or pull it away.

Coach's Corner

Some players like to try to step on the ball when it's arcing downward toward them. When done correctly, this is an excellent trap, because it immediately stops the ball and places it right at your feet. The catch is that there's a large margin of error. An instant of bad timing and you're stepping on air. Another drawback is that when you step on the ball you stop the ball dead, and will need to take an extra touch before making the next play. This takes time you may not have.

You'll find that a majority of your traps will be done with your foot. But there are other parts of the body that can be used as well.

The Thighs Have It

In the *Women's Dictionary of Annoying Body Parts*, the thigh is defined as an enormous persistently fleshy area at the top of the leg. And even the most muscle-bound men have to concede that there is quite a bit of truth to that definition. The good news is that it's a prime spot for trapping a ball that's coming out of the air.

If the ball is arcing downward, you can wait for it to drop way down, so you can use your foot, or you can stick your thigh underneath it. The beauty of the thigh is that it has built-in "give." You don't have to worry about timing your trap and pulling your body away at the last second, because the ball essentially dies on the thigh. You just have to be careful not to let the ball hit your knee instead.

If the pass is more of a bullet than an arc, you can also use your thigh to trap, but this time you'll want to use the inside of your thigh, rather than the top.

Tummy Trap

If the ball is slightly higher, you can stop it with your midsection. As the ball hits you, you want to cave in around it, rounding your shoulders, bending your head over the ball, and sucking in your stomach. You might even want to do a little jump backward. As you can see in this figure, this trap is much more likely to be popular with women than with men.

Trapping with the midsection.

Chest Do It

If the ball is really high up in the air, you're going to have to use your chest to trap it. For this trap, you want to bend your knees and bend backward at the waist, essentially doing your best to get your chest area close to parallel to the ground rather than perpendicular. You want to create a little platform for the ball to land on, as you can see this figure.

Then as the ball hits your chest, you bend your knees and sink your body lower, to take the momentum off the ball. This trap is much more likely to be popular with men than women.

Trapping with the chest.

71

Coach's Corner

Nobody traps perfectly every time, so you have to expect the ball to rebound a bit when it comes off your body. To minimize the damage, get in the habit of running through your traps, especially if you're trapping with the chest or midsection. Make the trap on the run and if the ball bounces out in front, you're already following it.

Moving without the Ball

It's one thing to stand opposite your teammate and receive a pass during practice. It's quite another story to get a pass during a game. As much as your teammate might want to pass to you, if you're not in a position to receive the ball, he'll never be able to get it to you. There are a number of things you can do to put yourself in a good receiving position, however.

Keep on Trucking

Movement is your best weapon against the defense. You know where you're going and they don't, so you stand a good chance of losing your defender if you're moving. If you're standing in one spot, on the other hand, the defender will have no trouble getting between you and the ball.

A caveat to this rule is to *meet the ball*. Even if you've managed to outrun and outmaneuver your opponent enough to get yourself open, if you stand and wait for the pass to come to you, then it will be intercepted nearly every time. That defender you evaded will be coming after you, and I guarantee he's moving. So if you see the ball coming toward you, move in to get it.

Two's a Crowd

Don't get too close to the ball. You're not going to be in a better position if you're only three feet away. Your teammate won't even bother to pass to you. One defender can take care of you both. You need to get in a position that is open but is far enough away so that a pass to you might actually be beneficial.

You also don't want to be too close to other teammates who might be possible receivers. Remember, the idea is to give your teammate many passing options. If you all bunch together, there's only going to be one option. Move off on your own. As your level of skill increases, try to constantly think about where the next pass will need to go. It's not good enough to connect one pass—your pass must set up the "receiver" for his next play. In other words, if you do not have a clear vision regarding where everyone is on the field your passes will not add up to much.

Be a Space Cadet

There are two types of spaces on the soccer field. One type is the six square feet of space wedged between other bodies that would be similar to the space you might find at the Jersey shore on a hot August day. The other kind is a wide-open space, something akin to a Minnesota golf course in January. Guess which one you want?

In soccer, wide-open spaces are the best kind. The defense collapses into the middle to cut off angles to the goal, so you're likely to find spaces out to the side. Spread your offense wide and you'll find you have many more passing opportunities.

Know Your Teammate

Going wide is usually a good option, but you need to consider the abilities of the passer first. For instance, if you're a kindergartner (which I know you're not), you may want to reconsider racing out to the sidelines. In fact, you may want to reconsider racing more than five yards away. Your fellow kindergartners are not going to have the strength to pass the ball more than a couple of yards.

The Thrill of the Drill

This is a good exercise to teach movement when you don't have the ball. It involves four players in a 10' × 10' square (or thereabouts). Three players stand in three of the corners. The fourth player is defense. The object of the game is to make sure the player with the ball always has two passing options, which helps foil the defense. She is not allowed to pass across the middle of the square, so the other players have to shift position to make sure that the two corners adjacent to her are filled. When she makes her pass, the players have to shift for the new person. The defense is there to put pressure on the passers to make it more gamelike.

While kindergarten soccer is an extreme, players at every level need to assess the ability of the player who is going to be passing the ball. If she can't use her left foot well, don't expect her to consider you an option if you are to her right. If she can't loft the ball, don't sprint down the wing behind two defensive players, because she won't be able to get the ball over them.

Creating Options

Much of the talk so far has been negative: don't crowd your teammates, don't go too far away from the passer, and so on. So you know where you *shouldn't* be, but that doesn't automatically translate into knowing where you *should* be. There are five places that passers can look for a receiver, so it stands to reason that you want to put yourself in one of these five places. If you keep these places in mind, you'll have a good sense of where you should be. By places, I don't mean an actual physical spot on the field, but more of a relationship to the passer.

1. Square
2. Wing
3. Wall
4. Overlap
5. Back

Of course, it would help to know what these mean.

Square

A *square* pass is a pass that goes directly out to the side, be it right or left. To communicate this pass, some people yell "square left" (assuming the pass is on the left). Some people say "square," figuring that the passer can interpret the left side from the direction of the voice. Others just say "on your left," which implies that it would naturally be a square pass because otherwise it wouldn't be directly on your left. Whatever you call it, teams should try to be consistent, so everyone knows just what the receiver is trying to say.

Try to call for the square pass before you are actually in position, because it's not a pass that leads the runner. That way you can run onto the ball rather than stand there, not moving, waiting for it, and making it easy for the defense.

Learning the Lingo

Just in case it seems odd to you that a pass, which is technically a line, should be referred to as *square*, here's a quick tip to help you get the concept and remember the term. Architects use a tool called a square to make sure they are creating a right angle. As a receiver, you want to place yourself at a right angle with the passer and the direction the passer is facing.

Wing

Spreading your offense wide is an effective way to thwart the defense. One way to do that is to run down the sidelines toward the goal. The wings do this all the time, but other players can take up this role as well, letting the passer know they are making a *wing* run by yelling "Wing!"

Generally a wing pass would be a long lofted ball that would lead you, because there would probably be defensive players between you and the passer. If not, of course, then the ball can be on the ground, again leading you so you can run onto it without breaking stride.

Wall

A *wall pass* is also called a *give-and-go* or a *1–2 pass*. This is an extremely effective play for evading a defender and is usually initiated by the passer, which is why it is included in Chapter 5 as well. While it's most effective when the passer calls the play, either the passer or the receiver can do it.

For those whose short-term memory fails them from chapter to chapter, in this pass, the passer sends the ball to the receiver and then becomes a receiver herself after sprinting around the defender. As soon as she's past the defender, she gets the ball back. It's as if the receiver is just a wall for the ball to bounce against and rebound back to the passer.

Learning the Lingo

Mark up means to guard a specific player closely.

Overlap

Generally teams play a mostly man-to-man defense, where defenders mark up against forwards and midfielders are with midfielders. Technically, the forwards should also be marking up against the defenders when the other team has the ball, but in reality this rarely happens. As a result, this presents quite an opportunity for a defender who's willing to run.

If a fullback sees a wide open space down the wing, and if the midfielder or wing in front of him either has the ball or is pulled out of position, he can shoot forward, *overlapping* the line of players in front of him, as shown in this figure.

The overlap pass.

Wing

Midfielder

Fullback

Because fullbacks generally don't have someone playing tight defense on them, he should be wide open and remain wide open until someone else picks up the slack. And that presumably would free up someone else for a nice pass, creating a favorable imbalance with the offense.

The drawback to this pass, however, is that the fullback is pulled way out of position and has to hustle back if the tide turns against him.

Back

Just because the goal is ahead of you, it doesn't mean that you have to always progress in that direction. Often your team's best option is to go *back*. Say, for instance, that your team is bunching on the right side of the field. You're the center midfielder and you see your left wing wide open and waiting on the other side of the field, but your teammates can't get the ball to her through the wall of defensive players that have gathered around. This is your moment.

Move behind your teammate and call "Back!" When she passes the ball out of the fray and back to you, you can turn, maybe dribble a little toward the left side and boot a long one down to the wing. Even though that initial pass was not toward your goal, you've quickly advanced the ball down the field and placed it in a position where your team has a wide open space and the other team has its defense all out of position. So be sure to let your teammates know when you're back there.

Open Your Big Mouth

Every successful relationship depends on open lines of communication, and as you may have figured out by now, the passer/receiver relationship is no exception. You have to talk. In fact, you should be communicating throughout the entire game, but it's especially important if you're trying to receive a pass. While ideally a passer should be keeping her eyes up, looking for her options, the truth is that this isn't always the case. Even if it is, it never hurts to have a little verbal assistance.

Heads Up!

It is considered poor sportsmanship to yell misleading directions to the opposing team, such as "I'm square" or "Pass it back" when they have the ball. Any ref worth his stripes will call you on it and give you a yellow card.

Let your teammate know where you are, and be specific. Don't just shout ìI'm open! I'm openî or call her name. She already knows she's the center of attention; she needs to know where you are on the periphery. If you've moved into position for a square pass, yell "Square!" If you're behind her and you see she's in trouble, yell "Back!"

You also don't want to fall into the trap of calling for the ball automatically. If there's a defender between you and the ball, keep your mouth shut until you've moved into a better position. If you're the chatty type and need to talk, you can, however, tell your teammate what his options are, even if you're not open to receive a pass yourself. It does no harm to yell, "Jay is down the wing, and you have Cory on your left!" and you might be giving him some new information. You can also tell him when he has time to get the ball under control and when he has to get rid of it quickly.

Finally, you want to make sure that your team speaks the same language. If one person, for instance, learned to yell "Wall Pass" where another person learned to yell "1–2" you're going to end up with a whole lot of yelling and not much give and go.

Stealing the Ball

There will come a moment in the game where you happen to be receiving the ball, but it certainly wasn't intended to go to you. You've sneaked in and stolen a pass. There are a number of ways you can achieve this:

➤ Anticipate where the opponents might be passing.

➤ Listen to what they're saying. If someone calls for a square pass, step in before it gets there.

➤ Keep moving. If you're running and they're waiting, you're going to get the ball.

➤ Be really, really fast.

Some players are going to be naturally faster runners than others, but you can still make a difference by giving it your all. A slower player who hustles or a smart player who anticipates is going to steal more balls than a lazy speedster does.

The Least You Need to Know

➤ No matter what part of your body you are using to trap the ball, you want to make sure that you "give" with the ball so that it will drop gently in front of you rather than rebounding off.

➤ Don't stand still. Move to get open and move to meet the ball.

➤ Fill the open spaces, by moving out to the sidelines or moving out away from the player who has the ball.

➤ Always communicate, describing your position and the situation as you see it.

How do I STOP?

Budda Budda Budda

Chapter 7

The Trouble with Dribbles

In This Chapter

➤ Moving the ball down the field

➤ Avoiding the defenders

➤ Knowing when to dribble

➤ Juggling the ball

Two steps forward. One step backward. A fake to the left. A shift to the right. And swing your partner and do-si-do. Dribbling the soccer ball is an art form, a dance, an athletic endeavor. The ball becomes an extension of the foot and the dribbling soccer player must step lightly and creatively to move it from point A to point B, without defender C stepping in and putting a stop to it.

It's virtually impossible for a player to single-handedly move the ball from one end of the field to another, but there are times when a player is on his own and has to get the ball rolling. The act of tapping the ball repeatedly with the foot is called *dribbling*, and accomplished dribbling can make a tremendous difference in a game.

Forward Progress

Obviously, any soccer player out on the field knows what the ultimate goal is: the goal. Nonetheless, while the shortest distance between two points might be a straight line, it's not the likeliest manner for the ball to get there, at least when there are defenders on the field. If that's the case, better hone your dribbling skills.

Dribbling is a combination of simple and complicated moves that can have the ball going in any direction at a variety of speeds. The beauty of it is that it's one of the few skills that you can practice on your own in nearly any space. Even your room!

Toe Tapping

At its most basic level, dribbling is really quite simple. You want to tap the ball with some part of your foot to get it moving.

The parts of your foot that are useful in dribbling are

➤ Inside of your foot

➤ Outside of your foot

➤ Sole

➤ Toe

➤ Heel

➤ Instep

In other words, you can use every single part.

Most players seem to prefer one foot over the other, or even one part of one foot to everything else. Don't fall into the trap of only using this one part. Force yourself to dribble with all parts of the foot no matter how awkward it seems. The game situation should be what's dictating which part of the foot you're using, not your particular comfort level.

Coach's Corner

If you find that you're shying away from using a certain part of the foot, isolate it. If you don't usually use the outside of the foot, then dribble down the field using only that part. Of course, this advice is just for practice, not for a game.

When you tap the ball, try to hit the ball in the middle. A ball that's hit slightly underneath will pop up, and a ball that's hit on top won't move. Now get out and practice. You've got to know your own strength and figure out just how hard you need to touch the ball.

You don't want the dribble to be so forceful that the ball gets away from you (and is therefore stolen by someone else), yet you don't want it so soft that you're tripping over it as you try to move.

Here's a good rule of thumb to follow: If you're dribbling straight down the field, keep the ball one step away from you. For example, if you're sprinting, then your tap needs to be a little harder than it would be if you were slowly jogging, because your one step will obviously be much bigger when you are sprinting. There are times when you can let it further out in front, but the one step guideline is a good one to keep in mind.

The Ball Is Your Buddy

A beginning dribbler is accomplishing a lot just getting used to the strength needed for each touch on the ball. But that takes time and constant contact. It's worth it, though. The more familiar you are with the ball, the better you'll be. Try to dribble the ball whenever and wherever possible.

As long as you can deal with odd looks from people passing by, try taking a walk through your neighborhood while kicking the ball in front of you. If that's not possible, go to a park or some other similar area. Take the ball to bed with you if that's going to make you more familiar with its foibles.

Once your feet have gotten the hang of things, spice things up a bit. Pick up your speed or dodge around trees. You can vary the speed, too, for another nice dribbling effect. Move quickly down the field for five taps, then slow down for three, picking up the speed again for five more.

Players of any age, but young players especially, get bored with the repetitive aspects of practice. If you can get a group together, playing traditional games with the added challenge of a ball can make practicing the dribble much more fun. Games such as Freeze Tag, Duck, Duck Goose, or Red Rover, Red Rover are very adaptable and are a great way to get a feel for the ball.

The Thrill of the Drill

Red Light, Green Light is an excellent way to get used to dribbling. One player is the traffic light and turns his back, saying, "Green Light." At this point, everyone starts dribbling toward him. A few seconds later, the traffic light whips around, shouting, "Red Light!" Everyone freezes, with one foot on top of the ball. If the traffic light notices you moving, you go back to the beginning. The first person to reach the traffic light wins. You can't let the ball get out too far in front, or you'll have to run to catch up with it when Red Light is called, and you can't move the ball so delicately that you lag behind and have no chance of winning.

If there are only two of you trying to practice, you can still make it fun. One of you is the dribbler and one is the defender. The dribbler should try to get from one end of the field to the other without losing the ball to the defender. Switch roles and then head back.

Heads Up

Watch out for that tree! Unless you're auditioning for a remake of *George of the Jungle*, you're going to want pay attention to where you're heading. So get your eyes off the ball and look up! It's as simple as that . . . in theory, anyway.

The temptation when you're first starting out is to have your eyes watch what your feet are doing. It's only natural because frequently you find that your feet aren't exactly doing what you planned them to do, and you have to adjust on-the-fly. If you're looking up the field, you're going to do more stumbling than adjusting.

Nonetheless, you do have to practice dribbling while looking up. There are a couple of very compelling reasons why:

1. To begin with, you don't want to dribble directly into a defender. This is a sure way to lose the ball.

2. You need to know who's out there. Passing moves the ball up the field much faster than dribbling, so you want to take advantage of open teammates if you can.

If you can get a friend to help you with your dribbling, have her hold up a certain number of fingers as you move across the field. Shout out the number of fingers as she changes them. Ask her to speed up the changes as you get better. You can also get special shields to put under your eyes, so you can't look down.

Control Factor

Just because you're not looking at the ball, it doesn't mean that you can relinquish all control. This is why you have to get your feet familiar with that black-and-white sphere. You have to have a really good idea of the direction in which the ball is going and how fast it's moving.

Fortunately, humans are blessed with peripheral vision, so you will have a general idea where that ball is if you don't let it get to far away from you. But you don't want to do that anyway.

Evasion Tactics

Simple dribbling is vital, but after you've mastered that it's time to let your feet dance. The dribbling skills for straight dribbling are a mere shadow of the ones that you'll need if you ever come up against a defender one on one.

Use Your Body

Effective dribbling uses the whole body. You're moving your feet to the disco beat in an effort to confuse the defender, but at the same time, you need to position your body so that defender has a hard time even getting close to the ball.

In other words, if you're in a tight clinch with a defender, you always want to keep your body between the defender and the ball. That way, the defender has to get around you first before he can get a foot on it.

Fancy Footwork

Dribbling when you have a defender on your back is not easy. You're going to have to catch him off guard before you can make any progress. Fancy footwork is the key.

You want to keep your feet within inches of the ball, if not in constant contact. You have to use every part of your foot, tapping the ball, dragging it, and sometimes missing it completely. You want to move the ball sideways, forward, and backward, or possibly not at all.

Here are some typical evasive moves:

The Thrill of the Drill

Bulls in the Ring can be played with players of all ages and abilities and is quite fun besides being helpful. Every player has a soccer ball inside the penalty box (the 18). The object of the game is to kick the other players' soccer balls out of the box while maintaining possession of yours. Players who have lost their soccer balls leave the box. The winner is the last one left inside the penalty box.

➤ With the ball in the center of your two feet, step over the ball sideways with one foot, without touching the ball and then quickly nudge the ball with the outside of that foot in the other direction.

➤ Step over the ball forward with one foot and then nudge it sideways with the other foot behind the first foot's heel.

➤ Make a hard move with your body one way, but keep your foot and the ball and send it the other way.

➤ Start dribbling hard in one direction, stop as if you're going to change direction, and then start up again in the same direction.

The key to good evasive dribbling is using your head and body to make the defender think you're going one way, while your feet are actually sending the ball another way. You better make sure you maintain your balance the whole time, however, or you're not going to be able to recover and move with the ball.

Fake Out

Occasionally, you'll be approaching a defender, but the two of you haven't gotten into a tight clinch yet. Or perhaps you are both sprinting down the sideline side by side, neck and neck, at top speed. It isn't exactly appropriate at either of these times to be doing small footwork moves with your body between the defender and the ball. In this case, you want to rely on some broader cuts and fakes.

The Cutback

If you're running down the sideline and a defender is coming toward you from the middle, she'll be approaching at an angle. Your instincts might tell you to move farther away from her. Fight those instincts.

If you move away from her, closer to the sideline, you'll be playing right into her defense. That's the way she's running, and it's away from the goal. Instead, just as she gets to you, cut in her direction into the middle. She will have to come to a full stop and reverse directions to keep up with you. This figure shows the cutback move.

The cutback move.

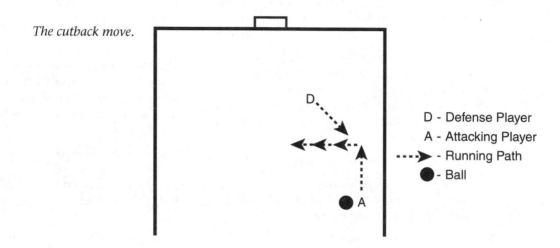

D - Defense Player
A - Attacking Player
┅➤ - Running Path
● - Ball

The timing on this move is crucial. If you don't wait until the last minute, the defender is going to have no trouble adjusting.

Stop and Start

If the defender is running along next to you as you sprint down the sideline, you're going to have to get rid of him somehow to make a cross or dribble to the center yourself. Odds are good that you cannot outrun him because you have the ball and he doesn't.

You're going to have to fake him out. Sprint as fast as you can and then stop. If the defender keeps going, then you have your moment. Dribble to the center or cross. If the defender stops with you, then try starting up again immediately, going in the same direction you were going. Maybe you can get a jump on him, which would free you up farther down. If this doesn't work, try it again.

Be careful not to start this too close to the corner. The end line cuts down your options considerably.

The Rock and Roll

But let's say you are stuck near the corner with a defender on your back. You need to get out of there quickly. Try the rock-and-roll move.

First, back in close to the defender and look over one shoulder. Then rock your body hard in the direction you're looking. If the defender buys into the fake, drag the ball in the opposite direction with the sole of your foot (while you are still leaning the other way to fake the defender out), and then roll off of her. Make sure the roll is right on top of her, so you put her behind you.

You can also do the double rock-and-roll. Rock one way, then start to roll the other without having dragged the ball back, and then go back the first way. This move is especially effective if you've fooled her with the other move recently.

Coach's Corner

For all the cuts and fakes you do, make sure you stay low with your knees bent, so you don't want the fake to work on you as well as the defender.

Choosing Your Moments

There is a time for everything, or so the saying goes, and dribbling is no exception to the rule. The game is going to dictate when you should dribble and when you shouldn't, and it's going to be vital for you to know how to take dictation.

Dribbling can take place on any part of the field, and every player should be capable of doing it. There are two ideal moments to be doing a lot of dribbling:

➤ No challenge by a defender

➤ On a breakaway

A dribbling player can touch the ball one time, two times, or fifty times. It all depends on what the defense is doing. If they challenge you, it is time to stop.

All By Myself

If you've somehow received the ball with no defense in sight, you've been given a gift. Unless you're in front of the goal, in which case you should be shooting, you can take your time, slow down the pace, and dribble to your heart's content. Think about it. If no one is guarding you, then the other team has 10 players guarding your nine teammates. Passing the ball off doesn't sound nearly as advantageous an option than keeping it to your little old unguarded self. Use this time to set up a play and make something happen on the field.

Coach's Corner

Besides keeping your eyes open, you want to keep your ears open, too. Listen to what your teammates are telling you. Are they saying, "You've got time!" or are they saying, "He's on you! Get rid of it!" to warn you of a defender coming up behind you.

As you move the ball up the field, keep your head up to see who is open for a pass. Someone might make a nice run, or a defender might leave his man to challenge you. If that's the case, you probably want to dump the ball off to the player that the defender just abandoned.

The Breakaway

Every once in a lucky while, you might get the chance to breakaway dribble. Most often this breakaway is down the sideline. You've stayed wide and gotten a pass out there, while the defense has bunched protectively into the middle. If this is the case, take the ball and head straight to the goal line. You are almost assured of maintaining possession, whereas a pass into the defense-heavy middle would most likely be intercepted.

Eventually, you're probably going to have to center the ball, but then you'll be down in front of the goal, and if you can loft the ball, a tall teammate might get her head on it no matter how many defenders there are.

If you somehow have evaded the last line of defense and end up with the ball on a breakaway in the middle, you're less likely to go unchallenged. You better believe that those defenders are scrambling to get back in front of you, and it's likely that their sprints without the ball are faster than yours with the ball.

Nonetheless, you still want to head straight to the goal with extra speedy dribbling.

No Thanks, I Think I'll Pass

As appealing as an unchallenged breakaway dribble sounds, this is not the game of soccer. The soccer ball makes more progress through passing than dribbling, and there are many reasons why you should make the decision *not* to dribble.

To begin with, dribbling is slower. Have you ever raced against a crisp, hard pass? You're going to lose. The ball moves much faster if it's not linked to a player's foot. The best way to score is to catch the defense out of position and the best way to do that is to get the ball moving quickly. Look for passing opportunities and take advantage of them as much as possible.

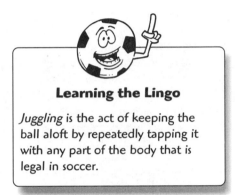

Learning the Lingo

Juggling is the act of keeping the ball aloft by repeatedly tapping it with any part of the body that is legal in soccer.

In addition, unless you know for certain that the defender in front of you is an incompetent klutz (or if you've developed world-class dribbling skills), then you're going to want to try to pass whenever you're challenged. Of course, sometimes that's not going to be possible, and you'll just have to rely on whatever dribbling abilities you've developed, but usually it's safer to evade an opponent by merely passing around her.

Juggling

Technically, *juggling* is not dribbling. But in a practical sense, good juggling skills are tremendously beneficial to dribblers. And once again, the ball familiarity alone will help you in infinite ways.

Juggling can be done alone, which makes it a great practice possibility. The idea is to keep the ball from touching the ground by using your feet, thighs, and even the head to bounce the ball back up into the air.

Start Me Up

There are two ways to start juggling—the easy way and the hard way.

For the easy way, you hold the ball in your hands and then drop it onto your foot or your thigh. The thigh is probably easier than the foot, because it's closer and it's a bigger target.

Or you can do it the hard way, by trying to get the ball up in the air using only your foot. This takes some practice. Step on the ball, drag the ball backward with the sole of your foot, then quickly slip that foot under the ball and give it a little pop upward.

Thrill of the Drill

It might sound like juggling is a pretty dreary way to practice ball-handling skills, especially if you're not accomplished at it. But there's something you can do to keep it interesting. Just turn it into a game. Set a goal for yourself. In the beginning, for example, you might want to achieve five consecutive juggles. Then try to beat that goal each time you juggle. If another player is with you, compete.

This might be something you want to save for when you're a little more experienced.

Group Therapy

If there are lots of players, you can try something called group juggling. Get in a fairly small circle and use only one ball (to start, anyway). One player tosses the ball to another to begin the play. When the player receives the ball, he juggles it as many times as he wants. It might be only once. Then he sends it off to someone else in the group. This continues without, you hope, the ball ever touching the ground. Just like hacky sack, if you are familiar with that game.

You can turn this into a competition as well. If there are enough people, you can have two groups. The group that can keep the ball aloft the longest is the winner. Or, if you only have enough for one group, you can play the elimination game. If the ball hits the ground, the person who is responsible for it hitting the ground, leaves the group. The winner is the one person still left juggling when every one else is eliminated.

The Least You Need to Know

➤ Use all parts of your foot when you dribble.

➤ Keep your head up and the ball under control.

➤ Be convincing with your cuts and fakes.

➤ Know when passing is a better option than dribbling.

➤ Juggling is a great way to improve your ball handling skills.

Chapter 8

Heads Up

In This Chapter

➤ Heading mechanics

➤ Easing into the skill

➤ Game situations

➤ Diving headers

Most people think of soccer as a foot game. In fact, in nearly every country in the world, the game is known as football. But don't let this fool you. Soccer is a game that involves nearly every part of the body (even the hands and arms are used in throw-ins and by the goalie), and one of the most powerful weapons a soccer player has is his head.

Any player, for play on any part of the field, can use the head. The head can shoot, pass, and defend. Without good heading skills a player is not going to progress much beyond recreational league soccer.

Getting a Head Start

Many kids think that heading the ball is great fun . . . until they get that first face ball. Then good luck getting them to try it again. Because of this, you really don't want to start them off with head balls until they're old enough to master the skills necessary to do them correctly.

Bet You Didn't Know

Soccer in England during the Middle Ages added a new meaning to the term "head ball." While the sport was already popular, the English defeat of an invading army of Danes brought the sport to a new level. In celebration of their military victory, the English used the severed heads of their victims as their soccer balls in the game.

Fortunately, this is not a problem. Most young players are incapable of getting the ball up off the ground in the first place, so heading is not part of their game.

But then players get older and better, and there comes a time in every young soccer player's life where the ball starts rising, the games start to matter more, and he's going to have no choice but to put forehead to ball.

As you sense this starting to happen to you or your child, it's time for you to begin the heading drills. You want to get familiar with the concept and skills for heading before you ever find yourself face to face with a ball in a game.

Go to the Head of the Class

Now its time to learn the basic skills of heading. There are six steps:

1. Get into position.
2. Watch the ball.
3. Keep your neck stiff.
4. Lean back.
5. Snap forward.
6. Contact the ball with your forehead.

Sounds simple, right?

Coach's Corner

A young player should also practice keeping his tongue in their mouth so he doesn't bite it.

Saving the Best for Last

Let's deal with that last step first, because if you're concerned with the ouch factor—and most novice headers are—then this is the most important lesson to learn. Even if you can't master anything more, if you can at least contact the ball with the forehead then you can be confident that you're going to face a head ball with no pain.

Many novice players, especially ones who have tried head balls and failed, are con-vinced that hitting the ball with the forehead is going to hurt. This is absolutely not true. I promise. Hitting the ball with the face will hurt. Hitting the ball with the ear will hurt. Hitting the ball on the scalp will hurt. But hitting the ball with the forehead won't be any more painful than hitting the ball with the foot.

Move into Position

And now back to the beginning. The first step in executing a successful head ball is getting into position. Don't you think the odds of hitting the ball squarely on your forehead are going to improve dramatically if you're underneath the ball than if you're leaning sideways to get it? And inch can make all the difference in a head ball.

Keep an Eye On It

Watch the ball. It may be incredibly tempting to shut your eyes at the last minute, but please resist. You need to see the ball come out of the air and connect with your head. After all, you might have miscalculated slightly when you moved into position and wouldn't you like to find that out visually rather than physically?

Some players like to use their hands to guide the ball into their forehead. They hold their hands up in the air as if they're going to catch the ball and then bring them in toward their forehead as the ball comes in. this figure shows you what that looks like. You don't want to hold on to this technique for too long, however. At some point you will also need your hands for balance and to hold off defenders. Also, as you progress you want to attack the ball and get to it before the defenders, thus guiding it in with your hands does not make sense.

Guiding the ball with your hands.

Using your hands is nice because it's both a reminder to keep your eye on the ball and a way to locate your forehead, because your eye-hand coordination is probably a little more developed than your eye-head coordination. Just don't touch the ball with your hands by mistake.

Keep a Stiff Neck

Some players think that the head ball's power comes from the snap of the neck. Nothing could be farther from the truth. The neck needs to remain absolutely stiff, with the snap coming from the body.

Not only do you want to avoid whiplash, which will almost certainly happen when a rocket ball connects with a head perched on a wobbly neck, but you also get more power this way. Your neck is not strong enough to withstand the force of anything more than a lightly tossed ball. If your neck isn't stiff, you're going to end up with a head trap rather than a head shot.

Bend and Stretch

Because your power is going to come from your body, you really have to lean back to create something to snap. This figure shows the bend and the snap.

If you don't lean backward and you try to snap, the ball is going to head straight down to the ground.

The many stages of a head ball.

Snap

Snap to It

Finally, we reach the climax: the snap. Just as the ball is about to reach you, snap your body forward into the ball.

For a straightforward head ball, you want to hit the ball square in the center. This sends a line drive shooting off your forehead. If you want to angle the ball down to the ground, try to contact the ball slightly above the halfway line. Careful, though. This can be a recipe for a face ball if you're not skilled in this maneuver.

Bet You Didn't Know

You're actually less likely to get hurt if you're snapping forward to meet the ball than if you're passively waiting for it or, even worse, shying away from it.

Soft Sell

Even if you see the facts on paper, even if you constantly repeat the "hit it on the forehead" mantra, you're not going to be able to do a perfect head ball immediately. So you want to start the process slowly. Different coaches swear by different ways of teaching the head ball.

Balloon Ball

Much to the delight of the children involved, balloons can be a great way to teach heading. For at least a portion of practice, you can substitute a balloon, or several balloons, for the ball. Players know the balloons won't hurt and can go after them with abandon.

There are a few ways to go about playing with the balloons. You can play actual soccer with the balloon, using the feet, too. Or you can tell your players that they must keep the balloon aloft using only their head. Divide the players into several groups, each with their own balloon, and have them compete. See who can keep the balloon aloft the longest, using feet and heads or heads alone.

Coach's Corner

If you can find punching balls, they're even better than balloons because they are slightly heavier. That way they don't float as much and they're easier to direct.

The advantages to using balloons is that it forces new players to use their heads as part of the game. If they wait for the balloon to drop to their feet, they are never going to get the ball. This is what would happen with a real soccer ball on a more competitive level. The other advantage, of course, is that a balloon face ball isn't going to hurt one bit.

Which brings me to the disadvantage. The problem with balloons is that they're really better for teaching a sense of heading rather than the skills of heading. Because they are so light, there's really little incentive (read pain avoidance) to contact the ball correctly. And even if a player is motivated to hit the balloon correctly, she can't tell if she did because balloons just don't react the way a ball would.

The Drop

Another way to train the head ball is the drop. This is a method that players can do by themselves, at home, to practice. It's simple. A player holds the ball up in the air above the head, using both hands, then he drops it onto his forehead in the proper head ball place.

Repeat this time and again, or at least until you sense the start of a headache. If you drop it on your forehead often enough, pretty soon your eyes and your brain will know exactly where the head ball is supposed to go.

This is an excellent method to use if you're the type of player who likes to pretend to "catch" the ball right above the forehead. This way, when you get into a real heading situation, you'll find yourself in the familiar position of hands over your head as the ball slips through and hits you on the forehead. You can't miss.

Unfortunately, this method can only take you so far. You can't exactly include a snap or a jump, and you can't make it any more difficult or gamelike.

The Pendulum

Another option is something called a pendulum, but this involves doctoring your ball or buying one that is already doctored. (And, or course, if you choose to do your own, then you need to replace it.) You want a ball with a string attached, which you then suspend from a tree or the crossbar of the goal, for instance. The ball should be at forehead level at first.

Move into the ball to get the feel of it hitting your forehead, then get it swinging a little so it has some movement to it. You can tell if you hit it correctly by the way that it moves. If you've hit it squarely it will come right back to you. If you've mishit it, then it will spin off to the side.

Once you feel comfortable with this, raise the ball. Now you're going to have to jump to get it, which makes it a little more matchlike. Keep it moving, because you'll never be hitting a stationary ball in a game.

Toss Turn

Probably the most popular method for teaching the head ball is the soft toss. Two players stand about three feet apart. One player is the tosser and the other is the header. The tosser throws the ball lightly at forehead level, and the header tries to connect with his forehead and send the ball back to the tosser. After 10 tries, they switch roles.

Coach's Corner

If you have some soccer balls that are deader than others, use them for learning purposes. Not only will they hurt less if they happen to hit the nose rather than the forehead, but the softer balls cut down on the general headache potential that comes with repeated heading practice.

Once the players have mastered the three-foot soft toss, move them apart a bit. Put them six to eight feet apart and then toss the ball. Then add the rest of the heading motion to the drill.

Pressure Build Up

As you can see, each method has its strengths, and it probably couldn't hurt to put all the methods together. Start with the balloons to get the players excited, add the drop to get them familiar with the feel of the ball on their forehead, move onto the pendulum and the soft toss, and then when the skill is mastered maybe go back to the balloons to show the players how the head balls actually come into play in a competitive situation.

Once you've reached this level, it's time to increase the pressure. Try to head the ball while moving.. Have the tosser throw the ball to the left and right of you. Move down the field with the tosser running backward in front of you.

Add a defender. First put someone in front of you who is just going to stand there. While this person isn't going to challenge you, they are going to force you to leap up to head the ball—the way you would in the game.

Finally, let the defender go live. Battle it out with another player, because this is the way you're going to be heading in the game. Think about it. If there's no one on top of you, you're probably going to let the ball drop to your feet, so more often than not, you'll be heading the ball because an opponent is breathing down your neck.

95

Coach's Corner

Because so many head balls are taken in high-pressure situations with an opposing player right on top of you, the black eye factor is high. Many is the time that two heads go up together and one head gets flicked back into the nose of the other. Ouch! Be extra careful during prom season.

Taking a Dive

One of the most spectacular plays in soccer is the diving header. This is almost a surefire way to get yourself onto the highlight films.

Diving headers are used when the ball is coming in low. Ninety-nine percent of the time the ball is going to be one that's handled with the foot, but every once and a while you're going to get some crazy player who wants to sacrifice his head for the sake of the goal. (By the way, you can expect to see this move a whole lot more when males—rather than females—are playing.)

Coach's Corner

Diving headers should be limited to balls that are in front of the goal. For one, it's not worth the bodily sacrifice for anything but a goal or defending a goal, and two, you don't want to end up on the ground as players proceed on with the game around you.

A player chooses to dive when he realizes that his foot won't get to the ball in time. Say he's in front of the goal and the ball is coming in about a foot off the ground. A defender is a step ahead of you. He knows he's got you blocked and he's just waiting for the ball to come to his foot. If you want to get to it first, you have to dive for it.

Just as in a regular head ball, you want to watch the ball, keep your neck stiff, and contact the ball with your forehead. You don't, however, get into position, lean back, or snap forward. You just can't.

One of the best reasons to do a diving header is the rarity of the move. You can bet that the goalkeeper will be completely caught off guard.

Every Which Way

Do you feel lucky? If you think you've mastered the straightforward head ball, it might be time to get a little creative. Your forehead is not merely a nod to your Neanderthal cousins. It's a many faceted, subtly variable weapon.

The Thrill of the Drill

If you want to practice diving headers, you need to see a shrink, but there is a good drill you can use. Get on the ground in a pushup position. Have someone toss you the ball and push off the ground into it. Because you are already low to the ground, this won't (really) hurt, and you'll get a sense of the motion you'll need to use a diving header in the game.

Heading Sideways

Sometimes you may get the urge to send the ball off to the side rather than straightforward. This comes in handy, for instance, when a corner kick is lofted in front of the goal. If you hit the ball straight on, it would just send the ball back out to the kicker and where would that get you? So how do you manage to head it to the side?

Basically, the first steps are all the same. Get into position, watch the ball, and keep a stiff neck. When you go into your stretch, however, the situation changes a bit. Instead of leaning backward, you want to lean to the side. Then when you snap, you snap sideways in the direction you want the ball to go.

You also have a slightly different contact point on your forehead. Still try to get as close to the center of your forehead as possible so you don't end up with an ear ball, but contact the ball slightly on the side of the forehead, the side closest to the direction you want the ball to go.

Going Backward

Believe it or not, you can even head the ball backward. I know it sounds a bit contrary to what you've learned previously about the mechanics of the head ball, but it can be done, and it actually comes in quite handy.

Picture this. You're standing in front of the goal with your back toward it. A defender is directly behind you. A shot comes in from farther out that's headed your way. It's probably not going to score, because if you let it go, your defender gets it. You're going to have to get to it first. What better way than a backward head ball.

In reality, the backward head ball is more of a flick than a real hard contact. It looks the same as a regular head ball until the moment of contact. At that point, instead of snapping forward, you flick your head and just your head (this is the one time you're allowed to have a wobbly neck) backward, contacting the ball again in the center of the forehead but maybe slightly closer to the eyebrows. This figure shows you how.

The backward head flick.

The backward flick doesn't have to be used solely in front of the goal. It can be used to nudge a ball over a defender anywhere on the field or to save time when you're passing to a teammate who has made a great run.

Use Your Head

But what's the strategy behind a head ball? When can and should it be used? The answer is any time you get a chance. Head balls can be used to take a shot, pass to a teammate, or clear the ball out from in front of your goal.

If you watch World Cup soccer, the players are constantly heading the ball. Youth league, high school, and college players would do well to take a lesson from them.

Heading for the Goal

Using your head to shoot the ball is probably the best and most common reason to learn a good, effective head ball.

Many, many times the ball will be airborne as it's centered from the sideline or a corner kick. You can't afford to wait for it to drop, because you can bet your shin guards that the defense isn't going to be waiting. Leap up and get your head on the ball. If you're tall, you have it made.

Bet You Didn't Know

Although he's extremely skilled in other areas, World Cup player Brian McBride won his spot on the United States National Team almost entirely on his outstanding heading ability.

Head 'em Off at the Pass

Head balls can be used in the middle of the field for passing. If you're skilled enough, you can redirect an airborne ball to land right at the feet of a teammate. And if you are battling for position with an opponent, you better leap into the air to get that ball first. As you get into position, try to have a sense of where your teammates are, so you'll know which way to head the ball.

Block Head

You have to use your head defensively, too, but be careful how you do it. On a corner kick or a cross in front of the goal, you want to jump up, box out the attacker, and head the ball away from the goal. That's not only a common use for the header, but it's really required of a good defender.

Another possible defensive use of the head is to block a shot. This is not recommended. Shots on goal can be coming in at speeds close to 100 mph, and your little head is going to be snapped back like a duck at a shooting gallery if it gets in the way. Notice how dainty human necks are. They weren't meant for this kind of abuse.

Heads Up!

I took a ball in my face when I was playing for the New York State League, well after I'd learned to head a ball correctly. Nonetheless, I got my head in the way of a rocket of a shot. Not only did it sting like crazy, but also I lost my vision in half my eye for about a week from a bruised retina.

If, however, you are far enough away from the shot (or pass) that you can judge its relatively mild strength and velocity, then you might want to use your head to block it.

Primarily, head balls are used in tight situations, when you need to get to the ball fast. If you don't use your head in situations like this, you're going to get beaten every time.

The Least You Need to Know

➤ Contact the ball with your forehead.

➤ Get into position, watch the ball, lean back, and snap your body forward.

➤ Head balls can go forward, backward, or sideways.

➤ You need to learn to head at every position, because head balls can be used to pass, score goals, and block shots.

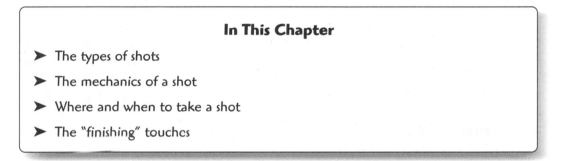

Chapter 9

A Shot in the Park

In This Chapter

➤ The types of shots

➤ The mechanics of a shot

➤ Where and when to take a shot

➤ The "finishing" touches

It's been 88 minutes of shutout play. The ball has changed hands (or feet, if you will) a thousand times. Tight defense, outstanding goalkeeping, and missed opportunities have been the name of the game.

Suddenly, your teammate gets the ball on a breakaway cut to the corner. You sprint to the center, getting open, and he sends you a clean, crisp pass. You sprint toward it, an all-out foot race with the goalie. Your foot reaches the ball a millisecond before the goalie does. You nudge it past him into the goal. Score! The game is yours!

No Shots, No Glory

Soccer is a real team game. The team shifts as one unit and works together passing toward one goal. The final touch may be the most spectacular, but without the preceding passes, it couldn't have happened. Nonetheless, it's still the shot that gets all the attention.

The shot is the glory play. In the low-scoring soccer game, it's the only thing that the news picks up on. Even if the shot misses, it will frequently make the highlight film at 11:00. And if the ball goes in . . . well, forget it. Then the clip is played over and over.

So what does it take to accomplish this ultimate high-profile play? How do you get your 15 seconds of fame on the field?

Learning the Lingo

Frequently you'll hear soccer players referring to *finishing* or a *finisher*. This is a fairly standard soccer term for a shot or the shooter.

Choose Your Weapon

A goal doesn't have to be pretty to win the game. There are any number of ways to get that ball across the goal line, and all of them look the same in the scorebook.

The Bullet

If you have a mental image of a shot on goal, it's probably a zinger of shot that flies into the corner of the net. This would be a shot that has been taken with the instep. And even though the shots in a game will come in all shapes and sizes, the instep shot will dominate. This is the hardest, fastest, and most forceful shot you can make, so in general players are going to try to score with it more often than any other kind of shot.

Slip 'em a Mickey

The big bang looks impressive, but sometimes a sneaky little tap past the goalie is going to get better results. If you're in a race to the ball with the goalie and you're lucky enough to beat him to it, a nudge is all you need, because he'll be way out of position and the goal will be wide open.

This tap, usually with the inside of the foot, is also what you want to use if you're right near the goal. If you have the opening, accuracy is a lot more important than speed. The last thing you want to do it use your instep and find that you've sent the ball flying right over the crossbar.

Be Heading

A coach wants smart players out on the field, but she also hopes that they can use their heads in more ways than one. Heading the ball into the goal is one of the best ways to score.

Very often, whether on a corner kick or a cross, the ball is going to be sent across the field in the air winding up five or six feet above the ground right in front of the goal. Do you think the defense is going to wait around until the ball drops to let you get your foot on it? Not a chance.

Knowing this, you have to be jumping like a frog on uppers. If you've read Chapter 8, which covers heading, then you already know how to connect forehead and ball. If you haven't read it yet, then I suggest stopping right here and going back there, because you're never going to be an effective shooter unless the head shot is part of your repertoire.

A Pass in Fancy Trappings

While you're going to have to learn the tricks of the trade when it comes to getting the ball into the net, physically, the shot is going to be nothing new. You already learned all the skills you're going to need when you learned how to pass. Think of the shot as a pass: you're just passing the ball into the net rather than to a teammate. But just in case you don't believe me, here's a quick nine-step overview of what you need to do for a shot.

1. Use the instep for power shots.
2. Use the inside of foot for more accurate, shorter shots.
3. Plant your foot on the side of the ball.
4. Point your planting foot in the direction you want the ball to go.
5. If you want the ball to be lofted, place your planting foot farther back.
6. If you want to make sure the ball stays on the ground, make sure your knee is over the ball.
7. Keep your head down.
8. Follow through.
9. Use your head to take the shot if the ball is in the air.

It's not just the physical motion of kicking a shot that's similar to making a pass. It's also the strategy. Just as in passing, you don't want to put every muscle into booting the ball if it only needs to be tapped.

This is especially important to remember because most of the time you're going to be shooting a moving ball. Just as a one-touch pass is going to be less accurate than a two-touch pass, the shot that's taken while a ball is in motion is going to lose some accuracy. If you can add accuracy by using the inside of your foot, so much the better.

The Thrill of the Drill

If you want to work on your one-touch shots, set up a game against a wall with a couple of other players. Mark off a goal area and then line up in front of it. The first player kicks the ball into the "goal" and then runs to the end of the line. The next player has to get the rebound and take a one-touch shot back to the wall. He then runs to the end of the line, and so on. If a player misses the shot, he is eliminated. The last remaining player is the winner. You can vary the difficulty by changing the size of the goal or the distance from the wall.

The only real difference between a pass and a shot is that a pass goes to a player and the shot goes away from a player. Don't forget this or you'll find all your shots ending up in the goalkeeper's hands.

Bet You Didn't Know

Major League Soccer prides itself on being one of the higher scoring leagues in the world, and they're averaging a mere 3.3 goals per game.

Pick Your Spot

Hit it where they ain't is an old baseball adage, and it works for soccer, too. The goal is a big area. It's eight feet high and 24 feet long. Your average goalie is five foot something high and only about a foot wide. That leaves quite a bit of extra space.

Nonetheless, soccer is a low-scoring game, with one or two goals a team being the average. Part of this is due to excellent goalie play. Let's not diminish their role. But another part often is the fault of the shooter.

When an inexperienced player takes a shot on goal, he's got three things working against him:

1. A natural tendency to kick the ball to another person (unfortunately, it's the goalie in this case);

2. A psychedelic blob (the goalkeeper's shirt) in the center of his visual field, drawing his eyes and therefore his shot in that direction;

3. An instinctual inclination to kick the ball in the center of the goal because then there's less chance of missing his target altogether.

As a result, when you work on your shooting skills, one of the main things you have to do is to train your mind to go against its natural tendencies. The first thing you need to do is to refigure the goal in your mind. It is not an eight by twenty-four foot rectangle. Instead, this figure shows, it's more of a combination of several two-foot wide sections, the shaded areas in the figure.

Areas of the goal to shoot for.

In other words, aim for the edges. Mentally block off the center of the goal. Your targets are the areas extending from the crossbar or goal posts to about two feet in.

If you like taking shots against a wall, then you can physically draw this "new goal" onto the wall. See how many times you can score. You can also use the regular goal, using colored string to mark off the edges. Play the game without a goalie. If the ball goes into the center of the goal, it's a goal kick. You can only score by placing the ball on the edges of the goal.

Practice, Practice, Practice

Just as with any skill, practice makes perfect, but practicing your shot can be a little harder than you think. You certainly can't go on your own in front of the huge goal and just take a few shots. Even my grandmother could score in that situation, and she's on a walker. You're going to have to make it more gamelike.

There are a few ways to do this, with the wall games mentioned earlier in this chapter being some of them. These games can narrow your goal options and force you to have quicker reaction times, both important shooting skills. The other advantage to the wall is that the ball is going to come right back to you. You're going to get a whole lot more shooting time in if you shoot against the wall than if you shoot into the empty goal.

Coach's Corner

Don't be lackadaisical when you're practicing your shots. Shooting in a game is a high-pressure situation. If you haven't practiced with that amount of intensity, you'll never be able to transfer what you've learned in practice to what you need on the field.

Adding a goalie helps some, but a goalkeeper alone hardly makes for a gamelike situation. If you find yourself in this situation, force yourself to shoot from outside the 18. Not only is the long-distance shot a good weapon for you to develop, but it also gives the goalie a fighting chance to stop the ball, thereby making you work a little harder. Or have your friend get out by the sideline and feed you crosses to give you practice at game speeds.

The Thrill of the Drill

If you only have two players to practice shooting, you might want to try setting up as two attackers rather than as an attacker and a goalie. This way you can practice shooting after a cross or a lofted ball. Or try receiving the ball with your back to the goal and then turning and shooting. To make it more difficult, however, reduce the goal area.

The best way to work on your shot, however, is with a defender on the field with you. You can work one-on-one or with a group. Sometimes it helps to make the sides slightly uneven, with one or two more attackers than defenders. That way, you're going to have more shooting opportunities, yet you'll still have the pressure. After you've worked out this way for a while, even up the sides and see how you do under gamelike conditions.

Thinking It Through

Shooting is not entirely physical. Your brain plays a huge role in getting off a good shot. Of course, any shot that scores a goal is undoubtedly a "good" shot, but some good shots are better than others, relying on strategy more than luck to get them into the net. There are a few tricks to learn that might help you increase your chances of getting that ball across the goal line.

Go Low

The pretty shots are the ones that sail into the uppermost corners, just out of reach of the keeper, but these are not high percentage shots. By aiming for the upper corners, you're narrowing your target considerably. If you loft the ball just a tad too much, the ball is going to go sailing right over the goal. So keep the ball low, that way if it rises, it will rise right into another part of the goal.

Coach's Corner

At the youth level, where small players are asked to play as keepers in a regulation goal, shooting high is often a sure way to score. This mindset has consequences when players get older and stronger though, i.e. shots sailing over the crossbar. Youth players therefore need to be in environments where keeping shots low is rewarded as much as higher shots.

There's another reason to keep them low, as well. The ones in the upper corners are probably out of the goalie's reach, but anywhere else in the upper half of the goal is an easy play for her. She can remain standing and catch the ball or she can reach up and punch it over. Because a high shot allows her to remain upright, shifting is easier, too.

But it's entirely different if the shot is a low one. Now the goalie has to shift and still have time to get down behind the ball. She might even have to dive to get it. On top of that, there's no way she's going to be punching a low ball. If she tries to punch it up and over, she's just going to punch it up and into the goal. Low balls don't have an option like that. They must be handled decisively or some attacker is going to have her toe on it, trying to put the rebound into the goal.

Careful Planning

When you take the shot, think about where you want to put it. If your mind isn't actively engaged in your shot, you're just going to send it right into the middle of the net, where the goalie will be waiting.

As you wind up, make a quick assessment of where the goalie is and where the defensive players are. Then analyze where you would have the most success and try to put the ball there. Your analysis has to be done in a split second or everything is going to change on you.

There is some analyzing that can be done ahead of time that might help you with your split second decision. Take some mental notes on the goalkeeper as he warms up or during the game.

Coach's Corner

Don't plan your shot too far in advance. You don't want to be waiting for a pass from a teammate, thinking you're then going to send it into the right-lower corner, only to find that when you do finally get the ball, there's a defender right there.

Does he have more trouble going in one direction than another? Is he reluctant to dive for low balls? What does he work on during warmup? If he's avoiding something, then maybe that area will be vulnerable. Does he hang back or is he aggressive, coming out to get the ball? You might be able to beat him.

Follow the Shot

It would be nice if we could all just sit back and admire a great shot as it sails toward the goal, but a good attacker wouldn't dream of it. Take the shot and then charge right behind it. Many a goal has been scored after the initial shot has bounced off a crossbar or a defender. Goalies can't always get their hands on the ball, either. If they have to punch or slap the ball away from the goal, you might get a gift if you've followed in that ball.

Choose Your Moment

There's a time to shoot and a time to pass to someone else and a smart soccer player better learn the difference. It's painful to see a team work the ball down the field with a series of well-planned passes just to see it fall apart in front of the goal because some overeager attacker tried to get a shot off when he was in the middle of a group of defenders. Don't take the shot if it's not there. If there's a group of defenders around you, then chances are that someone else is wide open.

That said, you also don't want to be a chicken. If you have the shot, even if it's not perfect, then take it. Don't play around with the ball in front of the goal, looking for the "ideal" shot.

Stage Fright

Some teams know how to finish. Other teams just can't get the shot in the goal no matter how many opportunities they get. The same is true for players. A player can have all the skills in the world, but if he's reluctant to take that shot, he's not going to be much of a scoring threat.

Coach's Corner

If your team is having trouble scoring, you might try to create that all-important desire to shoot by offering a prize of some sort if they can get the ball into the goal. The successful players might get out of wind sprints the next day or be treated to ice cream, and so on, depending on the level of play. This is only successful at the younger levels, however, because players at the higher levels have already developed their soccer personalities and presumably have an incentive to win and don't need any extra push to score.

The drive and desire to put that ball in the goal is a real personality trait. It has got to be first and foremost in a player's mind as he approaches the goal. Coaches need to be aware of which players have that deep-down burning desire to score and which of them don't.

Finish with a Flourish

If you find yourself frustrated in front of the goal, there are a number of things you can do. The simplest thing to do is to train your brain to think of the goal as the exclamation point at the end of your soccer statement. Put a goal at the end of every drill you do.

For example, if you're practicing your dribble by doing a slalom weave through some cones, put a goal at the end of the slalom course. This way, rather than merely dribbling through the course, you dribble and then shoot. If you're doing a passing drill, then pass down the field and shoot at the end of the drill. If you're learning how to trap out of the air, then trap the ball, settle it, and shoot. Pretty soon it will be ingrained.

Shooting at Point Blank Range

The other way to beef up your shooting skills is to put yourself into a game situation where you have no other choice but to shoot. There are a couple of ways to do this.

In the first, you want to set up a game situation where you don't have any choice but to shoot. If you have a portable goal, place it on the 18, opposite the regular goal. The penalty box now serves as the playing field, and the ball is out of bounds if it leaves the box. Put a goalie in each goal and two teams of forwards into the penalty box. Each team has a goal to defend and a goal to shoot on. Throw the ball up in the air and start shooting. With the dribbling and passing options removed, you are forced to take the shots no matter how reluctant a shooter you are.

If you don't have a portable goal, there's another shooting situation you can set up. Using the 18 again, set up four smallish goals (about eight feet) using cones, one on each side of the penalty box. You should also put cones in the regular goal to make it smaller, keeping things even. This figure shows the setup.

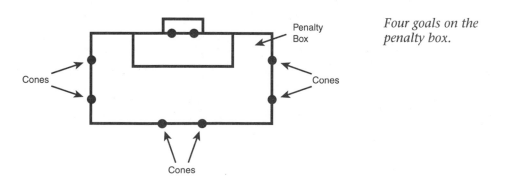

Four goals on the penalty box.

Bet You Didn't Know

This four goal situation is also an outstanding opportunity to indirectly hone the defensive skills of the forwards. They really have to be aware of sticking with the opposing player because the second he's open, he's going to be taking a shot.

There are no goalies defending. Again, place two teams of forwards in the box. This time, each team is defending two goals and shooting at two goals. With more shooting opportunities, you'll be tempted to take more shots.

In most sports, you want your reactions to become second nature. Even though shooting has a lot of strategy to it, you need to first make sure that you have the mentality to ìgo for itî already imprinted on your brain, so that you don't waste any scoring opportunity.

The Least You Need to Know

➤ Shots can be taken in a variety of ways, with various parts of the body, at varying speeds.

➤ A shot is a pass dressed up, with the only difference being that you're shooting away from a target rather than to a target.

➤ Watch the goalie and watch your defenders to make sure that you're not forcing the shot or missing a shooting opportunity.

➤ Practice makes perfect, but make sure that the practice is going to replicate gamelike conditions.

Chapter 10

Minding the Goal

The goalkeeper. The last line of defense. The handman. The netminder. The tender. It's a scary job, but someone's got to do it.

Like the soldier who dives on the grenade to save his buddies in the foxhole, the player who chooses to play in the goal must be a special type of player. Self-confident and selfless at the same time, the goalie is someone who's willing to risk the blame for a shot at glory. He's someone with good eyesight, good judgement, and no fear of falling. He's a team leader, and he's got a very tough job to perform.

The End of the Line

Many people think of the goalie the same way they might think of a pitcher in base-ball or a quarterback in football, and in some sense this is true. All three positions require leadership and a certain desire to be in the spotlight.

But that's where the similarities end. The fielders on a baseball team can't do their job without a good performance from the pitcher, and a football team can't score unless the quarterback makes the plays, but a soccer team would love it if its goalie never even got within 20 feet of the ball. Technically, if the rest of the team is doing its job, the goalie won't have to do his. Unfortunately, this is rarely the case.

And because you're going to want to play the odds, you're going to want to learn what skills and strategy a goalkeeper needs to excel in the net. You're going to need to be agile, quick, and physically fit. You're going to need to dive, catch, kick, and throw. You're going to have to be a physics major and a student of the game. And you're going to have to be a loudmouth.

Take a Stance

The stance seems to be the logical place to start. Before a goalie can do anything on the field, she has to be prepared to catch the ball. If the ball is at the other end of the field, the goalie can be upright and loose, yet on the alert for a quick change in the tide. Then, as the ball is approaching, she needs to get into the ready position.

Eyes following every move the ball makes, the goalkeeper should stand about three or four feet off the goal line, ready to move forward or sideways, depending on how the ball is approaching. Her weight should be slightly forward, with knees bent and feet about shoulder width apart and her arms loose and relaxed. As the ball gets nearer, she moves into position and gets up on the balls of her feet and brings her hands up to about her midsection, so that all parts of the body are ready to spring into action. On some more advanced teams goalies will be out of the 18 when the ball is at the other end. Some coaches consider goalkeepers field players who can use their hands.

Narrowing the Angle

So now, as your team's goalkeeper, you know *how* you should be standing, but you're still ignorant as to *where* you should be standing. It all depends on how the ball is approaching you and how far away it is.

You should be aware of where the ball is and what's happening to it, even at the other end of the field. If a long ball suddenly comes, you should already be in position to scoop it up. Thus little adjustments may need to be made even when the ball is in the other half.

However, until the ball crosses the center line, you don't have to react to it. Save your energy. But once that orb is heading your way, get moving. If the ball is coming down the side, you have to do something called *narrowing the angle*.

In its simplest terms, narrowing the angle just means getting your body between the ball and the goal, but it's slightly more involved than that. Here is a diagram of narrowing the angle, but it basically means that the shooter has a narrower area to shoot for on the nearest side to him.

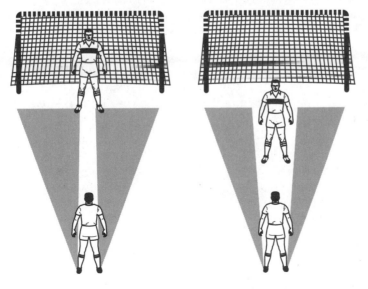

Narrowing the angle.

To put it another way, if a shooter is coming at the goal dead on, he can go to the three-foot gap to the right or the three-foot gap to the left of you, and there's little you can do about it. If you move two feet to the right, for instance, you narrow the gap to one foot on that side, but you leave a tempting, hard to defend five-foot gap on the other side.

But if the shooter is coming at an angle, it's a whole different story. If you move two feet to the right this time (assuming that the shooter is approaching that side of the goal), then you essentially limit that easier shot and force him to go wide for the far side of the goal. Not only is this a much longer shot for him to take, but it also gives you extra time to react to it. You can also narrow the angle if the ball is coming straight toward you by moving out on the ball, as you can see in this figure.

But limit how far you move. You really don't want to go out farther than the 6.

Narrowing the angle on a straight approach.

Moving forward puts you in a good position for a number of reasons:

➤ You narrow the angle.

➤ You can psych out the approaching player who might attempt to take a shot too quickly, thinking you are coming after him.

➤ You are nearer to the ball if the dribble gets too far out in front, enabling you to snatch it away before the player gets a shot off.

The more you play, the more you'll realize how much of the goalkeeper's game is a head game. If you can intimidate an approaching shooter, you've got her. She'll rush her shot or lose the ball altogether. Also, if there's a breakaway, move out and then move back, both to throw off the attacker, but also to slow her down, so your team-mates might have a chance to catch up. And the more talk, as long as it is constructive, the better.

Getting the Scoop

Eventually, however, the shot is going to come and that means it's time to catch the ball. If you don't know by now, the goalie is the only player on the soccer team who can use her hands, and that is a tremendous advantage in a game where feet and heads rule. Whether the ball is flying high in the air or rolling along the ground, the goal-keeper can reach in and snatch it away from danger.

Where you pick up the ball is going to determine the way you pick up the ball. Grabbing a corner kick that's high in the air is going to be a little different than scooping up a dribbler headed for the corner of the goal.

Merrily We Roll Along

As part of the soccer team, and because you were most likely a field player at some point, your first instinct when you see a ball rolling along the ground is going to be to stick your foot out to deal with it. Don't! You've been given the gift of hands. Use them.

To pick up a roller, you first want to get into position. Move your entire body behind the ball, and get down on one knee. This is just a little extra insurance in case the ball hits you wrong, takes a bad hop, or slips out of your hands. Your body is still there to keep it from rolling into the goal.

As the ball comes in, scoop your hands underneath the ball and hug it up to your chest.

Coach's Corner

Just because the ball is a lazy roller, don't get complacent and bend over to get it rather than getting down on one knee. It just takes one little clump of dirt to bounce the ball away and your legs are a fraction of the blockade that your body provides. Not to mention the fact that it's a whole lot harder to get a good scoop when you're not at ball level.

A Shot in the Gut

A waist-high ball is probably the easiest shot to handle, provided you have good hands and you've gotten yourself into position. You want your hands facing out toward the incoming ball as is shown in this figure.

When the shot comes in, you catch it with your hands, giving a little with your arms to take the edge off it, and then immediately scoop under the ball with both hands and hug it to your chest, as shown here.

Ready hands.

Scooping under the ball.

Hugging the ball to your chest ensures that you'll hold on to it. If you have the ball out in your hands and an attacker happens to bump you, there's a good chance that ball will come bouncing out. You don't, however, want to catch the ball in that underhand scoop method because that method has no give. If you try to catch the shot that way, the ball will probably just ricochet right off your chest.

Reach for the Sky

Sometimes, however, the scoop is going to be impossible. When the ball is coming in high on a cross, you're going to have to leap up and grab it between your two hands. Of course, as soon as you have a good grip, you're obviously going to bring it down and hug it to your chest, but the movement isn't quite as smooth.

You're really going have to work out in the weight room to be able to perform this play. The ball might be moving upward of 80 m.p.h., and you are planning to use only your two hands to stop it. Those two hands better be attached to some pretty strong arms.

And don't forget, you won't be alone. Just as you're jumping up to grab the cross, the opponent is jumping up to head it. Just because you can stretch a little more and get the ball in your hands doesn't mean you won't have a head crashing into your bicep an instant later. Bring that ball down to your chest ASAP!

Coach's Corner

Sometimes it's just a little too crowded in front of the goal for a goalie to grab a ball that's being crossed. The odds of an attacker or even a teammate knocking his arm are too great. Instead, the goalkeeper may choose to punch the ball out of the way. The punch gives him a little extra reach, more than a two-handed catch would, just to make sure he gets to the ball first.

You don't always want to get into the fray, remember. If your defensive back who is a great header is right there, let him take it and you stand back ready to react to the rebound. Because if you do try catch the ball and fail, then you're going to be caught out of position when someone else goes after the loose ball. This is where communication is vital.

Big Tipper

With an opening eight feet high and twenty-four feet wide, there are going to be times when you just can't grab that ball. Let's hope, however, that you can at least get a piece of it.

Goalkeepers have to practice tipping the ball over the crossbar or around the goalposts. This tip can be done with the entire hand (more like a slap), with the fingers, or with the fists. The fists obviously have more power behind them, but the fingertips have more reach. Use what you need.

Yes, tipping the ball over or around the goal is going to result in a corner kick, but it's better than a goal. In practice, spend time tipping balls rather than scooping them, even if they're very catchable. You need to get a good feel for just how hard you need to flick your fingers.

But be careful. Don't get into the habit of tipping balls you can catch.

Coach's Corner

If you can't get the ball up or out, consider slapping at it to direct it toward a teammate. This has got to be a last ditch effort, however, because the last thing you want is a loose ball in front of the goal.

And if you end up flicking the ball into the goal, instead, don't beat yourself up. Remember that for the ball to even reach you, every single person on the field failed in some way.

Dive Right In

A good dive is essential to a goalkeeper. If you can't bring yourself to throw your body on the ground, then maybe you need to find another position. Oh, and did I mention that you're not allowed to use your hands to break your fall?

A goalkeeper's hands have to be free to catch the ball or slap it out of the way, so they can't be used to ease the crash of your body against the dirt. By the time they're done breaking the fall, the ball is going to be in the net.

Bet You Didn't Know

When you watch soccer on TV, you might think the goalies have it awfully easy. It seems as if the ball is always coming right to them and they don't have to dive all that much. What's happening is that they are actually so experienced that they know how to position themselves and are not caught unawares by too many shots. So actually, the better you are, the less you're going to need to dive to save a shot.

Bet You Didn't Know

MetroStar and former World Cup goalie Tony Meola got more than he bargained for when he dove for a shot drilled by Tampa Bay Mutiny player Alan Prampin. He crashed head first into the goalpost, saving the ball but getting a Grade 1 concussion. He blacked out for a moment and although he regained consciousness, he has no memory of the game, although he continued to play. Talk about using goalie instinct!

The dive is probably the hardest skill to teach a goalkeeper who is reluctant to try. A player either has the guts to throw his body on the ground or he doesn't, and it's hard to change that. There are some things you can do to make it easier, however.

To start, sit on the ground, facing another player who has a couple of soccer balls. That player is going to throw balls to the left and right of you and you're going to fall on your side to try to block them. Then, when you feel comfortable doing that, move up onto your knees. Again, have someone roll balls to your right and left and you dive on top of them. Another way is to get in a push-up position and leap out at a ball. All these tricks help you get comfortable falling onto the ground from a lower level, so it won't be so intimidating when you have to do it from a standing position.

Remember, goalies get to wear padded clothing, so diving doesn't hurt as much as you think it might.

After the Save

Once you've stopped that ball, whether it be by catching, diving, tipping, or punching, you can't just sit back and admire your own prowess in the goal. There are things to be done.

If you've tipped the ball out of bounds, then you have to deal with a corner kick. If you've punched the ball out of the fray, then you have to hope that a teammate has cleared it further downfield or you have to jump into position to defend another shot on goal. If you've caught the ball, however, you have a couple of options.

The Punt

One option is long ball. A goalie is allowed to *punt* the ball downfield as far as his foot can send it. Some pro players can probably send it 80 yards!

The punt is used when your team is at a disadvantage. The other team might be better and most of the play has been at your end. In that case, you want to get the ball to the other end of the field by punting because it appears it's not going to get down there any other way. You also might use the punt when your team is losing, whether or not there's an imbalance. The punt is the fastest way to get the ball from one end of the field to the other, and when you're losing, you don't want to waste any time. Finally, you can use the punt when the other options just don't seem to fit—for example, when no one's open or in good position.

The punt is used more at younger levels than at higher levels. Because the younger players don't have strong arms, their throws are not going to take the ball very long distances, so it's better to punt the ball and get it out as far away from the goal as possible.

Learning the Lingo

A *punt* is a kick that begins with the ball held about waist high between the goalie's two hands. The goalie then takes a couple of steps, drops the ball as his kicking foot is moving up, and boots the ball as hard as he can.

The Throw

The throw is another option. This is a one-arm throw that is a combination of a baseball throw and a discus throw. Because the hand can't get a grip on the soccer ball the way it can with a baseball, the goalie has to long-arm the ball more, but it's essentially the same motion.

When it's thrown, the ball has a slight loft to it, but it's more of a direct bullet than the punt is, so the throw can be targeted at a teammate. The top players can throw almost to midfield, so this is really an excellent weapon when you want to maintain possession. A quick throw can turn the tide from defense into attack mode.

The Roll

The roll is used when you're winning the game. It's a good time waster. You, as the goalie, have the ball. You wait a little (not too much, however, because you don't want to be called for wasting time), and then after the opponents clear out, you roll the ball out to your defensive back. He might dribble it slowly up the sideline, or he might even tap it back to you.

If you get it back, you have to remember that you may not pick it up with your hands. This is a new FIFA rule, designed to limit the back-to-the-goalie play. But, if the offense has cleared out, dribble the ball yourself up until about the 18 and then boot it down the field.

Special Circumstances

Those are the goalie basics, but the beauty of soccer is that it takes what is a simple game on the surface and throws you a few curves. Goalkeepers are given the extra challenges of corner kicks, direct kicks, and especially penalty kicks. On top of that, nearly every goalie should learn how to play the field.

Corner Kicks

Corner kicks are a big threat to a goalkeeper. The opponents have usually loaded the box—they have their best kicker in the corner and their best headers in front of you. What to do? The first thing you do is make sure you have a defensive player standing on the front post. Then you stand near in mid-goal, about three or four yards off the line, as you can see in this figure.

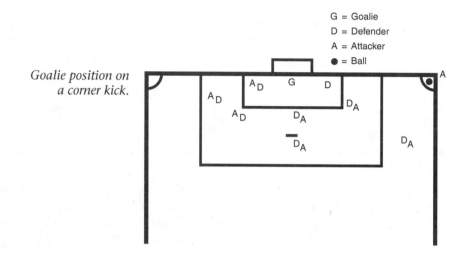

Goalie position on a corner kick.

You know the kicker is probably going to aim for the 6, so being a couple feet away from that allows you to move out and catch the ball if it's heading there. If it's short or farther out near the 18, then you have to step back into the goal and wait and see what happens.

Heads Up

Be careful of the other team taking a shot while you are trying to set up.

Direct and Indirect Kicks

On any direct or indirect kick in front of the goal, you're going to want to set up a wall of human bodies to help block off a part of the goal and therefore make your job a little easier. Stand on the post nearest to the ball and line up the first player in the wall. Make sure she's directly in line with the ball and the post, because you don't want to give the other team an opportunity to sneak the ball around the near side of the wall. This figure shows the how the wall should be lined up.

After the wall is set up on the near side, the goalie takes her position in front of the goal on the far side. If the wall holds, the size of the goal and therefore the chances of a score are greatly reduced.

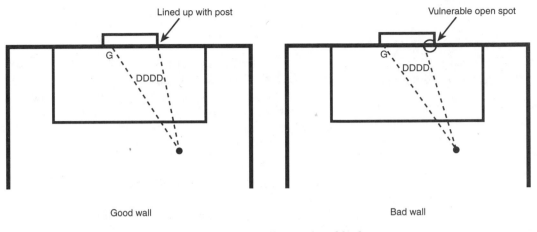

Lining up the wall—good and bad.

Penalty Kicks

Penalty kicks are few and far between—thank goodness. It's a one-on-one shot between a kicker and a goalie, with an immense amount of pressure on each. Fortunately, for the goalie, the kicker is in a worse position, because no one expects the goalie to stop the ball. If he does, it's all gravy.

Most keepers pick a side beforehand and start to dive that way as the ball is being kicked. It's a 50–50 chance, which is better odds than not moving at all until the ball is kicked. There are ways to improve the odds, however.

Study the opposition beforehand. If you know who the top player on the team is, chances are he'll be the one taking the kick. See which side he kicks to. If you don't know anything about the kicker, try to direct his kick one way or the other. Make an obvious move in one direction at the beginning of his motion. It may distract him enough that he changes his mind at the last minute and flubs the kick. One goalie in World Cup play started screaming about the placement of the ball. He didn't really care. He just wanted to get the kicker rattled.

Playing the Field

A goalie's job doesn't end with blocking the ball. One of the goalkeeper's biggest responsibilities is communicating with her teammates, especially the defense. With the entire field spread out before her,

Heads Up!

At high school level and below, it's helpful to have two goalies splitting the job. That way, the goalie who's off duty can get some field play when he's not in the goal. It also helps to know that if a goalie goes down with an injury, there's a reliable substitute.

121

Bet You Didn't Know

The Paraguay goalkeeper, Jose Luis Chilavert, is also the team's direct kicker if the kick is down near the opponent's goal. He races down the field, kicks the shot, and then races back to his post.

The goalie can work out at home by herself, too, as long as she has a ball and a wall. Throw the ball as hard as you can at the wall and catch the rebound. Move closer. This helps both your reaction time and your catching ability. Now spread your legs and put the ball in between them, holding it with one hand in front of you and one hand behind you. Switch hand positions without letting the ball drop to the ground. This is another agility improver.

the goalie has the best visual sense of the game of anyone on the field. Let the defense know what's happening.

To really understand what the field players have to do, however, you need to have played the field yourself. To help your defenders, you need to put in some time as a defender yourself. And if you can play some offense, too, then it will help you better understand the attackers who are coming at you.

Not only will personal knowledge help you to direct your teammates, but you'll also better understand which parts of your goal are vulnerable and you'll be more aware when your team starts to malfunction.

Another reason to be familiar with field play is that some teams like to have their goalkeepers come out of the goal and play the field in the last few minutes of the game if the team is down by one goal. This gives the team an extra man on the offensive end, which might result in the tying goal. And if a goal is scored against them because of the open goal, it's not going to really make a difference if they lose by one point or by two.

Be the Best You Can Be

While a good team should be able to keep the ball away from their goalie, a great goalie can save a mediocre team. You need to improve your stamina, agility, and reaction time by working on them every single day.

While the goalkeeper is a vital part of the team, her practice really should be slightly different. The first part of practice, she should work with the other goalie on the team, rolling then later kicking the ball to either side. Work on diving, tipping, slapping, and catching.

The second part of practice should be with the team, so you become familiar with game situations. Presumably, your coach has saved the small-sided games and the full game for the end of practice, so this jibes nicely. You need some match conditions to practice your mental and tactical game. The best dive in the world isn't going to be much good if you've judged the shot all wrong.

The Least You Need to Know

➤ Your first job as goalie is to narrow the angle as the ball approaches you.

➤ You can block the ball from going into the goal by catching it, tipping it, slapping it, punching it, or kicking it

➤ Once you've caught the ball, you can send it back out into the field with a punt, a throw, a roll, or a kick.

➤ Diving should be done without the hands, because you need your hands to stop the ball.

➤ All goalies should learn to play in the field as well.

Part 3
The Game Plan

At the beginning stages of the game, you might think that just mastering the footwork will be enough to turn you into a soccer superstar. But you're not even close. Soccer is a game of carefully planned strategies, devious tactics, and mental toughness.

Chapter 11 starts you off easy. The basic positions are described, along with what type of player would be best for each. Then comes the hard part of combining those players into a formation that would best emphasize the skills of your team.

But that's just the beginning. There's a whole lot of strategy to be worked out right from the starting whistle. Chapter 12 deals with the offensive and defensive strategies for each start and restart, while Chapter 13 goes into the game's strategy in general. Knowing where to run and how to move when you're nowhere near the ball is a large part of being a top player.

In Formation

A successful soccer team is so much more than a group of 11 athletes all wearing the same color T-shirts. It's a careful balance of aggressive defenders, generous playmakers, skillful finishers, and a tenacious goalie.

Who goes where, and how do they all fit together? This is one of a coach's greatest challenges. It's one thing to teach a group of players the nuances and skills of soccer, but it's quite another to put 11 players with varying skills together into one cohesive unit.

Who Does What Where?

According to the rule book, there are really only two positions on a soccer team: the goalkeeper and the field player. The field player can't pick up the ball with his hands (unless it's a throw-in situation), and the goalkeeper may use his hands within the penalty box. Nonetheless, most teams classify their field players into three distinct, yet overlapping, groups:

1. Forwards
2. Midfielders
3. Defenders

Despite these assignments, the positions in soccer are fluid. Except for the goalie, any player might find himself on any part of the field. The defenders can score, and occasionally do, and the forwards can be all the way back in front of their own goal defending on a corner kick. Nonetheless, there are characteristics and expectations associated with each position.

Forward March

The forwards are the finishers. Like a baker with colored icing in hand, the forwards take all the carefully measured passes, detailed plays, and mundane cuts that have been made all the way down the field, and put on the all-important decorative garnish. They put the ball in the goal.

Forwards begin the game at the center line and generally spend most of the game on the other side of it, close to the opponent's (or attackers) goal. This figure shows a typical lineup.

A typical soccer lineup.

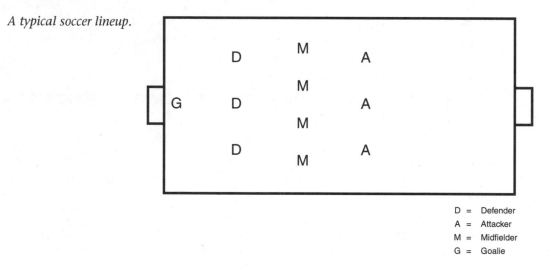

D = Defender
A = Attacker
M = Midfielder
G = Goalie

A forward's task is to score. The number of forwards usually ranges from one to possibly five, but the majority of teams like to have two or three players in this position.

Are You a Forward?

If a player has the drive and desire to put the ball into the goal, that's the only characteristic she needs to be successful at the position. But other traits help as well. You'll make a good forward if you are

➤ fast, the better to outrun the defense,

➤ a good dribbler, the better to outmaneuver the defense,

➤ a good header, to beat the defense to those high balls crossed in from the sideline and corner kicks, and

➤ a top notch shooter, the better to score.

Looking at the position in a negative sense, the ball hogs and weakest passers can be placed on the forward line, because this is less crucial to the position. Of course, wouldn't it be nice not to have to worry about weak players at all?

When You Don't Have the Ball

If a teammate has the ball, forwards should be making short cuts and long runs to get open and to lose their defenders. They have to be aware of how far their midfielders are capable of passing the ball, and alert to being offside.

When the opponents have the ball, defensive responsibilities include chasing and putting pressure on the other teams backs so they cough up the ball in a dangerous part of the field. They also might need to defend for a midfielder who was caught up. They also want to cover a fullback to make sure that he doesn't get the ball. This, however, is rarely an issue because if the other team has the ball, it is going to be doing its best to send the ball away from its goal.

A forward also frequently has to come back and assist the defense during corner kicks or direct kicks, to stand in the wall, or guard any free-floating opponents.

Caught in the Middle

Midfielders generally find themselves in the middle, between the forwards and the fullbacks.

Like the forwards, the number of midfielders varies quite a bit, ranging from two all the way up to six. Three, four, and five, however, seem to be the norm. When you have more than three, some are more offensive midfielders, while others are more defensive midfielders.

Have You Got What It Takes?

Their position naturally makes midfielders a link between offense and defense, so not unexpectedly, a midfielder's main duty is to make sure that link doesn't break.

Learning the Lingo

If you ever hear a player being referred to as a *halfback*, it means that he's a midfielder. Two names, same position.

Learning the Lingo

You might hear coaches referring to players as *creators* or *playmakers*. These are the set-up players who take the ball from the defense and set up scoring opportunities for the forwards. Almost without exception, these playmakers are midfielders.

A midfielder is often called upon to move the ball across the field horizontally. If most of the play seems to be on one side, and the defense all seems to be drifting over that way, a quick switch to the other side by a few well-placed midfield passes can find a wide open forward with a free run ahead of him.

That's not to say the midfielder won't be scoring himself, because frequently he'll be down as close to the goal as any forward. On top of that, the midfielder has to be a top notch defender, because when the ball is at the other end of the field, he has to be back helping out, marking up, and defending the goal.

With all these roles to fill, clearly a midfielder needs to be multitalented and many faceted. He also needs to be

➤ in great shape, because he'll be running from one end of the field to the other,

➤ skilled at passing—forward, backward, and side to side—which is the main way he provides that link, and

➤ a leader and a talker, to communicate with and direct the rest of the team and

➤ able to see the whole field clearly and process information quickly

Many coaches like to put their most skilled players at midfield, because they are involved in all aspects of the play. But on the flip side, this is also a good position for the least skilled players because they aren't quite as vital for scoring or defending as the forwards and fullbacks, respectively. Ideally, of course, a coach would like to have top skills at every position.

Off the Ball

When a teammate has the ball, a midfielder should be looking to get open to receive a pass. He should be thinking about where he can run to throw the defense off balance and set up a forward for a shot or perhaps get into position to take a shot himself. He should drop back behind a teammate who's having trouble and give him the back pass option. If an opponent has the ball, however, the midfielder needs to drop back quickly and mark up on his assigned man.

On many teams that do not have assigned men. Midfielders are thus often asked not to drop back, but to press forward on the person with the ball especially if he has cover behind him.

The Last Line of Defense

The defensive backs, also called fullbacks, are the main line of defense before the goal. They are responsible for

➤ putting a stop to any run made by the attacking team,

➤ beating the attackers to head balls during corner kicks and crosses, and

➤ clearing the ball out from in front of the goal.

Most teams like to have three or four defensive backs, but occasionally you'll see as few as two or as many as five. Over the years soccer has become a more and more defensive game, so coaches don't want to leave the ranks too thin in front of the goal.

Fulfilling a Fullback Role

While the main job of the fullbacks is to stop the attack, they are also considered the beginning of an offensive assault. With both these duties to perform, fullbacks should be

➤ skilled at stealing or intercepting the ball,

➤ athletic and fit enough to stay with their player in a match-up defense,

➤ smart passers,

➤ good headers, and

➤ strong enough to clear the ball out of the danger zone in front of the goal.

This position might be the place for your weakest dribblers. Because you want the ball cleared out of the backfield as fast as possible, any fancy footwork back there can only be viewed as needless dilly-dallying.

The Support System

All players also need to learn how to move on the field when they don't have the ball, but it's especially crucial for a back to have this knowledge. The defensive backs need to shift as a unit. If one defensive back moves out to confront the player with the ball, the others need to drop back and be support in case the attacker slips by.

They are also instrumental in getting offsides called on the other team. The backs need to push forward as a line. One fullback hanging too far back is going to allow any number of forwards to be down there with her, which can create a three-on-one breakaway, for example, for the other team.

Fullbacks can be offensive players, too. They start the attack forward, they can make overlap runs, or be back for support if a midfielder wants to make a back pass. On a corner kick in their favor, they might move way up to put on the pressure near the opponent's goal.

It's a Numbers Game

Now it's time to put all the players together into one cohesive unit. How many forwards do you want? How many defensive backs and how many midfielders? The answer depends a lot on the skills of your players, the strength of the team compared to your opponents, and where your strongest players are going to play.

131

Before you deal with specifics, however, it might be nice to know what your options are. There are quite a few combinations that have been made over the years, but here are a few of the most common.

The formations are referred to by numbers, describing the number of players at each position. The order of the numbers goes from defenders to midfielders to forwards, and the goalie is not included. So in a formation described as 3–5–2, there are three defenders, five midfielders, and two forwards.

4–3–3

The 4–3–3 setup is extremely common at the high school and college levels. The field is somewhat balanced, and the roles of each position are clearly defined and simple to understand. This figure shows a 4–3–3 formation.

The 4–3–3 lineup.

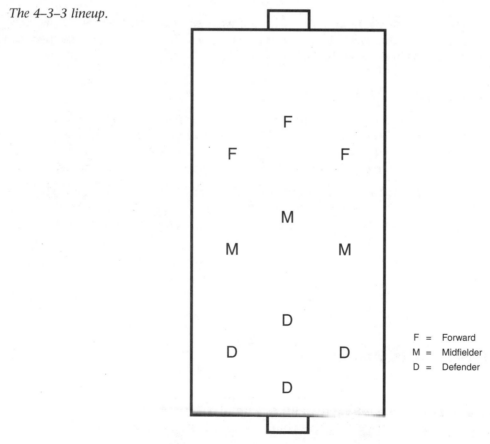

F = Forward
M = Midfielder
D = Defender

Let's begin with the four defensive backs. Usually these backs set up as a diamond. There are two on the wings and there are two in the middle. The one standing back nearer the goal is called the sweeper, while the other one is up closer to the midfielders and is referred to as the stopper.

The sweeper is a strong defensive player who moves back and forth across the field, following the ball, and helping out where he's needed. He doesn't usually mark up a man but remains free to back up in case the opponent slips by the other defenders, and to go for loose balls near the goal. The stopper marks up on the forward striker if the other team has one or follows the center midfielder if the opponent's setup has one of them.

Defining roles such as sweeper and stopper doesn't happen until players are older. Putting younger players behind the rest of the defense as a sweeper can hurt their development. They stay so deep that they are rarely under pressure and do not become comfortable with the ball in traffic.

Learning the Lingo

Sometimes it's hard to remember which of the defenders is the stopper and which is the sweeper. Think of the *stopper* as someone who tries to put a stop to things before they get too serious, and think of the *sweeper* as someone who has to "clean up" after everyone else has made mistakes.

The two wing fullbacks are responsible for the wing forwards. They are also the ones who make most of overlapping offensive runs, although sweepers and stoppers can also make runs.

The midfielders and the forwards set up in two lines of three straight across. They each have two wings and a center.

4–4–2

At first glance, the 4–4–2 seems a little more heavily defensive than the 4–3–3, but actually it's not. It's just a lot more running for the midfielders. This figure shows the setup, which you find at college and pro levels.

In this setup, the fullbacks remain the same as in the previous setup, two wings, a stopper, and a sweeper. The forwards' roles remain basically the same, too, although they are responsible for more territory, because there are only two of them.

It's in the midfield where you see the largest difference. The two center midfielders each are responsible for their half of the field. Even though there are wing midfielders out by the sideline, the center midfielders will frequently have to cover that territory, too, if the wing midfielder is breaking down the sideline. The other center midfielder then shifts over to the middle of the field.

Which brings us to the job of the wing midfielder. This player is sometimes a forward, sometimes a midfielder. If there's an opening on his side, he can make the run toward the goal. If the other midfielder is making the run, instead, then he drops back and shifts over as the two center midfielders shift over.

133

The 4–4–2 lineup and shifts.

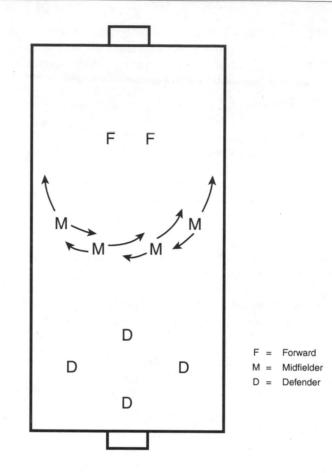

F = Forward
M = Midfielder
D = Defender

The advantage to this setup is that it really provides a lot of motion and shifting and changing of positions on the offensive end, which is what you need to throw off the defense.

3–5–2

The 3–5–2 setup is an even more fluid formation than the 4–4–2, and therefore it is used only at the higher levels. The roles are flexible and don't fit into precise categories, so inexperienced players might have a little trouble executing this formation. This figure shows the lineup before everyone starts shifting.

The beauty of this formation is that it can shift from being a balanced formation to a heavily defensive formation to a heavily offensive formation with relatively little difficulty. Because all opponents are not created equal, this can be a real plus.

The defensive backs are made up of a sweeper and two wing defenders. The midfielders stagger themselves across the middle of the field, with the two inners playing slightly more defensively than the center midfielder and the two wing midfielders. These three have a slightly more offensive bent to their play, but all five of the midfielders are responsible for both ends of the field. The forwards again are each responsible for their half of the field.

The 3–5–2 lineup.

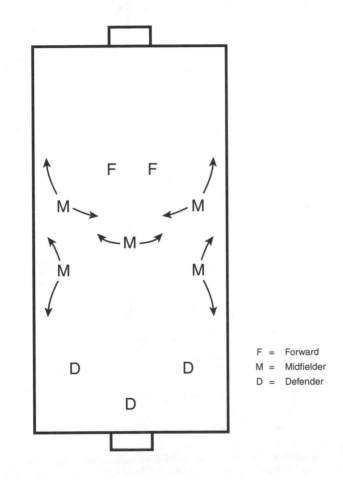

F = Forward
M = Midfielder
D = Defender

Those Crazy Americans

As he approached the 1998 World Cup season, coach Steve Sampson used a soccer formation that seemed outrageous to most of the soccer world (and to some U.S. players as well). It was a 3–6–1. This figure shows the lineup.

The idea was to have a more defensive team, because the United States was an underdog against Germany, who it met in the first round. The fullbacks were in a fairly traditional three fullback mode, with the two wing fullbacks covering each side and the sweeper free to roam, and they had help from the midfielders.

135

The 3–6–1 lineup.

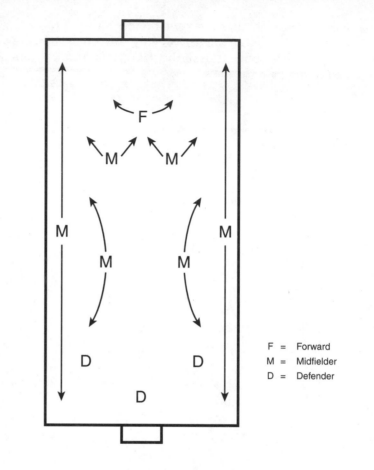

F = Forward
M = Midfielder
D = Defender

The set-up brought four midfielders back defensively to help the three fullbacks, but it allowed two of the midfielders to play a largely offensive game. The other advantage was that one of the strongest players on the team, Claudio Reyna, was not a defensive-oriented midfielder, so this arrangement freed him from that responsibility.

The real sufferers were the forward and the wing midfielders. The forward was on his own up front and had to worry about maintaining possession long enough for the midfielders to catch up, and the wing midfielders had to travel the entire length of the field, responsible for the sidelines from end line to end line.

But the big question remained. Would it work? The answer was a resounding "No!" as Germany trounced the U. S. team in its first match. The score was only 2–0, but the game was largely lopsided with an embarrassingly small number of good offensive possessions by the Americans. Sampson switched to the slightly more traditional 3–5–2 lineup for the next game.

Putting It All Together

It's one thing to identify the best players on the team. It's a quite another to figure out where they should play.

Many coaches of younger teams align their players based on the traditional body types. The heavier tanklike players are the tough defenders, while the tall, skinny speedsters end up on the forward line.

This is not a great idea. Coaches need to be open to other possibilities:

➤ If the heavy defensive back is dying to be on the front line, give him a shot. Maybe in his eagerness to prove himself there, he'll get the ball in the goal.

➤ If you find yourself constantly yelling at a midfielder to get back on defense, then change his position to either forward or defender. Presumably you put him as a midfielder because he was competent in both areas, but perhaps he doesn't have the stamina to do both.

➤ And if you find you have a forward who seems reluctant to shoot, despite an outstanding heading ability, try him on the defending end. You can always use those head balls as a defensive maneuver rather than an offensive one.

Bet You Didn't Know

Eddie Pope, of the U.S. National team, is an extremely fast runner and a rather tall player. Initially, his coaches thought that he'd be ideal up on the attacking line, to outrun and outjump the defense. But something wasn't clicking and he wasn't scoring goals. Finally, one of his coaches had the foresight to move him back to defense and bingo—an outstanding player was born!

Coach's Corner

Just because you have your top header playing defense doesn't mean you have to forgo all scoring opportunities for him. Bring him up into the fray on corner kicks and indirect or direct kicks coming from the sidelines. Just make sure he can scramble back on defense when the tide turns.

After you figure out the relative positions of each player, then it's time to set up the formation. There are a number of factors to take into consideration:

137

➤ The age and ability level of players

➤ The teams you'll be competing against

➤ Your best players' skills

➤ Your goalkeeper's skills

Let's take each item one at a time. At the early levels of soccer, probably up through junior high, it's best and easiest to go with a balanced line-up, like the 4–3–3 or 3–4–3. These lineups don't involve a lot of shifting or creative runs, and the roles of each player are traditional. This saves a coach a lot of explanation and headaches. At higher levels, you can experiment more. Your players are more knowledgeable and can understand the more advanced concepts that go along with a less balanced lineup.

You also want to take a look at your competition. Has your team traditionally come out on top in your league or conference? Or have you had a couple of goose eggs in the win column? If the competition is tough, beef up the defense, because that's where you're going to find most of the playing being done.

Coach's Corner

Sometimes if you're playing against a team that's much stronger than you are, you might want to load the box with defenders and have a double sweeper lineup. That enables two players to roam and help out where needed.

And what formation do the opponents play? If they have two forwards, then you're going to probably want to play three fullbacks, two to play man-to-man on the forwards and one sweeper. Why have an extra guy back there who really doesn't have a role to play? If they have three forwards on the other hand, then you might want to have four fullbacks.

You also need to figure out who your best players are and how you can maximize the time they'll be touching the ball. Let's say you have four players who have a good sense of the game and are good passers. You might want to go with four midfielders and only two forwards rather than moving one of these top players to the forward line or back on defense where she'll see the ball less. Or if you find that you have an outstanding sweeper, then you might be able to reduce your defenders to three and get a more offensive lineup.

Take a look at your goalie. Are you nervous every time the ball gets near him or do you think he can handle what he's given. If you're suffering from anxiety attacks because he has the stopping power of a sieve, you better beef up your defense and make sure that there are so many defenders that the ball doesn't make it to the goalie. Or you could just find a new keeper.

Coach's Corner

You don't have to follow any set lineup, although there's a reason that certain lineups are popular or unpopular. Go with what works for your team, even if it means challenging some accepted practices. Some other lineups that weren't described in this chapter are the 3–4–3, the 4–2–4, and the 2–3–5, which is one from a few decades ago when the teams were heavier on offense than on defense.

Figuring out a winning combination isn't easy, both with the players and the formation. But that's part of what makes the game exciting and challenging.

The Least You Need to Know

➤ Teams are made up of forwards, midfielders, defensive backs, and a goalie.

➤ Players can be grouped in a variety of formations.

➤ Formations are referred to by numbers, such as 1-1-2, with the number of defenders first, midfielders second, and forwards third.

➤ A coach needs to find the position that suits each player and the formation that suits the team.

Chapter 12

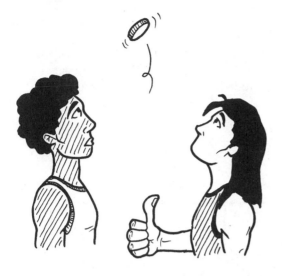

Starts and Restarts

In This Chapter

➤ Rule recap for the restarts

➤ Tricks for the offense

➤ Defensive strategies

➤ The wall

The whistle blows. Foul on the field. Now what? Who takes the kick? Where do you stand if you want to defend against it? Where do you stand if you want to help out your teammates?

In Chapter 3, you got a general idea of what happens during kickoff, when a ball goes out of bounds, or if a player fouls. You know whether to throw the ball or kick the ball, but that's about the extent of your knowledge at this point. Not surprisingly, there's quite a bit of strategy associated with each *start* or *restart*.

This chapter briefly recaps the rules and reasons behind each start or restart and then gives you offensive and defensive strategies.

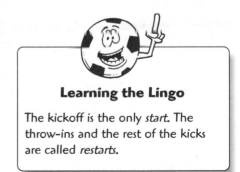

Learning the Lingo

The kickoff is the only *start*. The throw-ins and the rest of the kicks are called *restarts*.

Starting with the Kickoff

The start of the game begins with a kickoff. The kickoffs are also used at the start of the second half, any overtimes that might be played, and after each goal. The team that did not kick off the first half will kick off the second half, and the team that was scored on is the one that kicks off after a goal.

The ball is placed on the center spot in the center of the field, as you can see in this figure. Each team lines up on their side of the field.

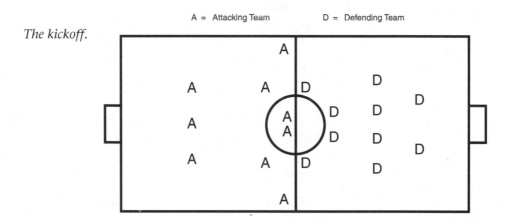

A = Attacking Team   D = Defending Team

The kickoff.

When the whistle blows, a player must move the ball forward, and then she may not touch it again until someone from either team has touched it.

The defense must remain outside the center circle until the ball is touched. It is not the whistle that releases them.

Heads I Win, Tails You Lose

The team that wins the coin toss at the beginning of the game kicks off. Because the player who touches the ball first is not allowed to touch it again until there's been an intervening touch, most teams put two players close together in the center of the field (see the previous figure to see an example). That way the first player can tap it forward to the other who can then do a variety of things.

A popular option is turning around and sending the ball back to a midfielder. This is appealing because it allows the team to retain possession of the ball.

Picture the position of the players at kickoff. One entire team is on one side of the field, while the other entire team is on the other side. If the players kicking off opt to continue to kick the ball forward, they are entering deep into enemy territory without the benefit of any advance forces clearing the way. However, if they send the ball backward, then the teams start to spread out a bit, and a foray into the danger zone doesn't look quite so bleak.

That doesn't mean that a direct attack won't work. Another popular option is to send the ball back to the midfielder, but have the midfielder move closer, within the center circle. Then the minute the ball is tapped forward, one or two wings break down the sideline. The ball is passed back to the midfielder who then boots it to the breaking wing.

Finally, a rather unappealing and generally unsuccessful method of kicking off is to just go for it. The two players in the center play a little game of give and go as they evade defenders and move toward the goal. Unless you know you have some skilled players facing some relatively inexperienced opponents, this will probably not be your best option. You really don't want to waste this free possession by giving the ball away on the third touch.

Charge!

Defending the kickoff is pretty simple. For one thing, you begin the kickoff with 11 players between the ball and your goal. There are not a lot of teams who can get through that quickly. Secondly, there isn't a whole lot you can do other than attempt to gain possession.

The best way to gain possession is to have several players charging the kickoff. Players must stay out of the center circle until the ball is touched, but they certainly don't have to wait for the second player to touch it. So line up a few players around that center circle. The minute that ball moves, you want to charge in to try to interrupt whatever play they might be trying to do.

Because the ball frequently goes backward, you'll want to have at least one player placed at the junction of the center circle and center line (refer to the previous figure), who can sprint back to interfere with the midfielder. And depending on how slow the midfielder is, you might be able to intercept the ball. Remember, the other team has to use three people for that play.

Just remember to leave some players back. You don't want everyone charging the ball or the other team will just feint around you. And defensive backs should keep an eye on those wings sprinting down the sideline. If they make a run like that, chances are they're expecting a pass, and you should be expecting it, too.

The Goal with Goal Kicks

When the attackers kick the ball over the end line, it's time for a goal kick. This is a ball that is placed anywhere within the goalie's box on the side of the goal where the ball went out, as shown in this figure.

The goal kick.

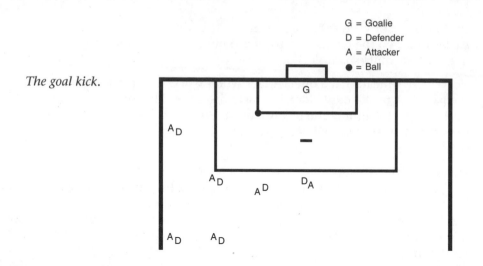

Any player from the defending team may kick a goal kick, and the ball must clear the penalty box before anyone—including the kicker—can touch it again.

Get It Out of Here!

Although the ball can be placed anywhere in the goalie box, most players choose to place it on the corner of the six, to maximize the distance away from the goal.

The strategy for goal kicks varies depending on the abilities and strength of the players. At the youngest levels, the basic strategy is to kick the ball to a teammate who is standing out near the sideline. You are not going to be able to send the ball a long distance, so you want to do whatever you can to get it away from your own goal.

As you get stronger and better, the tactics change a bit. You can still head out to the sideline, but if you have a kick that can get the ball close to midfield, then you can feel relatively comfortable kicking it up the middle as well, if that's where you feel you have the best chance of winning the battle for the head ball to retain possession.

At the highest levels, the goalie usually takes the kick, allowing the rest of the team to clear out and help fight for the ball. At the younger levels, this is not a good idea. Let the sweeper or another defensive back take the kick and keep the goalie in front of the net just in case the kick doesn't get too far.

Mark Up

Defending against the goal kick isn't complicated. You're going to want to just take care of a couple of things. First, if you're playing at the lower levels, send some players out to the sideline, because you know that's where the ball is going to go.

Secondly, you want to mark up, which means find a player and stick with him. Beat him to the ball whether it's rolling along the ground or flying through the air. Of course, if he runs to a spot where he does not have any chance of getting the ball, it does not make sense to stick with him.

And thirdly, place one or two players in the middle of the field near the 18, just in case they make a mistake and cross the ball in front of the goal.

At higher levels, the best you can do is just win the air ball.

Capitalizing on Corner Kicks

Corner kicks are awarded to an attacking team if the defending team knocks the ball over the goal line. As you can see in this figure the ball is placed in the corner arc on the side of the field where the ball went out.

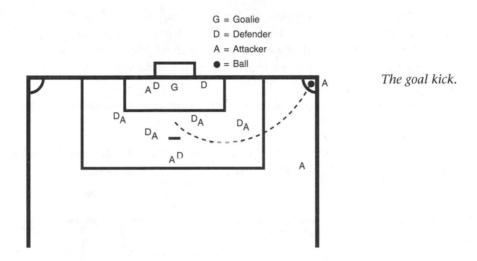

The goal kick.

Any player on the attacking team may kick the corner kick, and it may go directly into the goal for a score without anyone else touching it.

Time to Score

A corner kick is a terrific scoring opportunity, provided you have a kicker with a strong kick and some good headers.

Most corner kickers try to place the ball in front of the goal between the 6 and the penalty mark, in other words between 6 and 12 yards out. That way, if they're off a bit, the ball still goes roughly somewhere in front of the goal.

Frequently, teams set up prepared runs for the receiving players. Four of five might clump at the 18 and then as the corner kicker makes her move to kick the ball, they take off. One goes to the far post, one goes to the near post, one goes to the 6, one goes to the penalty mark, and one sprints across the 18 (or some variation similar to that). These set plays have the advantage of spreading the offense, and therefore the defense, making sure that players don't end up in the same place, and covering all the bases. Plus, at younger levels, it gets players making good cuts before they're aware of what good cuts are.

Coach's Corner

If you have a number of kickers on your team who are qualified to take the corner kick, you might want to try to get a left-footed kicker for the left side and a right-footed kicker for the right side. That way, when the ball is kicked, the arc will be away from the goalie, which makes it a little harder for the goalie to jump in and grab the ball.

Another possibility in a corner kick is to make a short pass if the defense doesn't send anyone out to guard for it. This figure shows where that pass might go.

The short pass.

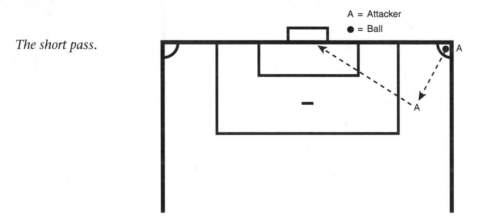

The advantage to this pass is that it puts a player in position for a clear shot on goal. Even if that player doesn't take the shot (or is physically unable to as is the case at lower levels of the game), it throws the defensive focus off to have the ball coming in at a different angle. This second kicker can then just loft the ball into the fray.

Defend at All Costs

Corner kicks are dangerous situations for the defense. The defense needs to be on top of its game. Most teams mark up man-to-man, leaving the sweeper free to go after loose balls. They also try to bring a player in to stand on the post nearest the kick, while the goalie stands more in the center of the goal.

Because you want to mark up every attacking player, while at the same time keeping the sweeper and the front post player free, you're probably going to have to have some forwards come back to help play defense on this play. It all depends on how many attackers the other team puts in front of the goal.

Coach's Corner

When you mark up, don't forget to send someone out on the player who might potentially receive the short pass, or they're going to take advantage of it.

When the ball comes flying through the air, it's the battle for the head balls again. Ideally, you always want to try to pass to a teammate, but in a situation like this, it's always more important to just get that ball out of there. So when in doubt, clear the ball high and wide. Then the team moves as a unit.

If you find that your team is losing these corner kick battles frequently, you either have a very short team, a very slow team, or your players aren't good at marking up. You can't do much about the first situation, but you can switch to a zone defense if the other two situations seem to be a problem.

A zone defense involves assigning a certain area, rather than a certain player, to each defender. Then, if an attacker ventures into the area, the defender can get on her until she leaves the area. With zone defense, your players don't need to be as quick because they don't have to keep up with another player who's racing all over the field.

The man-to-man defense works best for most teams, so you should practice it in nongame situations, and eventually go back to it when you think the team can handle it.

Directions When It's Direct

A direct kick can be awarded at any area on the field. It's given to a team when a player has been fouled by

➤ kicking,

➤ pushing,

➤ tripping,

➤ jumping at someone,

➤ hitting,

➤ charging,

➤ holding,

➤ tackling an opponent rather than the ball, or

➤ when a player on the opposing team, other than the goalie, touches the ball with his hands.

The direct kick is taken right where the offense occurred. A goal may be scored directly from the kick—hence the name. The defending team must stand at least 10 yards away and may not move until the ball moves. (If one of these violations occurs within the penalty box, a penalty kick is awarded rather than a direct kick.)

Look for the Goal

If the ball is within reach of the goal, generally about 30 yards away at the top levels of soccer and closer to the 18 at the lower levels, then you should go for the goal. After all, this kick can score, so take advantage of the fact that you're given time to set up and make a perfect shot on goal.

Coach's Corner

While you don't want to get yellow-carded for wasting time, take your time setting up your shot on a direct kick in front of the goal. You're in a position of distinct advantage here and have a good chance at scoring. Don't waste it by rushing your shot.

If the ball is not near the goal, then you're going to have to use the same strategy that you would use for other similar kicks. For example:

➤ on direct kicks down near your goal, play the situation the way you would a goal kick, that is, clear it out of there on a long, lofted ball;

➤ for direct kicks at the midfield, treat the situation like a kickoff and try to retain possession by using a short kick or passing the ball back; and

➤ for direct kicks that are near the goal but over toward the sideline with a bad angle for a shot, treat them as you would a corner kick and loft the ball into the center.

Finally, even though you can score directly from a direct kick, if you see an unguarded player nearby who has a better angle at the goal, pass the ball off and let her take the kick. But don't expect to have this opportunity too often.

The Wall

If the direct kick is awarded anywhere on the field (except in front of the goal), the defense is going to play its regular defense, going for head balls, marking up man-to-man, and so on. But if it's in front of the goal, it's *wall* time.

A free kick within 30 yards of the goal is a dangerous thing. Not as bad as a penalty shot, which is only 12 yards away, but still bad. Fortunately, unlike the penalty shot, the goalie can have some help from the defenders.

In this case, the defenders would be of little assistance marking up their opponents. The kicker is most likely going for the goal, so the only chance they'd have to get involved is on a ball that bounces off the crossbar or post, not a high percentage option. Instead, most teams like to use their defenders in a wall.

> **Learning the Lingo**
>
> The *wall* is a line of usually three to five tightly packed players (although it can be more or less) who stand 10 yards away from the kick and by their presence attempt to block off a portion of the goal.

The goalie shouts out how many players he'd like in the wall, usually three to five. The closer the shot is to the goal, the more players the goalie is going to want. One player raises his hand and lines up on a direct line with the post nearest to the kick. The others move in shoulder-to-shoulder next to him, crossing in front of the goal. It should always be as tight as possible so no ball can slip through.

The wall stands 10 yards away from the ball. Some teams try to stand even closer, hoping the referee won't push them back. The purpose of the wall is to block off the section of the goal nearest to the kick. The wall forces the kicker to shoot for the part of the goal that's further away or stops the ball if the kicker drills it at the players.

A wall.

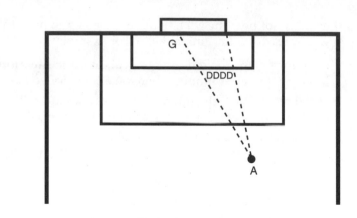

The goalie, if he has confidence in his wall, stands in the other part of the goal. If he has less confidence, he might stand closer to the middle, figuring if the kicker is going to the far edges of the goal, he'll have more time to react anyway.

The defenders who are not in the wall mark up man-to-man. They should be careful not to be any closer to the goal than the wall is, because an attacking player will be called for offsides if he tries to move in there without them. By holding with the wall, the defenders can keep the attackers farther out.

Indirect Information

The indirect kick is the trickiest kick of all, because the ball needs to be touched twice before it can go into the goal. This means that the offense can create a few options, and it keeps the defense on its toes.

Bet You Didn't Know

The only time a player is allowed a handball is when he (or she) is protecting a "sensitive" area during wall duty, because a 90 m.p.h. ball only 10 yards away can do some damage. You better believe the players take advantage of this. Watch the walls. The men have their hands cupped in front, while the women have their arms crossed over their chests.

Like the direct kick, the indirect kick is taken at the site where the offense occurred. The indirect kick is awarded when

➤ there's poor sportsmanship,

➤ there's an offsides violation,

➤ a dangerous kick occurs,

➤ an obstruction occurs,

➤ someone interferes with the goalie,

➤ the goalie takes more than four steps,

➤ the goalie touches the ball again after the release before another player does,

➤ the goalie touches the ball with his hands after it has been kicked to him by a teammate,

➤ the goalie touches the ball with his hands after it has been thrown to him by a teammate, and

➤ when anyone wastes time.

Unlike the direct kick, an indirect kick may be awarded if the offense occurs inside the penalty box, which results in the occasional close free kick. Again, the defense must stand at least 10 yards away.

Bag of Tricks

If the ball is anywhere on the field other than in front of the goal that you're attacking, don't worry about the kick being an indirect (versus a direct) kick. It's not going to matter. Chances are that not only one, but also two, three, or four players are going to touch the ball before it ever heads toward the goal. Just treat it like a direct kick.

But if the ball is in front of the goal, it's a whole different story. It's time to get tricky. Ideally, you want to take advantage of the free kick to take a shot on goal, so you have to figure out how to get the ball touched twice without giving the defense anytime to interfere.

Therefore, the most common play for an indirect kick is to have one player run by and nudge the ball while a second player comes in to kick it into the goal. Or one player can just tap it to another who then takes the shot.

If the indirect kick is at a bad angle, then you might want to involve a third player, who might have a better shot just four or five feet away. This can also throw off a defense who might be setting up a wall and looking at the second player to be taking the shot. This figure shows this option.

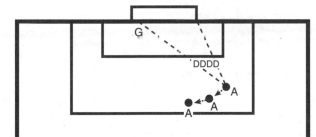

Indirect kick strategy.

151

Anything that fools the defense is going to be effective. Argentina, in the 1998 World Cup, found success in a beautifully executed indirect kick play, as shown in this figure.

Argentina's World Cup play.

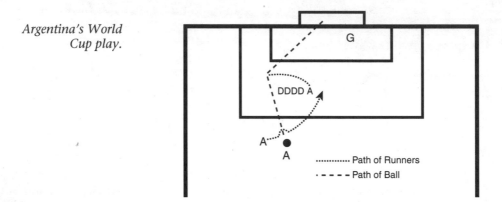

.... Path of Runners

· - - - - Path of Ball

Argentina placed a man on the inside of the wall. Then another player ran straight toward the ball, stepped over it without touching it (therefore not starting the play) and ran directly toward this man planted in the wall. All defensive attention was diverted to this area, because it looked as if they were trying to make something happen there. Meanwhile, the man in the wall, dropped back a step, then snuck behind the wall to the outside while people were watching the runner. He was the one who received the pass, after someone finally touched it, and being wide open, he took an easy shot that went into the goal.

Coach's Corner

You do not have to wait for a whistle to take either a direct or indirect kick. On an indirect kick, if you find that the defense is not moving quickly and you have a teammate wide open, pass the ball immediately, and get the shot off.

It pays to be tricky on the indirect shots. Chances are, however, that you'll practice these plays time and again in practice, and they won't come through for you in the games. But if they do, even once, as it did for Argentina, it's all worth it.

On Your Toes

Defending against the indirect kick can be tricky. On the one hand, you have a slight advantage over the direct kick because the other team is going to have to touch it twice, but on the other hand it can be closer to the goal and you never know where the ball is going to be sent.

Most teams also like to use a wall against an indirect kick.. Besides the wall, there should be one player charging the ball, in hopes of messing up the tap to the other player. The rest of the players mark up man-to-man.

Goalkeepers should be keeping careful count of the touches on the ball. If there's only been one touch, they can let the ball sail into the goal without a score. Then it's merely a goal kick. A bullet easily dodged.

Throw-in the Towel

A throw-in is awarded when the ball goes out of bounds over one of the sidelines. The throw-in is a highly stylized throw in which the thrower must use two hands, send the ball fully over the head, while keeping some part of both feet on the ground at all times until the ball is released.

The ball is thrown in at the point at which it went out of bounds. A goalkeeper may not catch a throw-in. No one is offsides on a throw-in. And no one may score a goal by throwing the ball in to the goal.

Toss Across

Like a number of the restarts, offensive strategy on a throw-in varies with the ability of a thrower. At the highest levels, the ball can be thrown in front of the goal like a corner kick. At the lowest levels, it can only go about five feet. Obviously, strategies would vary.

Bet You Didn't Know

Despite the restrictions placed on the throw-in, it's still possible to be creative. Some players master the skill of doing a flip before throwing the ball! That way they manage to generate a tremendous amount of body momentum, still keeping both feet on the ground at the point of release.

At the lower levels, the throw down the sideline is probably the best strategy. It keeps the ball from going in front of your own goal and the throw sends the ball in the right direction. At higher levels, the ball should go to an open man, if there is one.

If players are being guarded, they should try to break away from the ball and then break back, hoping to catch their defender off guard an get an extra step on him.

The throw should go to the feet of the receiving player. Often this player might want to tap the ball back to the thrower after he's stepped in bounds.

Get in the Way

Once again, the strategy is to mark up man-to-man. Stay with your player, beat him to the ball, don't let him turn on you, and don't let the ball go over your head. Also, don't forget that the offsides rule is "turned off" for throw-ins. The last thing you want is some player cutting behind you toward the goal to receive a throw just because you were too complacent, thinking the offsides rule would save you.

Two More

Penalty kicks and drop kicks are two more restarts that should be mentioned, although the strategy is minimal. Let's first quickly deal with drop kicks, which are like a face-off in hockey

To begin with, drop kicks almost never happen at the higher levels of soccer and are rare occurrences even at high-school level. So you really don't ever need to even practice them. The main goal, both offensively and defensively, is to be quick and get to the ball first.

Penalty kicks, fortunately, are a little more exciting, a little more common, and a little more strategic (but not that much). Both offensively and defensively, players want to line up around the penalty box, moving forward when the ball is kicked. They need to be ready for a ball that rebounds off the crossbar or goalposts. Otherwise, it's going to be a goal, or the goalie is going to catch it and they can all move away.

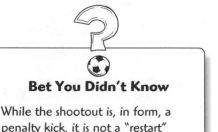

Bet You Didn't Know

While the shootout is, in form, a penalty kick, it is not a "restart" because even if the ball rebounds of the crossbar or goalposts, it's not in play.

On a penalty, the shooter can only score on a rebound if the goalkeeper touched the original shot. Any other player may score off of a rebound from the post, crossbar, or keeper.

The penalty kick shooter, however, does have a bit of strategy concerning the placement of the kick, and this strategy is mostly a personal (or coaching) decision. The majority go for accuracy, using about a half-speed kick to the edge. Some, however, prefer an all-out bullet, hoping the speed and the force of the ball will carry it into the goal.

There are two things you need to key on, however, no matter which type of shot you're going to take.

1. Decide ahead of time which side of the goal you're going to shoot at. If you don't, your indecision is probably going to send the ball straight up the middle into the goalie's hands.

2. Don't telegraph your decision. The goalie will be looking for all the clues she can get.

Other than that, go for it and follow your shot. You have the advantage.

The Least You Need to Know

➤ Take advantage of a free kick to either score or retain possession. Don't blow your opportunity on an undirected kick downfield.

➤ Both offensive and defensive players want to be thinking "head ball" for most free kicks.

➤ Defensive players should mark up man-to-man and battle for every ball.

Chapter 13

Thinking It Through

In This Chapter

➤ Developing a soccer brain

➤ Offensive tactics

➤ Defensive strategy

Soccer is a very physical sport, but it's also one of the toughest mental challenges around. Unlike basketball and football, where there are set plays to follow, soccer players have to react to the flow of the game and use their own instincts and experience to make the correct decisions.

And unlike baseball, there's no opportunity for a coach to be calling for the bunt or directing a player to slide. Soccer coaches have to do their job in practice. Then the players have to respond in the game. In fact, the coach pacing up and down in front of his bench screaming at the players on the field is probably doing more harm than good.

So a soccer player needs to be trained in the mental game as well as the physical game. She needs to develop the ability to react intelligently to every new situation that presents itself.

Soccer Smarts

It's not enough to have the strength of Arnold Schwarzenegger or to have the foot speed of Michael Johnson. You can't even rely on a Kareem Abdul Jabbar-sized body to enable you to reach the head balls long before anyone else. You have to have the smarts to get yourself in the right place at the right time.

Not every player has soccer smarts. Some truly gifted athletes are less than stellar performers when it comes to understanding the strategy and tactics behind the plays on the field. A bit of the mental game comes from instinct, a coach can teach some of it, but the majority comes from experience.

The Plusses of Pick-Up

Most kids in the United States who play soccer play on organized teams for the first decade of their lives. Most kids in the rest of the world play pick-up games for those same 10 years. Who do you think has the advantage? At first glance, you might think it's the kids in the United States. They're being taught the proper skills, they're playing real games at a young age, and they have coaches to guide them in strategy. But they are missing a crucial element.

The kids in the pick-up games play with different-aged kids. Usually it's a neighborhood that gets together, with players of varying sizes and abilities. The youngest kids aren't going to get the ball unless they start getting smart really quickly. This develops their soccer instinct early on. In the U.S. we seem possessed with fairness—that is equal playing time, playing with only the same age group, and so on. This hurts the development that is achieved through street soccer.

Training the Brain

Even if you grew up as one of those underprivileged United States youths who had to suffer through organized soccer and had to learn your tips from a coach rather than the street rats in your neighborhood, all is not lost. A careful player can pick up soccer smarts by paying attention to all that goes on around her.

Coach's Corner

When a team is playing a game in practice, the coach can stop the play occasionally to make a point, but he should try not to do this too often. Players learn more from and have more fun with the hands-on experience of playing rather than listening to a lecture.

For instance, if you are waiting for a pass to come to you and time after time it's intercepted, you need to start analyzing the situation. Why is the other team beating you to the ball? Are they faster? Are they in better position? Most likely the answer is that they are moving and you are just waiting for the ball to come to you. Start going out to meet that ball and your game will change radically.

Now let's say you've started to take this "meet the ball" philosophy to an extreme. Even when the other team has the ball, you're rushing out to meet it. Then every time that you are just about on top of the opponent, she sidesteps you neatly and continues on her way unopposed, while you are left trying to recover.

What's wrong here? In a defensive situation, you have to hang back and try to contain the player in a small area, while waiting for her to make a move, a pass, or best scenario, a mistake. That's when you make your move. By charging in, you're committing yourself and allowing her to react, which gives her the advantage. After you're beaten time and again, it will become another lesson learned.

The best way to train your brain in soccer smarts is to analyze and learn from your mistakes.

Frozen Concentrate

One of the hardest skills a soccer player has to learn is to keep his mind on the game. It's called concentration, focus, or alertness, and it needs to be going on for all 90 minutes.

Distractions are plentiful. Your grandparents might be in for the weekend—seeing you play for the first time ever. Resist the urge to wave in the middle of the game or even to commit the less offensive mistake of sneaking peeks over to see if they're watching you.

Don't listen to opposing players who might get frustrated and yell out unsportsmanlike remarks. Don't respond. Don't listen to the fans (or opponent's fans) who've gathered in the bleachers or along the sidelines. Your ears should be focused on what your teammates and coach are saying.

Even if you can easily tune out the off-field distractions, you have other concentration issues to contend with. It's easy for you to focus when you have the ball, when a player is approaching you, or when the ball is sailing through the air in your direction. But can you keep your mind on the game when the play is at the other end of the field? That is critical, and it is the mark of a disciplined player.

Just because you're not anywhere near the ball, you're not off the hook. Say you're a defender and your forwards have the ball down in front of the opponent's goal. You have to pay attention to

Bet You Didn't Know

During a women's match between Bowdoin College and Tufts University, the men's team from Bowdoin began heckling the star player on the Tufts team. They were relentless in their unsportsmanlike behavior, and it didn't take long for her to become rattled. With half the Tuft's star's attention on the hecklers in the bleachers, Bowdoin rallied to win the game.

opportunities such as where the other team's forwards are, what offsides possibilities you can create, or whether you're going to be needed quickly to give your team an advantage on a corner kick or direct kick, and so on. Soccer is a game that can go back and forth quickly and you don't want to be caught off guard.

Going for the Goal

Offensive strategy on the surface is simple. Put the ball in the goal. But there's a whole lot more going on out on the field. The ball is moved more quickly or more slowly depending on the score of the game. It can also go into the center of the field or out to the side, capitalizing on the other team's strengths and weaknesses.

Here are three offensive tenets:

1. When initiating the attack on the defensive end, go wide. You want to get the ball away from in front of your goal.

2. Bring the ball into the center when you're down in front of the other team's goal.

3. Switch the ball to the other side of the field if one side is getting too congested.

While there are exceptions to every tenet, these are good guidelines to follow most of the time, and they can be learned by even the youngest players.

The Big Spread

Staying wide is an offensive strategy that can be employed by even the most novice of players.

Coach's Corner

Little kids find it easier to grasp a concept if they can tie it to something concrete. If "staying wide" is too fuzzy a concept for them to grasp, try comparing the field to a small boat. "What would happen," you say, "if we all went to one side of the boat? It would tip. Pretend the field is our boat, and we don't want to tip the field. Stay spread out."

Aside from the obvious benefit of not getting in each other's way, staying spread out has the advantage of spreading the defense too thin in the middle of the field. Think about it. If you put players on the edges of the field, either they're wide open to receive the ball or the defense has to come out to guard them. If the defense moves out, the middle is left open, or at least semi-open, as you can see in this figure.

Spreading the defense.

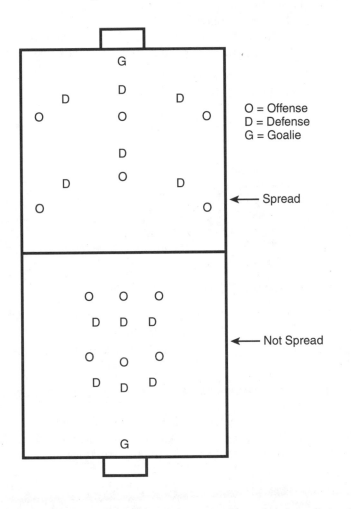

O = Offense
D = Defense
G = Goalie

← Spread

← Not Spread

On the other hand, if the defense is allowed to bunch in the middle because you're bunching in the middle, then they're going to have a much easier job guarding you, and you'll have a much harder job penetrating.

Crossing Paths

Now let's say you're a winger doing her job spreading the defense, which means that you're bringing the ball down the sideline. And if you bring the ball down the sideline, chances are you're going to cross it into the middle.

If you're the one doing the centering, then you want to aim for somewhere around the penalty mark. Any closer in, and the goalie will probably snatch the ball away. Any farther out, and it'll be too far from the goal for a header to score.

Learning the Lingo

Another term for crossing the ball into the middle is *centering*.

Some teams are better with crossing the ball than others. If you have a great heading team, then you should center the ball as much as possible. (This also assumes that you have players who can loft the ball into the box.) If you find that the defense is getting to the ball first every time, you need to try a different strategy.

So if your team is weak at lofting balls or shies away from the head ball, then you're going to want to move the ball into the center by short, accurate passes. Try some give-and-go passes and some through-passes to maneuver around the defense.

Coach's Corner

Many coaches of younger teams don't think to modify traditional soccer strategy for the abilities of their players. Coaches shouldn't tell their players to bring the ball down the sideline if the players aren't strong enough or skilled enough to get it all the way into the center.

If you're trying to work the ball into the penalty box using short passes and the defense seems to be stifling you at the 18, then try kicking the ball back to a midfielder. The defense is going to have to move out to defend the midfielder and it might open up something closer to the goal.

Easy Does It

More offensive strategies can be employed depending on whether you're winning or losing. If you're winning, you want to slow the game down. The more time you can take off the clock, the less time the other team is going to have to score a goal. And the only way you're going to control the pace of the game is to maintain possession. Possession is nine-tenths of the law in both the legal world and the soccer world.

So don't give the ball away any sooner than you have to. If you're the goalie, roll the ball out to a fullback, rather than punt it downfield. Let him dribble it slowly forward. Use small, controlled passes to move the ball upfield rather than long loopy ones, which move the ball quicker and are more likely to be intercepted.

Coach's Corner

Aside from slowing down the game, maintaining possession can help maintain your lead. After all, the other team can't score if they don't have the ball.

Pick Up the Pace

Of course, if you're down a goal or two, especially near the end of the game, your strategy should be just the opposite. You need to push the ball up to score. Punt the ball if you're a goalie. Don't play around with a dribble. Move the ball through quick passes.

If the end of the game does seem to be creeping up on you quickly, you can also increase the number of attackers you have. Pull your sweeper out of the defensive end, and replace her with an attacker, so you can outnumber the other team's defense and possibly have more opportunities to score.

If you do pull a player from defense to beef up your offense, make sure the remaining defensive backs are aware they have to mark up man-to-man, and there's going to be no one back there for support. For teams playing a zone defense, defenders need to be aware that there is one less player back there.

The midfielders are also going to have to give their bodies one last push to make absolutely sure they get back on defense and are there for offense as well.

The other way you can use a defender as an attacker is to have the defender make an overlapping run. Usually this is so unexpected that the defender is left totally unmarked or someone else is left open while the other team tries to adapt.

Don't do this run too often or the element of surprise will be gone. And don't do this run if the space in front is not open. You also have to make sure that you get back quickly rather than be sucked into lure of the offensive limelight. The other defensive players have to

Bet You Didn't Know

In the United States' 1998 World Cup game against Iran, the U.S. team pulled their goalie out of the box in the last few minutes of play. Their only hope of moving on to the next round was to win the game. If Iran happened to score again on the empty goal, it wasn't going to make any difference. Putting an extra attacker in the penalty box might, however.

adapt, too. They should be familiar with this play so they can compensate for the temporary loss of their compatriot.

Reading the Other Team

More advanced teams can take their cues from the opponents and tweak their offenses accordingly. Here are some easy offensive tricks that are dictated by the other team's defense:

1. If their defensive backs are slow, chip a lot of long balls over their heads. Your speedy wingers can race by the backs and leave them in the dust.

2. If their defensive backs are quick, on the other hand, use short passes.

3. If they're playing a zone defense rather than marking up, use a lot of short passes and give-and-go plays because one defender will have to try to cover two attackers in his zone.

4. If there's no sweeper, load the box with an extra attacker or two, because there will be no one to pick up the slack.

If you've practiced several formations, you can also change the number of attackers you have based on the number of defenders they have. For instance, let's say they're running a 3–4–3, assuming that you'll be running your traditional 4–4–2. They only need three fullbacks because you only have two forwards. The two wing fullbacks mark up man-to-man on your two forwards and the other fullback is the sweeper.

If you can quickly adjust to a 4–3–3 or a 3–4–3, then, you've taken away their sweeper. Their third fullback will have to mark up man-to-man on your striker. Throw a few middies in there and you've got them outnumbered.

On the Defensive

The defensive part of soccer is mostly reactive. Other than knowing that you're supposed to clear the ball as far as possible out of the backfield, you're not going to drive the action as much as respond to it. But there are still some tricks you can use to not only make your defense more effective but also to drive the offense in a direction you like. You should try to put the attacker on your terms. Force him wide, to where you have some help and know when to get in on a tackle and when to slow him down while support is coming.

A Good Fit

The first step for any defense is to try to match the offense the other team is playing. If they have three forwards, then you want four defensive backs, three to mark up and one sweeper. Likewise, if they have only two forwards, then you can get away with only three backs.

If you can, scout the other team when they play someone else to figure out what formation they use. If you can't that, you might want to go with the four backs to be safe rather than go with three and get caught outnumbered. You can always switch at the half if you're having trouble getting the attack moving or you can have your stopper familiar with taking more of a midfielder role if you find there are only two attackers on the other team.

Speed Assessment

Now you have to take a good hard look at yourself. As a player, are you fast or slow? And is the defensive line as a whole fast or slow? Be honest, because it's going to make a difference in how you play you defense.

If you're quick, you can play closer to your player. You cán try to intercept passes, and you know you can stay with him if he gets the ball and tries to make a move around you. Fast decisions can make up for slow foot speed.

If you're slower, you have to move off him more. Be about four or five feet away, which should be close enough to discourage a pass to him but far enough away to give you time to react if he does get the ball. You absolutely can't let that attacker beat you. Once he has the ball, he's going to be slowed down considerably, so that's when you move in and apply pressure.

Head's Up

The ball's movement should be the first thing that determines where you move as a defender. Too many kids are told to play man to man and they simply follow their opponent around the field even when they are not in the play.

If your team as a whole is slow, you might want to consider a zone defense rather than a man-to-man defense., In zone defense each player tries to cover an area instead of a person.

If you decide to use a zone, be sure to mark up when you're pushed back into the penalty box. Down there everything should be man-to-man.

Marking Up

Let's say your team does happen to be quick enough to use the man-to-man defense. Now you have to do it effectively. There are a few hard and fast rules to follow:

1. Get between your player and the goal.
2. If your player is one pass away, be as close as you can without being beaten.
3. If your player is two passes away, back off. His teammates must loft the ball to get it to him in one pass, at which point you'll have plenty of time to move in.
4. In the penalty box, be on top of your man.
5. If the attacker is in the corner, be on top of your man.
6. On the rest of the field, just be near enough to discourage the pass.

The corner might seem like an odd place to have a defender be on top of an attacker. It is, after all, two kicks away from the goal. There's not much threat down there. There are, however, two white lines that will help you out tremendously, which makes the corner a great place to trap a player.

Heads Up

If your team is going to use a midfielder for a double-team, the wing forward on that side of the field or another defender is going to have to be alert enough to mark up the attacking midfielder. Otherwise, when your midfielder moves off to double-team, she frees up a player in a rather dangerous position.

In the corner, an attacking player only has two places to go: into the center or backward, because the end line and the sideline prevent her from going anywhere else. If you play right on top of her, she's going to have difficulty moving in three of the four directions. You can easily force her back.

Many teams like to pull a double-team when the ball gets into the corner, as well. The midfielder on that side zips in and works with the wing fullback to double-team the attacker. Now the attacker is blocked in all four directions.

This strategy is a good one to use if you find that your team is especially vulnerable on crosses. A good heading team won't find it as necessary.

Offsides Is Your Friend

The offsides rule is a valuable weapon for the defense. It forces the attackers away from the goal (as long as you're away from the goal) and it puts the kibosh on many a breakaway. So use it. Try to trap the offense, and if nothing else at least push them back as far as you can. And if an attacker goes behind your defensive line and does not have the ball, don't worry about him—he is out of the play and in an offside position.

Every time the ball heads down to the other goal, you and the other defenders need to push up to the center line. Don't go any farther than the center line, because players cannot be offsides on their own side of the field. If you push into their side, they're going to get between you and your goal, and it will be legal!

As soon as the ball goes into transition, start pushing up immediately. Make it quick because you want to push those attackers away from your goal. If the tide turns and their team gets the ball back, they'll at least be close to the middle of the field, rather than at your goal.

And there's more! It's a two for one special if you buy into the special Offsides Plan. Offsides isn't just a handy tool for moving the offense out of the danger zone. It can also be a trap. If you see the ball is headed back in your direction, and there's a player who's hanging on the bubble, get him! Move forward as a line and leave him hanging out there, just before the ball gets to him. It's the easiest way to regain possession. In general, when the ball is moving forward, the back line is moving forward. When the ball is not moving and is being contested for, the line is holding its ground. When the ball is moving toward your own goal, the line is usually moving backward.

Coach's Corner

One player, usually the sweeper, should be in charge of telling people to push up, whether it's for an offside trap or just to get the offensive players out from in front of the goal. That way she can make sure everyone knows what's going on and get the players to do it all
at once.

You must, without fail, make sure that the entire line of defense moves together. Picture the disaster that would occur if one player isn't paying attention as the other defensive backs are pushing up to the center line. Just one defensive back is all the other team needs to keep their entire attacking line down near your end. So all of a sudden, the tide turns, the ball is popped over the heads of the fullbacks at the center line, and it's a three-on-one breakaway to the goal.

The Least You Need to Know

➤ Stay focused on the game.

➤ On offense, try to spread the defense and then get the ball to the center of the field.

➤ Capitalize on the other team's weaknesses.

➤ On defense, mark up man-to-man in the penalty box.

➤ Use the offsides rule to clear the attackers out of the backfield.

Part 4
All Aboard! It's Time to Train

In the beginning, it was all so easy and casual. There you were, a cute, little elementary school soccer player sometimes racing up and down the field, sometimes twirling your hair, watching a plane fly over.

But gradually, while you weren't even noticing, time slipped by and the game got more competitive. Now all of a sudden, you're going to have to be in top shape to just make the team, much less be a star. How do you go about doing it? Whether you're a young player about to step up the pace, or an old-timer who feels like getting back in the game, you're going have to prepare your body. So get set. It's training time!

Chapter 14 covers stretching, because without flexibility, you are seriously limited as an athlete. Chapter 15 goes into both anaerobic and aerobic conditioning, teaching your heart and lungs to withstand the 90 minutes of nearly constant running that soccer requires. Strength training, through weights and exercises, is described in Chapter 16. And finally, as much as you don't even want to think about the downside, Chapter 17 deals with common soccer injuries and their treatments.

Chapter 14

Down the Stretch

In This Chapter

➤ Why be flexible?

➤ Guidelines for stretching

➤ A part by part stretching trip

You might want to ask yourself, do you feel limber? Actually, whether the answer is yes or no, you're going to have to practice what is preached here in this chapter. It's stretching time.

Now don't get nervous. This is not going to be a yoga workout. No one's going to ask you to put your leg over your head. But you are going to be asked to get those muscles warm and loose before you play any kind of soccer. Not only does stretching prevent injury but the added flexibility makes you a better player.

Getting Loose

When you get out of bed in the morning, how do your muscles feel? Are they loose? Do you feel flexible? Or are you staggering across the bedroom floor trying to get them to function again? Yes, you're stiff, but by the time you get around to playing soccer, you probably feel pretty normal.

It would be nice if that were all your body needed, but it's not. Think of how you ease your muscles into the morning. You stretch them gradually by not moving too

Head's Up

The older you are the more you have to stretch. And conversely, five-year-old soccer players don't have to stretch at all, but they should do it anyway to get into the habit.

quickly. They don't have to do much more than get you walking smoothly, but still you take it easy at first. Now think of what you're asking your muscles to do when you step out on that soccer field.

Your muscles are going to be running, jumping, starting, stopping, and changing directions constantly. They'll be dribbling, feinting, kicking, and heading. Do you think the slow easy walk you've been doing all day has prepared them for this? I think not. It's time to put them to the stretch.

Get Those Muscles Toasty Warm

Before you play, you want to stretch, but before you stretch, you want to get your muscles warm by exercising them a little. Sounds a bit like your standard Catch-22.

Learning the Lingo

Warm is not just a euphemism here. Muscles do actually heat up when you use them and are more flexible warm than cold.

How do I exercise before I stretch if I'm supposed to stretch before I exercise?

The key is in the qualifier "a little." Do a light jog around the field dribbling the soccer ball first. You get an extra warm up with the ball without taxing your muscles too strenuously. Now your muscles are warm enough to stretch.

On colder days, keep moving until you feel that your body is warmed up. The same easy jog that worked in early September might not be as effective in late November.

No Bouncing Allowed

Theories on stretching have varied over the years, but the current trend seems to have quite a bit of support, especially because it has stood the test of several decades: *No bouncing allowed.*

When you stretch, you want to move into position and then hold that position for about 20 seconds or longer. Ideally you want to hold each stretch until you feel the muscle start to relax. Then you lengthen the stretch until you feel the resistance again. If you have time or you feel you need more stretching, you can even extend the stretch a little further. Always exhale when you are lengthening a stretch.

Head to Toe

So you're warm. The blood is flowing. And you know enough not to bounce. It's time to get down to the job at hand. I like to work from the feet up. Other people prefer from the head down. Some coaches like to have their players stand in a large circle, with each player leading a different stretch. Finding a routine such as this one is helpful for keeping track of what you've done and what you've forgotten.

Coach's Corner

To keep your body as flexible as possible, you should go through an abbreviated stretching routine at the end of the game or practice as well. If you just stop cold turkey, all your muscles will tighten up.

Whatever method you use to remember all your stretches, you're going to want to stretch the entire body. Picture a chain with one weak link. Where is that chain going to break when stress is placed on it? That one link. The same thing happens with your body. Forget to stretch one area, and that's the one that will be overstressed and most likely a muscle pulled.

A Leg Up

Because my personal preference is to stretch from the feet up to the head, that's the way the stretches are presented in this book. So first stop: legs.

Ankles Away

The ankle is probably the most used joint in soccer, so you absolutely must make sure that everything connected to it is loose and flexible. Not only does flexibility prevent an ankle sprain (which could put you out for the season), but also it gives you more movement in the joint, which automatically makes you a better player.

Despite the importance of the ankle, the stretch is a relatively simple four-step operation:

1. Point your foot and hold it.
2. Flex your foot and hold it.
3. Rotate your foot in a clockwise direction.
4. Rotate your foot in a counterclockwise direction.

Make sure you do this on both feet, of course.

173

Babying the Calf

The calf can be divided into two parts: the calf muscle and the Achilles tendon. Both of these can be targeted on the same stretch, however.

If you have a wall, a fence, or a tree nearby, face it and lean against at about a 45-degree angle. Stretch one leg out behind you as far as it can go while still keeping the heel on the ground. Keep the leg straight. This targets the calf muscle. Now bend the knee slightly. You should feel the stretch lower down in the Achilles tendon, which is just above the heel.

If you don't have a wall, you can do this same stretch on the ground. Put yourself in somewhat of a push-up position, although you'll want to stick your butt up in the air far higher than push-up purists could bear. Bring one leg forward under your body to support it and stretch the other one out behind, pressing the heel of the back leg to the ground.

Again, keep the leg straight to stretch the calf muscle, and then bend it to stretch the Achilles tendon. Switch legs and stretch the other one.

The Hamstring

The hamstring is the large muscle on the back of your thigh. There are a ton of stretches that can be used for this, but I'll narrow it to two.

The first hamstring stretch is done from a standing position. Extend one leg out in front of you. Bend the other leg fairly low, so you get good extension with the outstretched leg. Rest the extended leg on its heel with the toe up. Almost all your weight should be on the back leg. Now lean forward over the front leg. You should feel the stretch in your hamstring. Look at the figure that follows to get an idea how to do this stretch.

A hamstring stretch.

174

The other stretch for the hamstring is your basic toe touch, slightly altered to target one leg at a time. In a standing position, cross one leg over the other and bend down and touch your toes. Try to keep your legs as straight as possible without locking your knees. Cross the other leg over and repeat.

The All-Important Quads

The quadriceps muscle is the large muscle in the front of your thigh. Like the ankle, this muscle is important to a soccer player. You might have heard someone mention "soccer legs" or "soccer thighs." The quadriceps muscle gets the credit (or the blame, depending on who you're talking to), for the extra large muscle development in the upper leg.

The quadriceps is best stretched while standing. Bend the lower half of your leg back, and grab your ankle with the hand on the same side. Pull up on the ankle until you feel the stretch in the quad muscle. Hold and then switch to the other leg.

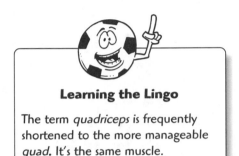

Learning the Lingo

The term *quadriceps* is frequently shortened to the more manageable *quad*. It's the same muscle.

If you have trouble maintaining balance in this position, you can hold onto a partner's shoulder or a wall, fence, and so on. If you're out in the middle of the field, you can try focusing on something on the ground about five or six feet out in front of you. This helps you stay upright.

In the Joint

Where the legs join the body, you have a few temperamental muscles. Perhaps this is because these muscles frequently get ignored. Don't make that mistake.

Be Hip

If you're a woman, you might think the hip is just a big bone designed to make a nightmare out of your search for a comfortable pair of jeans. But believe it or not that good old ball and socket joint has a few muscles attached to it, too. And here are two good stretches to take care of them.

The first is called the *pretzel,* primarily because you knot your legs up in an effort to isolate the right spot. This stretch is done seated on the ground, and because it's rather confusing, you'll definitely want to take a look at this figure.

First extend your right leg. Then bend your left leg and place it over the right leg with the left foot on the ground next to the right knee. Now reach your right arm across and place your elbow on the other side of the left knee. This should twist your body enough so that you feel a stretch in the left hip. Then switch and do the right hip.

The pretzel stretch.

The second stretch for the hip area is called the *hip roll*. You'll want to lie on your back for this one. Bend both knees and keep your feet on the floor. Then let your knees fall to one side and throw your arms over to the other side. The stretch is in the hip that's on top.

The Groin

The best stretch for the groin muscle is something called the *butterfly stretch*. For this stretch sit on the ground and place the soles of your feet together, so that your legs are bent and sticking out at the side like butterfly wings. Try to get your knees down to the ground. If you don't feel the stretch in the groin at this point, try moving your ankles out slightly away from the body and leaning forward.

Coach's Corner

If you're coaching a team that has a morning practice or game, you're going to get a lot of protest once you reach the midsection stretches. Dewy grass means soggy sweats.

Inner Piece

You might think the inner thigh stretch should fall under the category of leg stretches, rather than the midsection stretches, but the inner thigh area is close to the groin, and it also leads nicely into the next stretch.

To stretch the inner thigh, take a big step sideways with one leg, with your toes continuing to face forward and your knee bent. Make sure that the knee of the bent leg does not extend over the toe. Lean on the thigh of the bent leg and feel the stretch along the groin and inner thigh.

Hip Flexor

Hip flexor sounds like a villain worthy of a Superman comic book. And for people who have pulled a hip flexor muscle, it is a villain. A season-ending villain.

You can see the hip flexor muscle in this figure. It's the muscle that runs up the front of the leg from the top of the thigh to the pelvic bone. You can stretch it easily right after the inner thigh stretch by pivoting and shifting your focus.

The hip flexor.

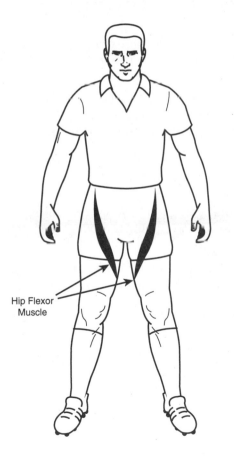

Hip Flexor
Muscle

177

While you're in that lunge position out to the side, pivot so your feet and body are facing sideways now. In other words, you're leading with your bent leg and the straight leg is out behind. Again, make sure that your front knee does not extend over your front toe.

Now, in this position, try to press the front of your thigh down to the ground. It actually shouldn't move any more than an inch or two closer before you feel the stretch, but that is the direction you should be pushing. Hold the stretch, and then switch and do the inner thigh and hip flexor on the other leg.

Up, Up, and Away

And finally, we get to the top half of the body. These muscles still need to be stretched even if most of your game takes place below the waist. How humiliating would it be to pull a muscle on a head ball or a throw-in?

Waisting Time

Head balls require you to snap your body forward, but basic dribbling, passing, and shooting involve a lot of body movement as well. To be your most flexible, you're going to want to stretch your waist and trunk.

To stretch your waist, start in a standing position. Raise one arm and then lean over to the opposite side. You should feel the stretch on the whole side of your body. Switch arms and lean the other way.

You're going to need a wall or a fence to do a stretch called the *torso twist*. Stand sideways to the wall and extend your arm out to meet the wall. Then reach your other arm around to that hand without changing the position of your feet. Then turn, face the other way and do the other side.

Reach for the Sky

Unless you're a goalie, you're really only going to use your arms during throw-ins, which means that the only area you really have to focus on during stretching time is the shoulder area.

There are two good stretches for the shoulder area, which is really the muscle group you're going to be using for a throw-in, both of which are done standing up. For the first stretch, extend an arm up in the air. Stretch it as far as you can to the opposite side of your body without bending your torso. You can even pull it with the other arm if you need to.

The second stretch comes across your body. Extend your arm straight out in front of you and then use your other arm to pull it across your chest, again without twisting your body.

Neck and Neck

Now you've stretched bottom to top and you've reached the head. This is it. You've reached the pinnacle. While some players like to work their jaw muscle, the neck is really the highest muscle you're going to have to stretch.

With good posture, face your head forward and then turn it to one side, as if you're bringing the chin to the shoulder. Hold it for a stretch, then bring it over to the other side.

A Few Goalie Extras

If you are a goalkeeper, you're going to use your arms, so you will want to stretch a few more areas, such as your forearms and your triceps.

Forearmed Is Forewarned

To stretch the forearms, raise your right arm over your head, then bend that arm at the elbow and let the right hand drop down to the back. With the left hand, pull that right elbow toward the back as well. Then switch and do the stretch on the left arm.

The Triceps

The triceps is the muscle on the underside part of your upper arm, opposite the biceps. People who do not have toned triceps often have what is referred to as "kimono arms" or, less kindly, "lunch lady arms."

To stretch your triceps, raise your right arm over your head. Then bend that arm at the elbow and let the right hand drop down to the back. With the left hand, pull that right elbow toward the back as well. Then switch and raise the left arm.

Learning the Lingo

Just in case you're not sure what the *biceps* is, it's the muscle in the upper-arm that little kids always try to show you, saying "See my muscle?" as they pump that fist up in the air.

The Least You Need to Know

➤ Warm up before you stretch.

➤ Stretch the entire body.

➤ No bouncing.

➤ Increased flexibility reduces the chance of injury and increases performance.

Chapter 15

Run for Your Life

Soccer is not like chess, where you can enjoy a challenging game sitting down. Soccer is not like golf, where you take a leisurely walk through beautiful scenery, occasionally swinging a club. Soccer is not even like basketball, which is an incredibly physically demanding sport, but where the movement is sprint, shuffle, jump, repeat. Younger players do not have to worry about training, however. This chapter is for high school and college students.

In soccer, you're going to have to do some long-distance running. There's no way around it. You have to be in great shape to be a good soccer player. There are 90 minutes of game with nothing like a foul shot or a huddle to give you a chance to rest.

Marathon Training

If you were to run a marathon, you'd train by running long distances, hoping to get yourself in shape to make it over the finish line in somewhere between three and four hours. If it were a half marathon, you'd be doing the same thing, but your time would be cut in half—to 90–120 minutes. Does that 90 sound like a familiar number?

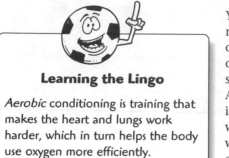

Learning the Lingo

Aerobic conditioning is training that makes the heart and lungs work harder, which in turn helps the body use oxygen more efficiently.

Yes, soccer is 90 minutes of running. Much of it is like marathon running, about three-quarter speed. Soccer, of course, has the occasional stops, but it also has a lot of full-speed sprints thrown in, too. That can make soccer even more difficult than running a marathon. And have you even thought about throwing a ball into the mix? Imagine trying to run a half-marathon with a ball in front of you. That's what happens when you play soccer, so you need to be in top *aerobic* condition.

So, if you're running a mini-marathon, shouldn't you be training for a mini-marathon? You couldn't imagine someone going out to run 13 miles without building up to it, so don't expect your body to act any differently when you ask it to play soccer.

Prep Work

Don't think you can just drag your potato-chip laden body off the couch, slip on a pair of old Keds, and take off for a five-mile jog around town. You'll kill yourself.

The first step is analyzing the condition you're already in. If you workout regularly, then you're all set, but if getting in shape is something new for you, you're going to have to start slowly. Choose a run that's maybe a mile long, tops. If there's a track nearby, you might want to try to run there because you can guarantee that you won't be surprised by a hill that you never noticed when you were climbing it in a car.

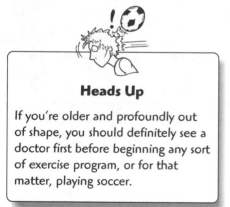

Heads Up

If you're older and profoundly out of shape, you should definitely see a doctor first before beginning any sort of exercise program, or for that matter, playing soccer.

And then you want to hit the nearest sneaker store to get some good running shoes. The proper footwear can really help ease the stress on your body. Good running shoes have lots of cushion in their soles to take some of the pounding off your knees. They also have a wide base at the heel, so you're less likely to twist an ankle if you step on uneven ground.

And finally, reread Chapter 14 of this book. You have to stretch. Get those muscles warm by doing some jumping jacks and then loosen them up with stretching before you hit the streets.

Good Form

Everyone over the age of two can run. It's one of those skills you never even have to be taught. Or is it? If you want to just move quickly, picking your feet up off the ground, then technically, no, you don't have to be taught. But if you want to be efficient with your running, maximizing your effort and getting the most speed and mileage you can, there are some things you should be doing.

First of all, relax. Why tense your shoulders or your arms when you run? Does it serve any running purpose? Yet many people persist in doing just that. Roll your shoulders back a few times. Let your arms dangle at your side. Feel relaxed? Okay, then let's begin.

Coach's Corner

If you know you're the kind of runner who tenses her upper body, try this trick. Do your running on a track and pick a spot on the track to be your cue. Whenever you pass that mark, notice your upper body. Is it tense? If it is, dangle your arms for a while as you run. Then pick them up again, keeping them relaxed.

Start with good posture. Keep your head up and shoulders back, yet in a relaxed manner of course. Don't hunch over. Your eyes should face front, not down. Not only does this help you maintain good posture, but it also prevents you from running into people as you make your way around town.

Now start moving. Are all your body parts going in the same direction? Or are your arms moving out to the side? Tuck those elbows in, and make sure that your arms are moving forward. Arms can actually help you move forward, especially when you're going up a hill, so if they're not going in the direction that you want your body to go, you're losing out on a lot of energy.

Coach's Corner

If you find you're having trouble fixing this arm problem, get someone to videotape you running. Once you have a visual image of a flaw, it's often easier to fix.

When you land on your feet, try to land on your heel and roll forward onto your toe. Avoid running solely on the balls of your feet, and avoid landing flat footed.

183

Keep your hands in a loose fist or dangling open if that's more comfortable. Remember you don't want to tense anything unnecessarily so a tight fist is not a good idea.

Rack Up the Mileage

Ready to run a marathon? Not quite is my bet. You want to start slowly. Ease into the longer runs. If you find that a 1-mile run is pretty easy, push it to two or three. If you're finding the one mile difficult, however, you're going to have to stick with that until it gets more manageable.

But don't get too complacent with your 1-mile run. You have to push yourself to run farther or you'll never be a good soccer player. Your goal should be regular five-mile runs, with the occasional 10-mile run thrown in.

All this should be accomplished before your soccer season even starts. You can't expect to perform well in a game when you are gasping for breath. And you also can't expect that the two weeks of practice leading up to that first game is going to be enough to get you in top condition. Here's a good weekly workout plan for the month before your soccer season.

Monday: 5-mile run

Tuesday: Sprint workout, 2-mile run, weight training

Wednesday: 5-mile run

Thursday: Sprint workout, weight training

Friday: 10-mile run

Saturday: Sprint workout, 2-mile run, weight training

Sunday: Day of rest

Notice how tough this schedule is. It means that you're going to have to get into at least minimal shape even earlier. Then in this final month before the season starts, you'll get into top shape. Finally, in-season workouts will maintain the conditioning base you built up in preseason.

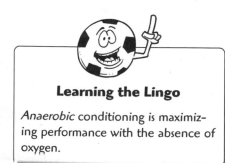

Learning the Lingo

Anaerobic conditioning is maximizing performance with the absence of oxygen.

A Few Sprints

Even though most of the conditioning you're going to need is aerobic conditioning, you'll still have to work on your sprinting ability, or *anaerobic* conditioning.

You'll have to sprint to get back on defense, sprint to outrun an opponent to get a ball, and sprint down the wing to get open for a pass.

But don't waste too much time doing sprint workouts, just because they're easier. A good rule of thumb to follow is to keep the ratio the same for games and practice. In other words, because 80% of your soccer game is endurance, then 80% of your training should be endurance, while sprinting practice takes up a mere 20%.

Racing Form

At first, sprinting style is similar to that of long distance running. You want your body to be relaxed, you want to have good posture, and you want to keep your head up with your eyes on your target. Tighten up your stomach muscles, and stand tall.

When you start sprinting, however, things change a little. You're going to want to get as much power out of your legs as possible. Here are some tips:

➤ Drive your legs into the ground as hard as you can.

➤ Stay up on the balls of your feet.

➤ Keep your knees high.

➤ Don't let your toes get out in front of your knees.

➤ As your leg moves to the back, get the heel up high.

➤ Make sure your arms are going forward.

The reason you need to have your knees high and your heel high is that the higher you get your legs off the ground, the more force they're going to have when they hit the ground. The more force you have pushing off the ground, the more speed you're going to have in your sprint.

The Workout

Sprint workout is a little tougher than long distance running, because you can't just pick a scenic route and go out for a long jog. You have to make the effort to go to a track or measure off a distance and have a watch ready to make sure you aren't resting too long or slacking off too much on your sprints.

Here's the deal. You pick a distance, say 50 yards. You sprint the 50 yards and take a minute's rest, including the time it takes you to walk back. Sprint the 50 again. Do this six times. If you can, you should time yourself to make sure that your sixth 50 is almost as fast as your first.

You should vary the length of your sprints in each workout. One day, do 50-yard sprints, and the next sprint workout, do 100-yard sprints. The longer the distance, the fewer reps you have to do, too.

Bet You Didn't Know

For an extra challenge, you can do your sprint training on a hill. This has the added benefit of building up your quads at the same time you're working out.

Hitting the Circuit

If all this running sounds dreadfully dull, you might be more receptive to doing *circuits*. A circuit is a training technique that gets people in tremendous shape without having to repeat the same old boring run. The circuit is made up of stations. At each station, you do the job at that station. Then you move on to the next.

Circuits can have any number of stations, although somewhere between six and ten is the norm, and the emphasis can change, depending on what you want to work on. There are three kinds of circuits you can create:

1. The fitness circuit
2. The sprint circuit
3. The skills circuit

Coaches love circuits because they keep all the players busy at once while getting them all in shape, and players like it because there's such variety.

The Fitness Circuit

The best way to do a fitness circuit is to do it with a partner, but you can just as easily do it alone as well. Let's assume you have a partner, however.

One of you is the timer, the other is the exerciser. The timer says "Go!" and the exerciser performs the task for one minute. Then you and your partner switch places. The one minute that you're timing is your chance to rest. (If you're doing it alone, you'll have to do the circuit somewhere where you can see a clock, and make sure that you only give yourself a minute between each station.)

Here are some good sample fitness stations:

1. Jump rope
2. Set up a five-yard square. Sprint one side, shuffle the next, sprint the third, shuffle the fourth, and so on.
3. Place the ball on the ground and jump sideways back and forth over it.
4. Push-ups
5. Sit down. Throw the ball in the air. Stand up and catch it. Sit down and repeat.
6. Sit-ups
7. Toe touches on the ball
8. Mountain climbers (your hands are on the ground—body in push-up position—and your feet are sprinting in place out behind you).

If you have a partner, you can also make a game out of the circuit. How many times can you jump rope in a minute? How many push-ups can you do? Have the timer also be the counter. Record the numbers and see who comes out ahead at the end of the circuit.

When coaches set up circuits, they put a group of three or four people at each station. Everyone does the specified work at the station, and then they all have one minute's rest before they move to the next station.

The Sprint Circuit

Sometimes, straight sprinting can get a little dull. By creating a sprint circuit, you can spice up that routine while still getting in good sprinting shape. Here's an example of a good sprint circuit. Your distance is 50 yards.

1. Jog halfway, stop, and run in place while pumping your arms hard, then sprint to the end.
2. Run backward halfway, then turn and sprint to the end.
3. Sprint halfway, do five jumps tucking your legs up under your body, and sprint to the end.
4. Skip a third of the way, lunge walk a third of the way, and sprint to the end.
5. Straight sprint the 50 yards.
6. Do high knees for the 50 yards.

The distance can vary, and as you can see from the example, in a sprint circuit, you really don't have "stations" per se.

The Skills Circuit

The soccer circuit is more of an in-season circuit, but it obviously can be used any time you want. In the soccer circuit, you definitely want a partner, because frequently you'll need to be doing the same exercise together. In this case, you're on for a minute and off for a minute. Here's a sample:

1. One-touch passing
2. Juggling solo
3. One-on-one dribbling offense
4. One-on-one dribbling defense, against the players at station 3. (Because you're working with a partner, one of you obviously does station 4 before station 3.)
5. Heading balls back and forth
6. Throw-ins back and forth
7. Juggling as a pair
8. Dribbling around two cones set about 20 yards apart.
9. Trapping balls out of the air

The minute on, minute off rule is flexible as you can imagine. With younger players, especially on the fitness circuit, that could be virtually impossible. Shorten the time period or lengthen it as you see fit.

Making It Fun

Older players who know that their game is going somewhere have little difficulty motivating themselves to workout. In fact, it's often easier to go out and take a five-mile run than it is to hone your skills.

But younger players have a harder time being interested in a basic conditioning workout. Fortunately, most of them are so full of energy they don't need too much conditioning. Nevertheless, there are some things you can do to make the workout more fun for them.

Having a Ball

The first thing you should do when working with younger players is include a ball in everything you do. That way, they think they're playing soccer even if what they're really doing is working on their conditioning.

For example, if you want them to take a lap around all the playing fields, have them take a lap dribbling the ball. If you want them to sprint 50 yards, have them sprint with the ball, do 10 toe touches at the end of the sprint, and then sprint back.

The beauty of adding a ball to everything you do is that the drill then works on the kids' skills at the same time that it's building their stamina.

Competition Can Be Good

There's a whole lot of psychobabble out there about how kids should play noncompetitive games. Let's not keep score for the youngest groups. Everyone's a winner. Everyone gets trophies. But the truth is that kids are just as competitive as the grown-ups who spawned them.

Every kid in that game that supposedly didn't have a score knows exactly which team won and which team lost, and they probably know how many goals were scored, too. And most of them are dying to win. So capitalize on that in practice. Set up some competitions.

Relays are probably the best way to get kids in shape without them knowing it. For those who cut out of gym class years ago, a relay race is two or three teams of kids who line up behind the starting line. The first player in each line does the race. She comes back and tags the next player in line, who then does the race. When a player in a line has completed the race, she sits down. The first team to have all players sitting down is the winning team.

Here are some good relay races:

➤ Dribble to one end of the field and back.

➤ Dribble through a slalom course, then sprint back.

➤ Dribble down to the goal, take a shot, and sprint back (you can also make them take the shot again if it doesn't go in).

➤ Do the line run that's described in Chapter 2.

➤ Have two players pass the ball back and forth to each other down the field.

➤ Have the two players stand closer together and pass using only the outside of their feet as they move down the field.

➤ Leap frog down the field.

➤ Run backward down the field.

You get the idea. The list can go on and on.

Of course, you do have to be careful not to rely on this all the time. There are kids who don't thrive on competition or are not skilled enough to succeed in this arena. That psychobabble about noncompetition did evolve for a reason.

Coach's Corner

If you have one player who is so weak that he is going to be a real handicap to a relay team, stack the deck occasionally. Put all the top players plus your one weak player on one team. Let that weaker kid know what it feels like to be on a winning side.

You don't want a kid coming in last every time. He'll start to hate the sport, which is exactly the opposite of the goal you were trying to achieve. To prevent this, make sure that your competitions are group competitions, so that no one player is singled out. However, at more advanced levels, be careful not to compromise the competitiveness

of the group. If someone is constantly holding the team back, she may be better off in a less advanced environment.

Go Crazy

Kids love silly, too, so really anything you do that is out of the ordinary will work for them.

Be creative and go with their interests. Tell them they are race cars, racing around the track. Periodically, as they're running, yell, "Head on collision!" which instructs them to put their heads on the ball. Then yell "Spin out!" which means they have to dribble the ball in a circle.

The most important thing to remember is that soccer should be fun, even the conditioning. Of course, the best way to become soccer fit is by playing soccer.

Bet You Didn't Know

During one especially rainy season, I told the kids that we needed to do an ancient tribal sun dance in order to get clear skies for the game that weekend. I led in a jog around the field, with all of us waving our arms in the air, and chanting, "No rain!" The weekend was gorgeous, and the kids, far from feeling like they had gotten a workout, wanted to do the Sun Run every week.

The Least You Need to Know

➤ Good running form means a relaxed body, good posture, eyes up, and all moving parts going in the same direction.

➤ Mix up your aerobic conditioning workouts with the anaerobic sprint work.

➤ Circuits are a great way to ease the boredom of training.

➤ Try to make conditioning work fun for the youngest kids through games and relays.

Chapter 16

Muscle Bound

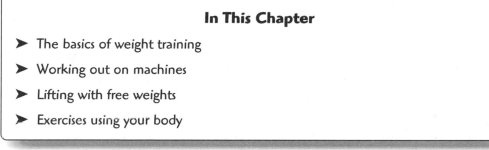

In This Chapter

➤ The basics of weight training

➤ Working out on machines

➤ Lifting with free weights

➤ Exercises using your body

When you see soccer players, you don't automatically think of muscles. They're not football players with big necks or softball players with big forearms. In fact, big is generally not what you think of when you think of soccer. Instead, you think of lean, athletic-looking, long-distance runners, because, of course, that's what they are.

But strength training has its place in the game of soccer, and if you've ever taken a good look at a soccer player's legs you'll know that there are some pretty big muscles being used and developed. Strength training, like flexibility training, can improve performance and prevent injury.

The Starting Line

You might be eager to get out of the gate and start your strength training immediately, but there are two factors you need to consider before you do anything:

1. Age
2. Knowledge

The first is easy. How old are you? Has your body completed most if not all of its growth? If so, then read on. If not, skip this chapter and wait till you're older. Strength training while you are still growing can cause serious damage to your ligaments and your muscles.

The next question is a little more complicated. What do you already *know* about weight training? Don't plan on getting all your knowledge from this book. This chapter covers the basics of strength training, but it cannot tailor a program to meet your specific needs. It cannot teach you how to work the Nautilus, Universal, and Cybex equipment that you might come across, and it cannot tell you when you're doing something incorrectly. Until the interactive version of this book comes out, your best bet is to read this, get an idea of what you need, and then consult a trainer.

Weight a Minute

If you have a school or gym available to you, then you probably have access to weights and machines. You probably also have access to a trainer, which is nice. Here's a brief description of what you're missing if you don't.

The Machines

Weight machines are everywhere. You must have seen them. Huge metal contraptions that have a baffling number of moving parts. They go by names such as Universal, Cybex, and Nautilus. These machines are excellent for weight training for two reasons:

1. They isolate the muscle.
2. They're safe.

The reason it's nice to have the muscle isolated is that you can go through a circuit of machines and be confident that you've covered all your muscles. Each machine is carefully labeled, so as long as you know your anatomy, you're in good shape.

The safety factor is another plus. The weights are usually attached to a pulley, which enables them to be somewhere far away from you. Therefore, if you suddenly feel you have to let go or if your sweaty palms suddenly lose their grip, you're not crushed or decapitated. You also don't need *spotters*.

The disadvantage to these machines is that they're expensive and bulky. One machine usually works only one or two muscles. To have enough equipment to work all the muscles on your body, you'd have to have Donald Trump's bank account for both the equipment and the house large enough to hold it.

Learning the Lingo

A *spotter* is someone who stands next to you while you're working out with weights to keep things safe. The spotter has his hands right next to the weights, just in case they look as if they're going to slip or in case you need some help.

Free Weights

Free weights have been popular strength builders for ages. These are considerably cheaper and smaller than the weight machines and they do the same things.

Disc-shaped weights of varying degrees of heaviness are placed on metal bars of different lengths. You choose a big bar with heavy weights if you want to use two hands, for example, for a bench press. You choose a small bar, with lighter weights if you want to do a biceps curl.

Whenever you work with free weights, you should always have a partner. This person can act as your spotter. Then after you've done your repetition, she can do her rep while you rest and act as her spotter.

Get Your Strength Up

No matter what kind of equipment you're using, there are two philosophies to weight training. You can either tone or bulk. Both of them make you stronger, although bulk training makes you a tad stronger than tone training.

For bulk training, you want to lift heavier weights for a small number of times. For instance, try putting 100 pounds of weights on a barbell. This is probably going to be tough for you to bench-press. If you can do it three to five times, this weight is good for you. As it becomes easier and you can do more, then it's time to add more weight to add more bulk.

Heads Up

If you're bench-pressing at your maximum, make sure you do this with a spotter. You don't want to be alone when you find out that your maximum was a little bit less than you thought it was.

On the other hand, you can strengthen your body without building bulk (women seem to prefer this) by doing less weight with more repetitions. In this case, you might want to bench-press about 50 pounds, but do it 40 times. Break it up into four sets of ten presses, with a rest in between each press.

No Equipment Necessary

If you don't have the weights handy, don't despair. There are quite a few exercises out there that use your own body as resistance. You may have heard of a few of them:

➤ Push-ups

➤ Sit-ups

➤ Abdominal twists

➤ Lunges

➤ Side lunges

➤ Calf raises

➤ Wall sit

➤ Squats

➤ Step ups

With the exception of push-ups, these exercises work on strengthening the lower body, which, unless you're the goalie, is what you're really going to need in soccer.

Push-ups

A push-up works the upper body, specifically the muscles in the chest, the shoulders, and the back of the arms. These are all muscles that you use when you're doing a throw-in, so push-ups are a good exercise for everyone on a soccer team, not just the goalie.

I find it hard to believe that there's someone out there who doesn't know what a push-up is, but I'll quickly describe it just in case I'm wrong.

You're going to want to lie down, with your stomach on the floor. Your hands, palms down, are just outside your shoulders. Your legs and body should be straight, with your weight being supported by your hands and feet. Now, press upward, lifting your body off the ground until your elbows are fully extended. Then lower your body as far as you can go without your body touching the floor. That is one push-up.

Girls luck out on this exercise. After their body starts maturing, their weight is distributed differently than boys, making even one standard push-up virtually impossible for the average muscled woman. Because of this, a modified version has been created, where the weight in the back is on the knees rather than on the feet. This is considerably easier, yet it still works the muscles that you're trying to strengthen.

⚽ Bet You Didn't Know

If you are convinced that you use your stomach muscles all the time, there's a good test you can do. Do sit-ups until you feel the burn in your stomach. Then do 20 more. In other words, really give your abdominal muscles a workout. The next day you'll feel them in nearly every movement. Guaranteed.

Sit-ups

Like the push-up, the sit-up is a common exercise. It works the stomach muscles, which you'll need for nearly every movement you perform.

To do a sit-up, lie on your back with your legs bent and your feet flat on the floor. Place your hands loosely behind your head. Lift your upper body off the floor, making sure you exhale as you do this. Inhale as you go back down.

Keep your lower back on the ground during the whole sit-up. People used to go all the way up, but this strains the lower back, and it's not really necessary because you get most of the muscles in the first part of the lift.

Ab Twists

Another way to work the stomach area, with a few of the muscles on your sides thrown in, is to do abdominal twists. An ab twist is a sit-up with a little extra thrown in. In other words, you can think of the ab twist as a sit-up with a twist.

Follow the same instructions as with a sit-up but when your upper body is off the floor, twist first to one side, then back to the center, then to the other side, and then go back down. That's one ab twist.

Lunges

Now it's time to work those legs. The lunge specifically targets your quad muscle, which is the one that runs down the front of your thigh, and it also works your derriere.

Stand tall with your hands on your hips. Maintaining good posture is key for this one, so make Emily Post proud. With your head up facing forward, take a giant step with one leg. This step should be so big that your thigh is parallel to the ground. Do not get the thigh parallel by letting your front knee go out in front of your front foot. Return to standing and repeat with the other side. This is one lunge.

Side Lunges

A lunge to the side works your hip muscles and your backside.

Begin the same way as you would for a lunge, but instead of stepping forward, you step sideways, while your trunk remains facing forward. Again, keep good posture and make sure that your knee doesn't get out in front of your foot. Return to the standing position and lunge in the other direction. And that is one side lunge.

Calf Raises

Not surprisingly, calf raises work the calf muscles. This is a simple exercise, but one that is important to a soccer player. Don't ignore it.

Stand with both feet on the ground. Lift up onto the toes, hold, and then slowly return your heels to the floor. That's one.

Wall Sit

The wall sit is a favorite among skiers, because it really isolates the quad muscle, which is a muscle they rely on. It's also fun as a party challenge, once you've gotten really good at it. It looks easy, but boy, is it painful.

You want to create the illusion of sitting against the wall. Press your back up against the wall and then slide down into a sitting position. Pretend you have a chair beneath you. Your thighs should be parallel with the floor, and your feet flat on the ground.

Your level of strength determines how long you can hold this. If you're just beginning, try about 20 seconds the first time. Rest for 20 seconds and then do it again. Repeat it three times. If this seems too easy, increase the time against the wall to about 30 seconds. And at parties, you'll want to hold the wall sit as long as you can.

Squats

Squats are good exercises because they work a number of leg muscles at once, but they are a little hard on the knees, so if you have knee problems, go easy. Squats work the muscles in the front and back of your thigh, plus your backside.

Stand with your hands on your hips and your feet shoulder width apart. Maintaining good posture once again, bend your knees, keeping your feet in place. And, like before, do not let your knees get out in front of your feet. Return to standing position. This is one squat.

Step-ups

Step-ups work the same muscles as squats, so you probably don't want to do these exercises one right after the other or even in the same workout.

To do a step-up, stand in front of a one-foot-high bench or in front of some stairs. Step up onto the bench (or second step if you're using stairs), and then bring your other foot up. Step down with the first foot and then step down with the second foot. Repeat for the set, then change the leg that you lead with for the second set. You'll want to do four sets of this exercise, so that each leg gets an equal workout.

A Few for the Goalkeeper

Just because the goalkeeper wears a different color shirt and isn't bound by the no-hands rule it doesn't mean we can ignore her when it comes to working out. Certainly every goalkeeper can benefit from the leg, abdominal, and chest exercises described here, but here are a couple of other exercises that might work her upper body.

Bench Rowing

This is a good exercise for the shoulder muscles, or deltoids. There are three deltoids; one is in front, one is on top, and the other is in the back. Bench rowing works them all.

Place your knee and the arm on the same side on a bench (or coffee table or something of that nature). Place a dumbbell (or a small bag you've filled with cans or books or something heavy) on the floor. Reach down with the other arm and pull straight up. Do repetitions on both sides.

Reeling

A goalie must have strong wrists and forearms to snatch that ball out of the air and hold onto it, and reeling is a good way to work on them.

Tie a three-or four-foot length of string to some kind of weight. Anything mildly heavy will do. Then tie the other end of the string to some sort of stick, such as a broomstick. Hold the stick out in front of you, with your palms facing down and reel the weight up. Unreel it. That's one repetition. Do it six times and then rest. Then hold the stick palms up and reel it up again for the second set. Do four sets.

Timing Is Everything

You're probably wondering how you're going to figure out how many of each exercise to do. One rep? Two? And what's a *rep*, by the way? And while we're at it, how often do you do this? Every day? Once a month? What's the answer?

There's no exact answer as to how much weight training you want to do, but it's better to err on the light side. Whatever method of weight training you choose to use, you want to make sure that you don't overdo it or strain your muscles.

Learning the Lingo

Rep is short for repetition. And that means one execution of the exercise you're going to do. So, for instance, if you're doing push-ups, then pushing up and coming back down is one rep.

Planning the Reps

Whichever exercise you choose, you do it for a certain number of repetitions, and you do those repetitions three or four times. Say you choose squats, for example. A beginner might want to do five squats and then rest. Then do five more. And then a third set of five more. A more advanced player might do four sets of six or eight.

Coach's Corner

You'll know it's time to move up to more reps when you find that the third or fourth set is becoming as easy as the first one.

After the four sets, you then move on to the next exercise. Try to pick one that doesn't work the exact same muscles. In other words, you don't want to go straight from squats to step-ups or the wall sit. All these exercises work the quadriceps muscle. Try side lunges or abdominal twists instead.

Try to do at least six or seven different exercises in a workout. A beginner's workout should last about 20 minutes for it to be worthwhile, and a more advanced strength trainer should work out for about an hour.

The Weekly Schedule

Muscles actually have to rip to get bigger. That's what you're doing when you push them in these weight training exercises. So you have to let them heal. You can't just rip, rip, rip, with no repair time.

Work out with weights about three times a week, and make sure that you take a day off in between each weight day. In other words, don't make your weight days Monday, Tuesday, Wednesday, with the other four days off. A Monday, Wednesday, Friday schedule or a Tuesday, Thursday, Saturday schedule is better.

You can alternate your strength training and your conditioning training. For instance, on Monday you might run for long distance, five or six miles. On Tuesday, you hit the weight room. On Wednesday, you run a shorter distance, maybe only two miles and you run some sprints. Then on Thursday, it's back to the weight room for some more muscle work.

Ideally, you can also alternate which exercises you use in each strength workout, so that your different muscles get worked out in different ways.

Down Time

You also want to do your weight training in the off-season. If you build your muscles to their peak in the off-season, then the work you do playing soccer in practice and games will maintain this peak during the season. There are a some reasons for this:

➤ *You don't want to overwork your muscles.* If you're ripping your muscles in the weight room one day and then racing around the soccer field the next, there's no down time.

➤ *You don't want to throw off your touch.* If you keep getting stronger, that simple pass to a teammate 10 feet away might end up as a bullet across the field.

➤ *There's no time.* Unless playing soccer is your job, you're either going to be working or going to school during the time you're not playing soccer. When are you going to fit in the weight training?

Unfortunately, it never occurs to players to do weight training in preseason. Let's hope this is enough to give you a push in the right direction. If not, maybe your coach will step in

The Least You Need to Know

➤ Don't strength train until you've stopped growing.

➤ Heavy weights a few times for bulk. Light weights lots of times for toning.

➤ Alternate strength training days with conditioning days, so your muscles have time to heal.

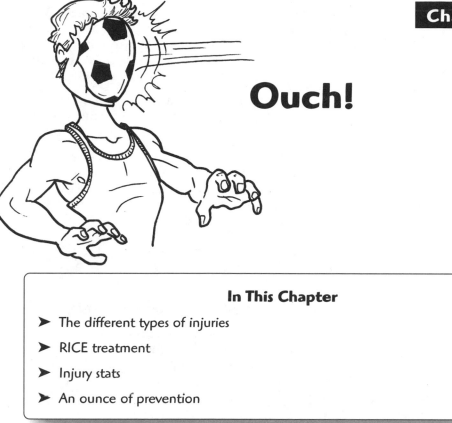

Chapter 17

Ouch!

In This Chapter

➤ The different types of injuries

➤ RICE treatment

➤ Injury stats

➤ An ounce of prevention

It was a perfect October Saturday. The sky was cloudless, red and gold leaves covered the hillside near the field, and the temperature was about 58 degrees, perfect for 90 minutes of soccer. We were about 20 minutes into the play when the opposing half-back let her dribble get a little too far away from her. I scrambled to get it, and as she tried to recover, our feet connected with the ball at the same time. Everything stopped but my knee. Pop! Tear! Three ligaments and some cartilage ripped as my knee continued to charge forward without me.

That injury was a fluke, just as many sports injuries are, and there was nothing I could do about it. (I did recover fully, by the way.) However, there are a few things you can do to prevent injury or at least minimize its impact. This chapter talks about the most common kinds of soccer injuries, what you can do to heal them as quickly as possible, and how you can prevent them from happening in the first place.

Injury Inventory

No one likes to get hurt, and soccer certainly has its fair share of injuries. There are sprains, strains, pulls, breaks, and snaps. Blisters, concussions, and heat stroke round

out a checklist that no one wants to complete. But fear not. An entire game can go by without an injury to a team. An entire season can go by without an injury to a player. Soccer may give you some bumps and bruises, but in general, you can stay healthy playing it.

Sometimes it's hard to tell just how serious an injury is. Is it just a twist of an ankle or is it a sprain? Is it a bone broken or is it just a bad bruise? The Five Minute Rule is a good one to follow:

The Five Minute Rule: If you rest for five minutes and feel fine, you can go back to playing. If the injury still hurts after five minutes, then it's something that's more serious and needs attention.

If you do find yourself with an injury, it's not the end of the world. Most injuries are not career-ending or even season-ending. Here are a few of the most common.

Twist and Shout: The Sprain

The sprain is probably the most common soccer injury. And if you're playing soccer, the ankle is usually the joint of choice for this type of injury. You step on the ball accidentally, the ankle turns sideways, and all your weight comes crashing down on this mispositioned foot. No doubt about it. You've got a sprain.

The sudden and violent twisting of a joint causes a sprain. This in turn causes the ligaments that hold the joint together to stretch or tear. A ligament is a tough strand of fibrous tissue that connects the bone to bone in a joint.

There are three degrees of a sprain.

➤ In the first, the ligaments are stretched so that the fibers just begin to pull apart.

➤ In the second one, the fibers actually start to tear as well.

➤ In the most severe sprains, the ligament tears completely.

If the fibers tear, you have a severe sprain, which could be season ending. If they stretch, you'll just be out for a few days to a week.

Once you've sprained a joint, it's going to be weakened. Take care to let the joint fully heal, so that you don't tear the ligament again. If you tear it completely, you'll have trouble with that area for life.

Pulling Muscles

A muscle looks like a whole lot of heavy threads stuck together. If you make one of your muscles—and you have many of them—do something it doesn't want to do, these threads are going to start pulling apart. This creates a *pulled muscle*, one of the most common injuries found in a soccer player.

Oddly enough, it's also one of the most preventable. All you need to do is stretch the muscles before you play. Time to read Chapter 14 again? After you get the muscles loose, they'll be more willing to make any movement.

Head Case

Because head balls are such a huge part of the game, head injuries are, too. Fortunately, the brain is well-protected by the skull and the fluid inside it. Therefore, most head injuries aren't serious, just surface bruises that never reach the brain. But injuries can result in the more dangerous *concussion*, where the blow does reach the brain and can affect its functioning.

Learning the Lingo

A *concussion* is the mild or complete loss of function due to a blow to the head.

Even when a knock to the head is the more serious concussion, it's still usually not something to worry about. Most concussions are gone by the next day with slight disorientation and a headache being the only really annoying symptoms. A number of concussions are more serious, however, and you should be on the lookout for other symptoms that might indicate that you should call a doctor or rush to the emergency room.

Signs of a concussion:

➤ Vomiting

➤ Unequal dilation of the pupils

➤ Unresponsive pupils

➤ Unsteady walk

➤ Numbness

➤ Dizziness

➤ Incoherent speech

➤ Seeing stars

➤ Hearing bells

➤ Unconsciousness

If you have one or more of these symptoms, then your concussion is more serious, and you should get it checked out by a doctor. You could have a crack in your skull or bleeding in the skull, which needs to be operated on immediately or there will be permanent brain damage.

If a player has a serious head injury in the game, take him out for good, even if he passes the five-minute test. A second blow to the same damaged area could cause some serious problems.

Hot Enough for You

Ninety minutes is a long time to be racing around an open field, especially if the day is a hot one. So soccer players always need to be on the alert for heat exhaustion and heat stroke. These are not to be taken lightly.

Heat exhaustion is less serious and is caused by dehydration. The player should replenish the fluids and take a rest in a shady area.

Heat stroke can be life-threatening, and if you see a player who has turned beet red, is running a fever, and is acting irrationally, cool him down with ice and water and get him to the hospital immediately.

Heads Up

Children don't develop efficient cooling systems for their bodies until close to puberty, so they're more prone to heat problems than adults are. They also are more eager to play despite discomfort or exhaustion, so you really have to keep an eye on them on hot days.

Knee Knowledge

Ligament damage in the knee (my personal favorite) is on the rise for athletes, and in scary numbers among girls playing soccer. Oddly enough, this isn't as common among boy soccer players. This figure shows the ligaments in the knee. The most common knee ligament injury is the tearing of the anterior cruciate ligament (ACL).

No one is absolutely positive why girls are getting what used to be a common football injury, but many people in the sports medicine world feel that a girl's quadriceps muscle is considerably smaller than her male counterpart's. Therefore even though both the boy and the girl are playing soccer, the sport is putting much more stress on the ligaments. The ligaments are doing far more work holding the joint together because the girl doesn't have the muscle power to help out. (So if I'd only had beefier thighs . . . sigh.)

Cartilage damage is another knee problem that shows up in athletes. The cartilage is a cushion under the knee cap that helps reduce the stress of the joint. If the cartilage is ripped or worn away through injury, then it can be painful, because it's bone hitting bone. The pain can be relieved through minor arthroscopic surgery.

The knee ligaments.

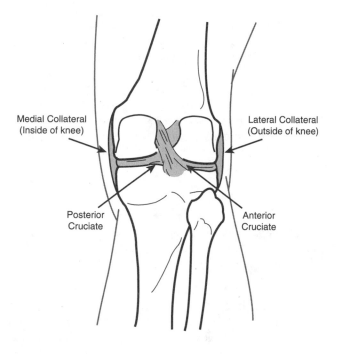

Medial Collateral
(Inside of knee)

Lateral Collateral
(Outside of knee)

Posterior
Cruciate

Anterior
Cruciate

Break Dance

Sticks and stones will break my bones, or so the old saying goes, but unless you're 80-years-old with a calcium deficiency, it's actually quite difficult to break a bone. Two-thirds of a bone is actually not "bone" at all but rather *collagen* and water. Collagen is kind of like the gristle in meat, and it makes the bones much more flexible than you'd think.

Nonetheless, you will find the occasional broken bone in soccer, but more often than not, it's of the less serious type. You probably didn't know that there are actually three types of fractures:

Learning the Lingo

Technically, *collagen* is a protein that takes the form of white fibers of tissue when it's in the bone but turns into gelatin when it's boiled. Collagen is the substance that is injected into people's lips to make them look fuller.

1. **A complete fracture**, where the bone is actually broken in two. In this case, the treatment is to reset the bone and immobilize in a cast.

2. **A stress fracture**, where the bone is just cracked. Treatment for this is rest. This is also sometimes called a hairline fracture.

3. **A greenstick fracture**, which is a crack on one side of the bone. This is found almost exclusively in children, whose bones are much more flexible (like a green stick on a tree), so rather than breaking under stress, the bone just bends a lot and cracks on one side.

Bone can heal itself by creating new bone material to fill in the gaps. The cast helps the bone remain immobilized to speed up the repair, to make it heal properly, and to reduce the pain that more movement might cause, but technically even a complete fracture can heal without help.

Easy Does It

Back in the dark ages of childhood, kids used to play a little of this and a little of that. A little street hockey one day and stickball the next. Sometimes they'd play an organized sport, but it was only for one season, and then it was on to the next or back out into neighbors' backyards for pick-up games.

Well, things are a little bit different now. Parents are not as comfortable sending their kids out to play for hours on end, not having any idea what they're doing and where they are. The United States is not as rural as it was, and more people and less open space mean a higher potential for danger. Kids have one or maybe two kids over at a time, and who can play a full game of soccer like that?

So with little to do with free time, it's not surprising that there was a boom in organized sports participation. But here comes the problem. Rather than just playing whatever they feel like playing, kids are being directed into one or two sports, with soccer topping the list. They play these sports not just for one day or even one season, but sometimes all year round.

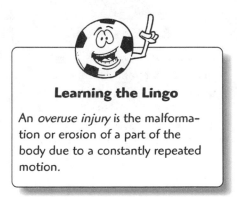

Learning the Lingo

An *overuse injury* is the malformation or erosion of a part of the body due to a constantly repeated motion.

So instead of just playing soccer in the fall, when the local school offers it, kids are playing indoor soccer in the winter, spring soccer, and going to summer soccer camps. What happens? An *overuse injury*.

Kid's bones are not fully developed. The areas at the end of the bones are soft because that is where the growth happens. When a joint is overused, the ligaments repeatedly pull on these soft bone areas, causing injury.

The most common overuse injuries for soccer are

➤ **Osgood-Schlatter disease**, which creates a painful bony lump just under the knee

➤ **Shin splints**, a pain in the front and sides of the lower legs that increases during exercise

➤ **Tendinitis,** an inflammation of the tendons

➤ **Stress fractures,** which occur due to repeated jarring of a bone

➤ **Bursitis,** an inflammation of the fluid-filled sacs that cushion joints, especially knees, elbows and shoulders

➤ **Sever's disease,** pain in the heel that usually happens when a lot of activity happens at the same time as a growth spurt

Aside from making sure that you don't play one sport excessively, you can prevent overuse injuries just by taking it easy when an area starts to hurt. Go see a doctor if you have persistent pain anywhere, and she can tell whether you need to cut back or if it's some other type of injury.

RICE Is Nice

If the dreaded event happens and you do finally get an injury, speedy and proper treatment can get you back on the field quickly. There are four steps to recovery and they can be easily remembered through the RICE acronym. RICE stands for

➤ Rest

➤ Ice

➤ Compression

➤ Elevation

Early action with the RICE treatment can mean an early return to the playing field.

R Is for Rest

Rest is a pretty basic idea. It means stay off your injury. If you have a sprained ankle or a pulled quad muscle, get some crutches. The more you can keep stress off the injured area, the quicker it's going to heal.

Then after a few days, you can see if you can put pressure on the area with something simple like walking. You don't want the area to build up scar tissue or get too stiff from inactivity, so light movement is what you need now. Finally, when you feel it is *fully* (this is the key word) healed, you can suit up for practice. If that works out, it's game time once again.

I Is for Ice

As soon as you injure *anything*, get some ice on it. If you bump your head, put ice on it. If you pull a muscle, put ice on it. When an area is injured, the blood pours into the

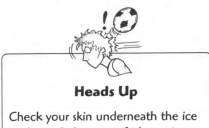

Heads Up

Check your skin underneath the ice pack regularly to see if it's starting to get frostbite. You can recognize frostbite by the fact that your skin is getting hard and white.

affected area, making it swell. The swelling is the source of most of the pain associated with an injury. Ice constricts the blood vessels in your body, thereby reducing the flow of blood, reducing the pain, and reducing the amount of time it's going to take to heal.

Ice should be applied as often as possible for the first 48 hours, with three times a day being the minimum. Ice should be applied no more than 20 minutes at a time, however, to prevent frostbite.

When you ice, you want to place a wet cloth between the ice pack and the injured area. Ice packs can be purchased or made. Here are the three most popular:

➤ Commercial gel pack found in first aid kits

➤ Ice cubes (or crushed ice for better fit) in a bag

➤ Frozen vegetables in a bag

Bet You Didn't Know

Many players continue the heat and ice cycle well after they're back in the game. They use heat before the game to loosen the muscle or ligament, and then they ice after the game when the area has been aggravated to reduce any swelling that might occur because of the aggravation.

After a few days of using ice, the area has started to heal, and the extra blood won't be flowing there. Then it's time to resume minimal activity and treat the area with heat. The injured area has probably become a little stiff from the ice and the immobility, and heat, in the form of heating pads, will get it moving smoothly again.

Any time you feel pain returning to the area because you've been using it, throw an ice pack on it, even if you're past the initial 48-hour ice treatment.

C Is for Compression

Wrapping an injury tightly also helps reduce the flow of blood to the injured area. In addition, it helps you to keep the area immobile. Many players continue to tape the injured area after they're back in the game, hoping that the tape will provide extra support for a weakened part of the body.

E Is for Elevation

Finally, you want to get the injured area higher than your heart. This slows down the blood-pumping effort, which in turn reduces the swelling and the pain. Prop up the injured area whenever you can.

And P Is for Physical Therapist

If, after a few days of RICE, things are not looking up, then it's time to see a physical therapist, a doctor, or a trainer if you're at a school. Your injury may be more serious than you think, and require more treatment. Trainers and physical therapists have weight machines that can strengthen the muscles around a weak joint and deep-heat machines that can penetrate much farther into a damaged muscle than a heating pad.

A Look Behind the Numbers

Soccer injuries have risen dramatically in the last few decades, and many worrywarts are sounding the alarm. Are kids bodies more fragile these days, are the programs too difficult, or is something else considerably more sinister afoot? The answer is: none of the above. With the exception of the overuse problems already discussed, several positive forces are changing the injury statistics. Think about it. The sports scene today is different from the scene just one or two decades ago.

1. Kindergartner
2. Recreational players
3. No more vacant lots

Sound a bit fishy? Let's take them one by one.

And They Just Keep Getting Younger

First of all, kids are starting to play at a much younger age. In the '60s, there was a 50/50 chance that a high school even had a soccer program, and even less to have a girl's soccer program. Same for a lot of colleges. In the '70s, the numbers began to grow, especially for girls after Title IX was enacted. Junior high schools and youth leagues began to have soccer teams.

By the '80s, many schools had soccer teams, and the ages of the players just kept creeping lower. Now not only did high schools and junior high schools have teams, but youth leagues had sprung up everywhere. By the '90s, if a kid didn't start playing in kindergarten, he was going to have a tough time catching up with his peers.

So we can safely conclude from this development that the numbers of players have gone up, because rather than just older boys playing, we have boys

Learning the Lingo

Title IX was a section of a 1972 federal education amendment, and it stated that "no person in the United States shall, on the basis of sex . . . be subjected to discrimination under any education program or activity." In other words, if there's a boy's soccer team at a high school, there has to be a girl's soccer team, too. Or else!

and girls from kindergarten through college taking up the sport. More numbers equals more injuries.

Rec League Lightweights

This brings us to the adult recreation leagues. These also have sprung up around the country. It used to be that your mental picture of the "aging athlete" would be a beer-swilling, paunchy, slow-pitch softball player. Not so anymore. Men and women are both joining amateur and recreational soccer teams by the truckload.

This is great news for soccer, but not so good for those soccer injury stats. Again, we have the more numbers, more injury argument, but now, thrown into that equation, are older, weaker, and less fit bodies playing the game.

Most recreational athletes are not anywhere near being as in shape as they once were when they played the game for their schools, yet they still push their bodies to perform the same way out on the field. At most, they have one practice a week, and outside conditioning is minimal. The situation is ripe for injury. Not to mention the fact that once you stop growing, the warranty on your body runs out. It breaks a whole lot easier and takes a whole lot longer to repair.

Just a Different Way to Look at It

Finally, there is the vacant lot syndrome. It used to be that kids took a ball over to a vacant lot, set up a few makeshift goals, and had a game. If someone twisted an ankle or banged their head for a concussion, they went home, told Mom, were taken to the doctor, and it was reported as "childhood injury."

But play on those vacant lots has declined dramatically in the past decade or two. Now kids have such scheduled lives that they have no need to create the pick-up games they used to. Now when they play soccer, they are playing in an organized league and when they get the exact same injury at the exact same age in the exact same way, it's considered a "soccer injury."

Bet You Didn't Know

How soccer (an average injury sport) compares with other sports in the injury department: football: high; basketball: medium; baseball: medium to high; tennis: low; golf: low; lacrosse: high for boys, medium for girls; ice hockey: high.

Prevention Is the Best Medicine

Injuries are certainly a very real part of playing sports, but you shouldn't let the fear of being hurt scare you away from participating, especially when the sport of choice is soccer, and you've now seen that the report of rising soccer injuries is just a myth.

Of course, medium isn't as comforting as low, and if you play soccer long enough, you're probably going to fall prey to at least one injury in your career, but there are a few things you can do to lower that risk. You can reread Chapter 14 and learn about stretching. You can check out the nutrition section in Chapter 21, you can have the proper equipment, and you can drink plenty of water. Here's a quick overview of the crucial points in case rereading isn't your thing.

Coming into the Stretch

Stretching can make a huge difference in injury prevention. The more flexible a muscle is, the less it's likely to tear when you make a peculiar or unnatural movement.

Equipment Check

The right equipment can make a world of difference. It's there for a reason. Just as it would be ludicrous for a football player to play without a helmet, you shouldn't ever consider stepping on a soccer field without your shin guards—even if it's just practice. The law requiring those little pieces of hard plastic dropped the bruise-and-break rate of the lower leg dramatically.

You also want to make sure you're playing with the right size ball. Little kids with little legs shouldn't be trying to propel a size-5 ball meant for adults. It's going to put far too much stress on their knees.

And finally, make sure there's water handy. It's important every time you play, but it can be critical on really hot days. Bring it yourself if you know there's no fountain near the field.

Know Your Limitations

It's an age-old story. When big kids and little kids play a sport together, the little kids get beat up on, even if it's not intentional. The littler ones get run into, knocked down, stepped on. It's open season for concussions, breaks, and bruises.

Even if you are playing with kids your own age, you have to be careful not to try to reach levels that your body is not prepared for. Most injuries happen early in the season. The athletes are not in top shape, yet they try to run the entire 90 minutes, sucking wind for the last 30. A tired athlete is not going to lift his legs nearly as high or change directions quite as sharply, and the resulting misstep can be a sprained ankle or a pulled muscle.

The key here is to get in shape before your season starts. You owe it to your team and you owe it to your body.

Take Care of the Little Problems

Finally, if you do get slightly injured, let yourself heal. A slight muscle pull that gets the RICE treatment for a few days will disappear. A slight muscle pull that goes right back into the game and is treated with inattention is only going to get worse and become a severe muscle pull, which might keep you out for the rest of the season.

The Least You Need to Know

➤ If you injure yourself, wait five minutes and see if you can play. If you can, it's a mild one. If you can't, you need to give the injury some treatment.

➤ The acronym RICE (Rest, Ice, Compression, and Elevation) is the best treatment for most injuries.

➤ Stretching and knowing your limitations can prevent quite a few injuries.

Part 5
A Parents' Primer

Many of you who are reading this book are newcomers to soccer, drawn to the sport through your child's involvement or potential involvement. Everyone seems to be doing it, but you still have a few questions.

Some parents have hesitations about the very nature of sports and soccer specifically. Do you want to put your child in this environment? In my highly biased opinion, the answer is a resounding "Yes!" But I'll support my conclusion in Chapter 18.

And then, just when I've convinced you that soccer is the most wonderful thing you can do for your child, I'm going to turn around and bring you back to earth in Chapters 19 and 20. That's when I tell you about all the demands the sport puts on both you, as the parent, and your child. And if your child happens to be quite good at soccer, there's extra fun in store for both of you, which I cover in Chapter 21.

Chapter 18

To Play or Not to Play

In This Chapter

➤ Why your child should play sports

➤ Or maybe they shouldn't

➤ How to handle quitting

Parents are polarized on the sports issue. Some swear by it, claiming that it builds character and good habits for life, and some are nervous about exposing their children to such a competitive and stressful environment.

Not surprisingly, I come down heavily on the sports-are-good-for-you side, and research supports me. The advantages and disadvantages of children's participation in sports has been consuming the American public almost as much as the sports themselves, and the overwhelming majority of studies conclude that participating in sports is a wonderful opportunity for young people. Here's why.

Physical Fitness

The physical part is the easy one. It's hard for anyone to argue with the fact that sports, running, and conditioning are good for general overall health. Because soccer has them all, you can conclude that at least on this one point, signing your child up for soccer is a good thing.

Bet You Didn't Know

Soccer is the pick of the sports litter as far as I'm concerned. It gives you more running than any other sport. It's played outside in the fresh air in a semicool season. It's easy enough for little ones to understand, yet complicated enough to be challenging at the highest levels. It's relatively cheap, and the injury factor isn't too bad.

Bet You Didn't Know

Air-conditioning also affects the way we eat. If it's hot, you don't feel like eating much. In climate-controlled houses, however, you lose nature's little diet plan. On top of that, summer foods used to mean light dishes, a lot of fruit, and cold salads. With air-conditioning, there's no incentive not to go ahead and make that roast with baked potatoes.

But not just soccer. Any sport is good. And not just good. As far as physical fitness is concerned, sports are vital! Because of the way things work today, many children have lost the opportunity to be in shape naturally, which could set a pattern for life. Organized sports need to step in.

Fattening Factors

Numerous studies have been done on children's physical well-being as the decades passed in the last part of the twentieth century. The results were all the same. Every decade the children got fatter and less fit. The reasons are varied and numerous.

Progress seems to be the big fitness killer, and I don't mean just television (which I will get to in a minute). Take air-conditioning, for instance. It can be blamed for a lot of the fattening of our youth (grown-ups, too, for that matter). It used to be that the summer months meant it was too hot to stay indoors. People went outside to the pools, the sprinklers, the swimming holes, and the beaches. Now the reverse is true: because the house can be kept comfortably cool, it's too hot to go out. Instead of all that athletic water activity, kids find indoor projects to keep them entertained.

And let's not forget television, as I mentioned before. The hours logged as a couch potato sitting sluggishly in front of the television are an obvious health hazard. The TV plays a part in another way, too. The media reaches far and wide these days, so while abductions and abuse are not necessarily on the rise, the reporting of them is. Many parents are no longer comfortable saying, "Go play outside. Just be back for dinner." A lot of physical exercise that used to go on in those woods and vacant lots has been lost.

Suburban sprawl has also sucked away a lot of the exercise that kids used to get. Children used to live in small towns. If they wanted to get to a friend's house, school, or the local movie theater, they walked or rode a bike. In today's vast and sprawling suburbs, a car is the only option.

Okay, enough is enough, you say. You get the idea. Physical fitness, which used to be an everyday part of life, does not come as naturally to our children any more. Reason numero uno to sign your kids up for sports.

Fit for Life

Every medical professional on the planet (and probably all those on other planets as well) will tell you that exercise is good for you. But did you know just how good?

It expands your heart and lung capacity. It keeps your weight down, your cholesterol down, and your blood pressure down. It reduces your risk of heart failure, arthritis, cancer, osteoporosis, depression, and, as was just recently discovered, Alzheimer's disease (bet you didn't know that one!).

While your child is probably not at risk for any of these ailments at the tender age of six or seven, physical exercise is still good for him, too. A fit child is less likely to get sick or to have the aches and pains that are associated with extra weight. Besides, if a child develops a love of sports early in life, chances are it will continue into old age when he really needs it. And that's reason number two for sports.

Bumps and Bruises

But what about injuries, you ask. After all, there is some physical danger involved with playing sports, all of which is detailed in the previous chapter. Sports are not entirely beneficial to your body, and have a tendency to create sprained ankles, torn ligaments, and a whole lot of bumps and bruises.

But look at it this way. A child who isn't physically fit and who tries to compete, say in gym class or in a pick-up volleyball game at a backyard picnic somewhere, is actually going to run a far greater risk of getting injured. A body that's pushed beyond the limit of what it's used to is going to break down. Not only that, but most injuries occur when a player is tired, which I guarantee will be the case rather quickly with your out-of-shape child.

Think back to those pick-up picnic games you joined in as a youth. Who were the kids who were always complaining of aches and pains? The unathletic ones, right? And, unlike what you thought at the time, it wasn't merely an excuse just because they couldn't keep up with more fit children. They probably were truly hurt.

So unless you make sure that your child never gets into a physically challenging situation, and that's unwise as well as unrealistic, she's better off being an athlete. We're cooking with gas now. Up to reason number three.

Mental Health

The battle of brawn versus brain still rages, but they mesh nicely when it comes to sports participation. Sports not only improve the body, but they do great things for the mind as well—building self-esteem and confidence in one's abilities.

If you have a good coach, then sports are a guaranteed self-esteem and confidence builder, at least at the younger levels. Because the sport is so new, improvements arrive daily and the support and praise of the coach is genuine. Even if a player is not the best on the team, she can be proud of the personal accomplishments she has made.

And This Award Goes to . . .

At the end of the season, many teams hand out certificates or trophies with a little comment about each player achievements. Kids love this and it really helps boost their confidence to know that they're the "best" at something.

Here are some good examples of awards that players can get even if they aren't going to win The Most Valuable Player award. You can suggest these awards to your child's coach if she hasn't already planned to do this.

➤ Best Midfielder

➤ Best Goalie

➤ Best Defender

➤ Best Forward

➤ Best Passer

➤ Best Dribbler

➤ Best Kicker

➤ Best Attitude

➤ Toughest Player

➤ Best listener

➤ Most Improved

➤ Most Well-rounded

And don't be concerned with the fact that these awards promote competition or comparisons. This is a part of life that your child will have to deal from the minute he starts preschool until the day he dies. You can try to make it as positive an experience as possible, but don't try to eliminate competition because that just doesn't reflect reality. Keep in mind that the reason for the award should be legitimate.

There is a sense that in the United States, everyone has to be the best. And unfortunately, not everyone is going to be the best. Some people use that as an argument *against* awards like these (why promote this be-the-best attitude?). They think that trophies should be given for participation rather than achievement. I use it as an argument *for* them (the attitude is there, so give the child a taste of accomplishment). Trophies are for achievement.

Academic Achievement

Study after study shows that kids who are involved in sports do better in school. If that's not a great argument for sports, then I don't know one. There are quite a few theories that go along with this.

➤ Sports teach a child how to be disciplined.

➤ The time demands of sport force a child to be organized.

➤ The desire to play on school teams keeps children in school.

➤ Scholarship opportunities raise the bar on academic achievements.

➤ Sports keep kids off drugs, which is a big reason for dropouts.

➤ Sports reduce teen pregnancy, another big dropout factor.

Most schools try to emphasize the importance of both academic and athletic achievement by giving scholar-athlete awards or by denying participation to students who don't make the grade.

So that's self-esteem, confidence, and academic achievement. Reasons four, five, and six to have your child play sports.

Social Security

But wait! There's more. Sports help your child make friends, keep friends, and work well with others. You can't beat that with a stick. The friend issue is a big one. By having an immediate common interest, two players who don't know each other can at least begin a conversation. On top of that, in soccer, each player is relying on the others, so many players develop close bonds that persist long after the season is over.

Good sportsmanship skills can also create friendships off the field. People who have learned how to treat others fairly, accept a victory without gloating, and muffle disappointment are well-liked by others. You can learn these skills without playing sports, but isn't it nice to have sports teach them?

The teamwork and leadership skills that soccer and other team sports provide are invaluable throughout life, whether it's for a group project in school or a presentation to a new client at work. In fact, many successful adults cite their sports participation as the greatest benefit to their achievement in the working world. Not only do you learn how to be part of a team, but you learn how to direct others, make quick decisions, win and lose gracefully, and set priorities.

Sports also emphasize following and playing by the rules. Again, this is a valuable lesson to learn for situations throughout life. Referees are going to be blowing the whistle at anyone who tries to cheat, so kids learn quickly that bending the rules is not the way to success.

Bet You Didn't Know

There's an added bonus for you that comes out of your child's involvement in sports. You get to make friends, too. Those hours in the bleachers make for some good bonding moments.

Finally, kids who get involved in sports stay out of trouble. This is partly because they don't have time to get into trouble, with boredom being the number one reason for juvenile delinquency, but also because many athletes have a respect for their bodies. They don't want to do anything that might hurt their bodies and therefore hurt their performance on the field.

So, there you have it. Ten great reasons to sign your child up for sports. A quick recap:

1. Source of exercise for kids
2. A lifetime love of fitness
3. Less injury prone
4. Self-esteem
5. Confidence
6. Academic achievement
7. New friends
8. Teamwork
9. No cheating frame of mind
10. Keeps kids out of trouble

Can't argue with that can you? Give your kids a leg up on life by involving them in sports. Don't push if they're not interested, but don't deprive them of the opportunity to play just because you have a few hesitations.

Dishing the Downside Dirt

Okay, all is not a bed of roses—there are a few negatives to sport. But just a few. And most of them are negatives for the parents rather than the players.

For parents, the big one is the time drain. Shuttling your child around to practices, games, and tournaments is time-consuming enough, but when you're trying to do it for two or three children, it borders on ridiculous. And if you work, it's doubly hard, because you need your weekends to get things done (such as the laundry, because you're going to have piles of dirty uniforms to deal with).

For the kids, one of the biggest downsides is the controlled organized environment at such a young age. Kids should be racing around, making up their own games, rather than being forced to stand in a line and follow FIFA's rules. Unfortunately, because so many kids start playing organized soccer at such a young age, your kid may lose out on the chance to play *ever* if he doesn't start at roughly the same time. The other player's will be leaps and bounds ahead of him by the time he wants to pick it up in high school.

Coach's Corner

Because organized sports aren't ideal playgrounds for the youngest children, coaches should have a loose practice with lots of room for variation, little standing in line, and good sense of play.

There are other factors that might create a negative experience for your young soccer player. Bad coaches, a competitive environment for a noncompetitive kid, and pressure to perform are a few. Some players get much too stressed out to make sports a healthy activity for them. If you can't get them to take it a little less seriously, then you might want to switch to a different activity. Sports are meant to be fun after all.

Quitting Time

Many parents are afraid that allowing their child to quit a sport is going to turn them into a quitter for life. But children are born dabblers. They like to try a little of this and a little of that. Think back to your toddler at play. Did he ever stick with anything longer than 15 minutes? It gets better as the kids get older, but it's really not until adolescence or even adulthood that true commitment to an activity becomes a possibility.

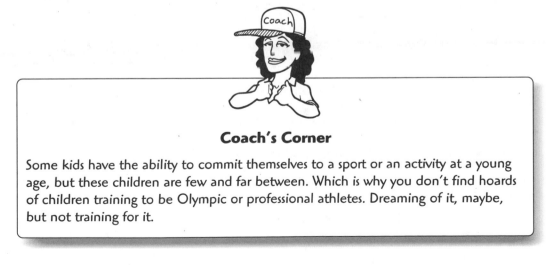

Coach's Corner

Some kids have the ability to commit themselves to a sport or an activity at a young age, but these children are few and far between. Which is why you don't find hoards of children training to be Olympic or professional athletes. Dreaming of it, maybe, but not training for it.

But aside from the fact that children are experimenters, your child might be looking to quit because he never really wanted to play soccer to begin with.

➤ Did you sign him up without first finding out if this was something he liked?

➤ Did he want to sign up because his best friend signed up?

➤ Is your child a perfectionist who is frustrated because he isn't the best player on the team?

➤ Does Saturday morning practice mean he misses his beloved Saturday morning cartoons?

If you take a look behind the curtain, there's a good chance there's a wizard who doesn't want to be there in the first place.

Soccer Blahs

Especially if you were an athlete yourself, the idea of having a child who wants to quit a sport can be quite painful. But sometimes, if you delve into the reasons behind the "I want to quit" statement, you might find out that it's soccer that's the problem, not sports in general. (I just hate saying that.) Just because soccer doesn't work out, doesn't mean that another sport will be equally as disappointing.

Find out why your child doesn't like it:

➤ **The coach.** That's easy. Switch coaches. He may love soccer after that.

➤ **Working with other players on a team.** Try a solo sport, such as tennis, golf, squash, fencing, swimming, diving, wrestling, skiing, snowboarding, figure skating, skateboarding, roller skating, biking, or running. The list is long.

➤ **Too much running.** Try nearly anything but soccer, but specifically baseball, golf, diving, and wrestling don't have as much of a heavy emphasis on aerobic conditioning.

➤ **Time commitment.** You might find a less demanding league, allowing your child to stick with soccer.

➤ **Competition.** This is a biggie for sports, because almost all of them have winning and losing at the core of their being. But something such as dance will give a child exercise without the pressure of competition.

Work with your child to find an athletic activity that's going to make her happy. You don't want to lose the opportunity for her to find something she truly loves just because of one bad experience with soccer. Experiment a little. If three or four totally different types of athletic experiences are failures, then maybe you can accept defeat.

Not for Me

Why accept defeat? Because it happens. Inevitably there are going to be children for whom sports are a bad fit. Any sports. No amount of tweaking is going to work. And parents are going to have to accept that whether they starred on the football field or tennis court in college.

Yes, that means your child is going to lose out on a lot of what athletics has to offer, but as long as he is interested and committed to some other activity, he will still reap many of the same benefits, such as confidence and self-esteem. Activities such as band and drama also develop the teamwork and camaraderie traits that sports provide. A hobby such as stamp collecting or watercolor painting can expand the mind and build self-esteem.

Coach's Corner

If you can, try to encourage your child to finish out the commitment before quitting as long as it isn't too long. Usually a soccer season is about eight to ten weeks, so a month or so more won't hurt, and it will give your child a lesson about commitment and responsibility.

The only time you really should worry is if you can't get your child interested in anything or if a normally involved child suddenly quits everything. The first trait will make her a less well-rounded and less-interesting person, and either one could signal depression or drug use.

The Late in the Game Quitter

Let me tell you about this guy I know named James who played soccer in all the youth leagues growing up. From kindergarten to junior high, he was high scorer on every team he played on. The soccer coach at the local high school was drooling in anticipation, just waiting for him to get to ninth grade.

Well, freshman year arrives, and over the summer James has had his growth spurt. The football coach, who knows he's a talented athlete starts recruiting him to try out for football. James is tempted. He's already proven himself on the soccer field. Wouldn't it be great to become a star on the gridiron, too. He makes the switch, much to the dismay of his parents and the soccer coach..

James doesn't become a star right away, but he does catch on quickly and the potential is there. He's hooked. And when spring season rolls around James ditches baseball for the new challenge of lacrosse. His parents are beside themselves.

Learning the Lingo

I call this the *Michael Jordan syndrome.* Just when you get really good at something, you quit to find a new challenge.

Why, you ask, would this bother his parents so much? To begin with, they're not wealthy. They've been counting pennies and setting aside money every year to send James to soccer and baseball camps. They knew there was a slim chance that he could make a living at these sports, but he was improving so much, they thought there might be a good chance at a scholarship to college. That's a potential $50,000 decision that James just made.

They're also concerned about James's character. Is their son a quitter? Is he going to have problems with commitment later in life?

And on top of all that, they remember the countless hours they spent driving to faraway games and the weekends they gave up because of tournament demands. Was it all for nothing?

No, no, and absolutely not. In the first place, James made a nearly decade long commitment to soccer at a stage in life when people are usually dabblers, remember? Does that sound like the personality of a quitter?

Secondly, he never quit in the middle of the season or quit because he got mad or quit because he didn't get what he wanted. He quit largely because he was burnt out and bored and wanted a new challenge. Transport those same feelings to his job twenty years later. Wouldn't you encourage him to move on?

Finally, was it waste of everyone's time and money? Hardly. Except for maybe some of the driving, the parents loved watching their son play and he loved having them as spectators. It was a totally positive experience. And even if James never goes back to soccer, his experience with the game will stay with him for life, and the lessons and skills he learned from the sport will help him in other endeavors.

A Sporting Chance

After the mostly positive spin this chapter has put on sports, you're eager to get your child involved in soccer, but he hasn't shown any interest at all. Do you sign him up anyway, or do you just wait for it to happen?

The answer is you just start playing soccer with him. Not surprisingly, the best way to get kids excited about sports is to be excited about them yourself. Play sports in the backyard with your children, watch the MLS and World Cup games on TV together. Things might change in the teenage years, but right now, your kids respect your interests and want to be like you. If you show them that you think sports are desirable and it's something you share with them, then their interests are going to be preset.

But sharing is the key. One couple I know took their love of sports to an extreme. One or the other of them was always playing something while the other was home with the kids. Or they'd get a babysitter and both go play tennis or golf. One day, they got a real wake-up call, when their four-year-old daughter, whom they'd always assumed would follow in their footsteps, said, "I hate sports." To her, sports meant that Mommy and Daddy were too busy to be with her. Realizing that she was old enough to begin to play some things herself, they quickly started involving her. Now she's more obsessed with sports than her parents.

Even if it's not much fun to kick a ball around the yard with a four-year-old, stick with it. It will get better, I promise. You can even take it a step further and coach your child's team. Not only will this give your kids a strong sign that you like soccer, but they're going to love the sport because you're there, whether they truly love the sport or not. By the time, you've done your stint and you're out of there, they're already hooked.

The Least You Need to Know

➤ Involvement in sports often helps people develop an interest in fitness all their lives.

➤ The lessons learned in sports can be used forever, in both personal life and work life.

➤ Quitting a sport is not a bad thing as long as the reasons are fully explored.

➤ Parents sharing their love of sports with their children is the best way to get those children enthusiastic about sports.

Chapter 19

Role Playing

In This Chapter

➤ Your life in the car

➤ A few pick-me-up tips

➤ Checkbook woes

➤ Bleacher behavior

You are the proud parent of a little soccer player. Not only are you eager to go to all the games, but you even want to go watch the practices, too. It's the part of parenting that you've always dreamed of, cheering from the sidelines as your superstar athlete scores the winning goal.

Well, wake up! The dream's a nice one, but the alarm clock is about to ring. The reality is that you're going to get to be the proud parent, but you're also going to be a whole lot more:

➤ Chauffeur

➤ Caterer

➤ Therapist

➤ Bank

Many people think it's all part of the dream. Some other people think it's a little closer to a nightmare. But either way, I think it's good idea for me to open your eyes a little.

The Chauffeur

The O'Malleys are your average suburban family with three kids, Katie (age 10), Pete (age 8), and Jack (age 5). It's spring and all three kids are playing soccer. Katie also takes gymnastics, Pete is in Little League, and Jack is trying T-ball. Here's the weekend sports schedule:

Saturday	
9:00	Pete's soccer practice
10:00	Katie's soccer practice
	Jack's soccer practice
10:30	Jack's T-ball game
3:00	Katie's gymnastics practice
4:30	Pete's Little League game

Sunday	
12:00	Jack's soccer game
3:00	Pete's soccer game
5:00	Katie's soccer game

Mom has Jack for the morning. She takes him to soccer practice on the dot of 10:00 to make sure he gets as much practice as he can before he's pulled away at 10:27 to go to the T-ball field for his game.

Dad takes Pete and Katie. He and Katie drive Pete to soccer practice first at 9:00 a.m., staying there until 9:45, when they drive Katie to her soccer practice across town. She has to be there a little early in order for Dad to get back across town by 10:00 to pick up Pete from his practice. They go home for a quick half hour or so before getting back in the car just before 11:00 to pick up Katie. Then the three of them head over to the T-ball field to catch Jack's game.

By noon, they're all home again for a few hours of lunch and relaxation, but at 2:30 Mom and Katie are back in the car to get Katie to her gymnastics school 20 minutes away. Gymnastics class is two hours long, just long enough to make it a difficult choice to stay. Mom drives 20 minutes back home. Just before 4:30, Dad, Pete, and Jack climb in the car to head to Pete's Little League game, and shortly after that, Mom drives back to gymnastics school to pick up Katie. They then head over to the Little League field to catch the end of Pete's game.

Sunday is the day of soccer games. Mom and Dad are somewhat grateful that games don't conflict with each other this weekend, so they can watch each of their kids play, but the 12:00, 3:00, and 5:00 schedules mean that they're hopping in and out of the car constantly, with half-hour breaks at home.

Coach's Corner

Carpools can be lifesavers, so do your best to set them up. Unfortunately, these really only work for practices, because many parents want to watch their children play in the games.

In sprawling suburbia, car time has gone big time. Fields are scattered around the town, and parents of the younger kids frequently don't feel comfortable sending them off on their bikes to get to the fields on their own. The older kids are often on competitive traveling teams, so even if they could use their bikes to get around town, they can't very well use them to get to a town that's 40 miles away.

Heads Up

If you're into soccer for any length of time, you're going to find yourself, at least once, driving across the state for a tournament, only to have it canceled because of rain 30 minutes after you get there.

And it's not just weekend driving, either. Once your child is playing soccer at the high school level, you're going to have to pick her up after practice because the buses are all done running for the day. Even if you're not in a busing district, you might feel you have to use the car just to save time. By the end of the season, too, after daylight savings time has ended, it's frequently dark by the time your child is heading home, so the car is needed for safety reasons.

Basically, soccer means a whole lot of chauffeuring. Many families limit their kids to one sport a season. The kids might protest, but it does help them set priorities. Do they love soccer enough to specialize in it, playing in both fall and spring, or is one season enough, so they can have other sports opportunities? Either way, one sport per kid per season helps reduce your driving.

The Bank

And then there's the money issue. Compared to most of the other sports your child might want to join, soccer is relatively cheap. But that doesn't mean it's free. Here are some things you might end up forking over big bucks for:

➤ Registration fee (perhaps twice a year if your child plays in fall and spring)

➤ Membership fee if your program is run by the Y or something similar

➤ Cleats (new ones every season for your growing child)

➤ Shin guards

➤ Soccer ball (in various sizes as your child ages)

➤ Tournament fees

➤ Camps

➤ Team outings to MLS games

➤ Gym time for indoor soccer in the winter

One of the most painful drains on your bank account happens when your child leaves his equipment behind somewhere. There are a few things you can do to prevent this. The first is the old laundry marker routine. In other words, put his name and phone number on absolutely everything, his cleats, his ball, the duffel bag, even his shin guards. Secondly, if your child is a repeat offender, make her take the time and effort to find a lost item and then if it can't be found, make her pay for it. I guarantee she'll start being more responsible once it's her money and time that's being spent and not yours.

Nonetheless, soccer is still the best bargain in kiddie sports, so you're better off sticking with the mildly painful soccer fees than taking out a loan so your child can play ice hockey.

The Caterer

Fortunately, there's so much more to soccer than driving and dollars, but the "more" is still both good and bad. One aspect of team sports participation that is rarely mentioned is the food that's involved. Why is this important? Because, girl, it's party time, and you're the cook!

This is not something to be taken lightly. Your soccer player is going to suck you into a variety of food-serving occasions, and while many of them are going to be fun events for you, too, they are all going to mean time in the kitchen.

The first requirement is the orange slices. You talk to nearly every soccer player you know, and they will all tell you they eat orange slices at halftime. And for some reason, parents buy into this and provide them. Usually parents figure out a schedule at the start of the season, or sometimes it goes game by game, but you're bound to be peeling oranges or rushing off to get the Gatorade early one Saturday morning.

Coach's Corner

Orange slices don't have the appeal with the youngest kids that they do with the older kids. Cantaloupe, watermelon, apple, and pear slices seem to be bigger hits. Yet it's not too long before those oranges push their way in.

And then there's the end-of-the-year party. Definitely potluck. And be careful or your kid will sign you up for the lasagne rather than the bread, because "my mom loves to cook lasagne."

As the players get older, the team meals seem to become more frequent. There's the team breakfast before a big game. There's the team spaghetti dinner the night before a big game. There's the after-game cookout, and let's not forget the fundraising bake sale. It might not seem like a big deal, but when you go back to the O'Malley family's three kids and six sports, you can begin to get a sense of kitchen claustrophobia.

The Therapist

You take the vows when you get married, but it seems like they should also be done in the delivery room. It's a parent's job to be there in sickness and in health, through good times and bad, and so on and so on. And although you pictured soccer to be one of the good times, and it *is* mostly, there are occasions when you're going to have to do some consoling.

It's All My Fault

One of the nice things about soccer is that when a team loses, it's usually the fault of the entire team and not just one person. And because the sport is low scoring, you don't have a situation like you find in basketball where someone misses a shot at the buzzer. Nonetheless, there are a few things to look out for:

1. **The penalty shots.** These are killers. It's just the kind of one-on-one high pressure situation that soccer usually avoids. Yet you might find your daughter kicking the ball over the crossbar on this freebie. Ouch! "All my fault."

2. **Breakaways.** Whether your son is the forward who gets a one-on-one chance against the goalie or the defender who lets the opponent slip by to get a one-on-one chance with the goalie, it's going to be painful. If your son the forward misses the goal, he'll be saying, "it's all my fault." If your defender son lets the opponent by, then same thing. "It's all my fault."

3. **Goalie.** Note that the goalie is totally differentiated from the rest of the team. She can use her hands, she wears a different shirt, and she shed the comfort of "team failure" when she took on the job. She better have some tough skin, or you're going to be mopping up the tears.

4. **The Martyr.** Some players take the entire burden of the loss onto their own shoulders, obsessing about every little misstep they made in the game, when in fact they put in a perfectly acceptable performance. These kids are the toughest to deal with, but chances are that this is a trait deeply ingrained in their personality, so you're already well aware of what you're up against.

5. **The Perfectionist.** Maybe you've been blessed with a child who wants to be an outstanding soccer player. He practices constantly, working diligently to perfect every skill. He watches the pros and knows exactly what he should be doing. But somehow this knowledge loses something in the translation from his brain to his feet. Even though he's busted his butt practicing in the backyard, he still makes mistakes in the game, and blames himself unnecessarily for the team loss.

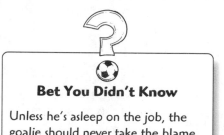

Bet You Didn't Know

Unless he's asleep on the job, the goalie should never take the blame. It takes complete failure by every single other player on the field for the ball to even get to the goalie, so it clearly can't be his fault.

So, if the car ride home from the game is full of gloom and doom, you're going have to start playing therapist. No matter what the game situation was, you can reiterate that soccer is a team sport. Her inability to score on that one opportunity didn't make or break the game. What happened in the other 89 minutes? Why wasn't anyone else scoring?

For a perfectionist, parents need to emphasize the progress he's making. Point out how much good the practice has already done, and look to the future.

Don't let your child off scot-free, however, by shifting all the blame to the team as a whole. We probably learn more from our failures and disappointments than we do from successes. Emphasize the need to practice and improve to avoid future fiascoes. Ask your child what went wrong in that situation and how she'd do it differently the next time.

And finally, remind your child that it's just one game and one minor mistake. Small potatoes in the whole scheme of things. The next game is bound to be better. If it's not, and week after week you're consoling a miserable child, then perhaps soccer is not the activity for her. The point of joining the team in the first place was to have fun, and if it's not fun, then the point is missed.

Bucking Up the Benchwarmer

Which brings us to the benchwarming issue. There you are on the sideline, waiting to see your child's euphoria when he scores that winning goal, but instead you find that in reality, he's right there on the sideline with you. And the euphoria you were hoping for looks a whole lot more like depression.

In the casual atmosphere of recreation league soccer, everyone gets to play, and technically everyone should play an almost equal amount. Who knows who's going to be a late bloomer, and it would be a shame to discourage some first grader just because he hasn't yet mastered the instep kick.

But as time goes on, it becomes pretty clear who is going to be playing regularly and who is going to be warming the bench, waiting until the team is losing or winning by a large margin to get his turn to play.

Learning the Lingo

Alternative to benchwarmer: sub, scrub, scrubeenie, reserve, pine rider, pine weasel, back-up, utility player, role player, low man on the depth chart, pinch hitter, splinter butt, waterboy, second string, practice squad, lumberjack.

This is not an easy situation for the therapist/parent. You can't use the "one game/one moment" argument, because reality is that every game has been like this and every game probably will continue to be like this. So what do you do about it?

It's best to confront the issue and take some action. Sit down with your discouraged soccer player and weigh the pros and cons. Then you can make a rational decision about what to do. There are really only three options:

1. Your child can accept his role of backup and just enjoy being on the team.

2. He can work hard to improve by practicing every day in the off-season or going to soccer camp. Be forewarned, however, most camps are not the cure-all they claim to be. Playing in good games is the best way to improve. Camps often do not provide this environment.

3. He can accept the fact that competitive soccer is making him miserable and perhaps he shouldn't tryout again. In this option, he may find that he still enjoys the sport on a rec league level.

Try to make him stick out the commitment, however, at least for the season. Tell him to always be ready to go in and be proud that he made the team in the first place.

The Fan

Finally, after all that, you get to be what you really want to be in the first place: the proud parent. You love the excitement of standing on the sideline while your happy and talented child runs up and down the field. The trees are starting to change colors, the sky is a vivid blue, and your new fisherman's sweater is keeping you toasty warm.

Then suddenly it's November. The trees are brown, the sky is gray and damp, and the thirty-three layers you've piled on underneath your parka still haven't stopped the wind from penetrating through to your bones. And then your child comes crying and limping off the field because the bullet of the soccer ball stung her ice cold thigh when she tried to trap it. Still having fun?

Except for a few bad weather moments, being a soccer fan is mostly what it's cracked up to be. It's a tremendous amount of fun to be outdoors in the fall (and spring if you're a two-season player), watching your child play and chatting with other parents. But being a good fan has it's responsibilities, too.

Athletic Supporters

Who knew that there were guidelines to being a good fan? Yet there are some basic rules that everyone should follow when they're standing on the sidelines or sitting in the bleachers. The National Youth Sports Coaches' Association (NYSCA) publishes a code of ethics that they encourage their coaches to distribute to the parents of their players. This is a good place to start.

Parents' Code of Ethics

➤ I hereby pledge to provide positive support, care, and encouragement for my child participating in youth sports by following this Parents' Code of Ethics Pledge.

➤ I will encourage good sportsmanship by demonstrating positive support for all players, coaches, and officials at every game, practice, or other youth sports event.

➤ I will place the emotional and physical well-being of my child ahead of a personal desire to win.

➤ I will insist that my child play in a safe and healthy environment.

➤ I will support coaches and officials working with my child, in order to encourage a positive and enjoyable experience for all.

➤ I will demand a sports environment for my child that is free of drugs, tobacco, and alcohol, and will refrain from their use at all youth sports events.

➤ I will remember that the game is for youth—not for adults.

➤ I will do my very best to make youth sports fun for my child.

➤ I will ask my child to treat other players, coaches, fans, and official, with respect regardless of race, sex, creed, or ability.

➤ I promise to help my child enjoy the youth sports experience by doing whatever I can, such as being a respectable fan, assisting with coaching, or providing transportation.

➤ I will require that my child's coach be trained in the responsibilities of being a youth sports coach and that the coach upholds the Coaches' Code of Ethics. (See Chapter 25.)

While the NYSCA is right on target defining the overall behavior of parents, I have a few more specific suggestions on how you want to behave in the bleachers.

1. **Don't draw attention to yourself, either positively or negatively.** Most kids are mortified when their parents do anything to distinguish themselves from the crowd.

2. **Stay out of it.** Your child is the one who is playing the game. Let him play it. He doesn't need you constantly yelling advice from the sidelines. You'll just distract him from the purpose at hand. Remember, you are just an observer to console or congratulate when the game is over.

3. **Pay attention to the game.** It's a lot of fun hanging out in the bleachers with other parents, comparing war stories about the drive home from the last tournament or complaining about the lack of time, but keep an eye on the game while you're doing your chatting. Soccer isn't a high scoring game. If you miss your son's one goal, there's probably not going to be another one to talk about. And you know his eye will be turned toward the bleachers the second after it happens. Don't disappoint.

4. **Cheer for the whole team, not just the superstars.** Learn the names of everyone on the team. The superstars already know they're great. Give an ego boost to some of the support players.

5. **Be a good sport.** There's no need to insult the ref, insult another parent, yell at the other team, or criticize a player who isn't up to speed.

Fortunately, most parents are wonderful fans, and acting properly at a game comes naturally.

All for One and One for All

The sportsmanship issue, however needs a little more elaboration, because it really embodies the essence of sports in the first place. In fact, it's one of the most cited reasons for having a child play sports. Unfortunately, quite a few parents forget to practice what they preach. How many times have you heard a Little League parent yell, "Get the pitcher out of there! He's losing the game for us."

Fortunately, in soccer it's a little harder to notice when one player is putting in an especially bad performance, so comments such as these are much rarer. But, in truth, they should be extinct. There's no excuse for a parent, player, or any other observer to be making disparaging comments about another player on the team. The only lesson that comes out of that is that winning is everything and it doesn't matter if you hurt a player's feelings as long as you get him out of the game. Is that why you signed your kid up for soccer in the first place? Good sportsmanship isn't just for the playing field.

It also doesn't apply just to your child's teammates. Be kind to the other team and their players. It's unsportsmanlike to be yelling, "Ref, number 6 is a dirty player!" And while we're on the subject of referees, they like to be treated nicely as well. "Ref, are you blind?!" is not a sportsmanlike comment.

So if the other team has a beautiful passing sequence, clap for them. No one's asking you to cheer as they score a goal against your child's team, but you can acknowledge a good performance.

Coach's Corner

Frequently in rec leagues, you're going to know players on the other teams because you'll all be from the same town. If that's the case, then go ahead and give your neighbor a big cheer, even if she did just score against your daughter's team.

Playing soccer should be a fun, happy experience for players and parents. Yes, winning is the object of the game, but it's not the only reason to play.

You're Not the Coach

Unless your child is on a school soccer team, the majority of soccer coaches that you'll come into contact with are volunteers. Some will know what they're doing, and some will be woefully uninformed. It's hit or miss, but even if you miss, you have to realize that this coach is there for your child out of the goodness of his heart. Keep your criticism to yourself.

That doesn't mean that you shouldn't *ever* step in. If you feel your child is being mistreated in some way, then it's your duty to have a chat with the coach to see if you can work it out. It could be something as simple as having a sarcastic coach who doesn't realize that her teasing is hurting a sensitive child's feelings.

The time to chat, however, is later, away from the game or practice. Call her on the phone or figure out a time you can get together. What you don't want to do is create a scene in front of the other parents and players because this will only mortify your child and probably put the coach on the defensive.

The other issue that might bring your out of your role as bleacher bum is an injury. Some coaches are from the "shake it off" school of sports injuries. Sometimes this is

Coach's Corner

It's frequently helpful to involve the child in the discussion with the coach, especially if you haven't been a witness to the difficulties. A child might be exaggerating to Mom and Dad to get sympathy, but when he's in front of the coach a more realistic picture comes out.

truly all an injury needs, but it's better to err on the side of safety and use the five-minute rule. If you can tell your child is still really hurting after five minutes, but an overeager coach is yelling, "Don't be a wimp!" it's time to step in.

But for the most part, let the coach be the coach. After all, he volunteered when you didn't, so don't be looking to finagle your way onto the field in the eleventh hour. You'll just have to accept the fact that your child is playing defense even though you want him on the forward line. Respect the coach's position, much as you would expect him to respect yours. You wouldn't want the coach criticizing your ability to raise your child in front of the entire town.

The Least You Need to Know

➤ Being a soccer parent is more than just being a bystander watching from the bleachers. Be prepared for a big time commitment.

➤ Driving and money issues may lead you to conclude that you're going to limit your children to one sport a season.

➤ Emphasize the team aspect of soccer to a player who thinks she just lost the game.

➤ Be a good fan by being a good sport and letting the coach do his job.

Chapter 20

The Juggling Act Off the Field

In This Chapter

➤ Learning to prioritize

➤ The academics vs. athletics debate

➤ Good eats

➤ Sibling rivalry

Parents perform a juggling act every day of their lives. Whether you're trying to balance your career and your home life or satisfy the varied demands of a family full of kids, the crazy scheduling conflicts will force your brain to work overtime. Add soccer to the mix, and you'll find yourself reaching for the Tylenol.

You have to get healthy, nutritious meals into your children when they're only home for about five minutes at a time. You're going to have to make sure that their grades are good enough to get them into college while they still maintain the soccer schedule that they love. And you are going to have to do all this amidst the bratfights more commonly known as sibling rivalry.

But it can be done. It's a matter of setting your priorities and not trying to have it all. Figure out what counts to both you and your child, and then don't sweat the small stuff. You just to have to find the right balance for your family.

Food for Thought

When your children's sports schedules are taking up every free minute of your life, you hardly have time to plan a meal, much less worry about making it a nutritious one. A bagel on the way to a Saturday morning soccer game an hour south of you, McDonald's for lunch on the way back. Then you leave money on the table to order pizza for that night's dinner because you're taking your youngest child to her swim meet.

This is no way to treat a body, but it's pretty standard fare for the average on-the-go family. With practices, games, and all the other time demands, family meals have became a quaint, but obsolete ancient ritual. It's time to bring them back, not just for family unity, but also so that you can make sure that your little athletes are getting the proper nutrition.

Pyramid Power

As you may recall, eating a balanced amount from each of the four food groups used to be accepted nutrition philosophy, but in the mid-nineties, the food pyramid, which you can see in this figure, took over.

The Food Pyramid.

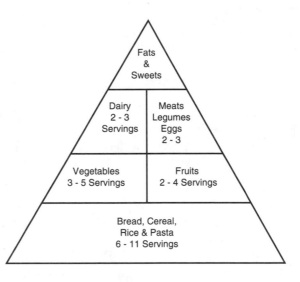

The pyramid gets its shape from the fact that you should be eating more per day from certain groups and less from others, rather than trying to balance the amounts from each. You want 6–11 servings of grains (breads, cereal, rice, pasta, etc.), 3–5 servings of vegetables, 2–4 servings of fruits, 2–3 servings of dairy (milk, yogurt, cheese), 2–3 servings of meats and legumes (beef, chicken, fish, eggs, beans, and nuts), and minimal use of fats (butter and oils).

Bet You Didn't Know

If you add up all the numbers in the food pyramid, you end up with 15–26 servings of food each day, which might seem like a ridiculous amount.. The key is to recognize that a serving is pretty small. A half cup of rice, for example, is considered one serving, when most people put about a cup and half on their plates for dinner. There's three servings right there.

It seems pretty basic, but many people, especially those with lives on the go such as the soccer playing son in the example, are neglecting major areas in the pyramid. Let's take a look at that example again.

Breakfast:	bagel	2 servings grains
	w/cream cheese	1 serving dairy
Lunch:	McDonald's	2 servings grains
	cheeseburger	1 serving meat
		1 serving dairy
	Large fries	2 servings grains
	Soda	
Dinner:	2 slices pepperoni pizza	2 servings grains
		1 serving meat
		2 servings dairy (cheese)
		1 serving vegetable (sauce)
	Large glass milk	2 servings dairy
	Chips	2 servings grains

So, let's add it up. That's 10 servings of grains. Right on the money there but pushing the outer limits. Meat is also right on target, but with the choice of hamburger and pepperoni, the fat consumption is high. Six servings of dairy is double the recommended amount. And one serving of vegetable and none of fruit is appallingly deficient.

Now let's take a look at the items that had fat in them, a category you want to have minimal amounts of:

cream cheese

hamburger

cheese on the burger

French fries (loaded with fat)

cheese on the pizza

pepperoni

chips

Milk (unless it was skim)

So with large fries being a double serving, that's eight servings of fat. Because fat is at the top of the pyramid, it's hardly on the same level as the grains.

This is a somewhat extreme example of a day of poor nutrition, but it's not at all unusual for soccer players and their families who spend half the weekend in the car, racing around to various sporting events. Let's hope that there were some orange slices during the game and not just sugar-laden Gatorade to refresh the players.

Water Works

One item that is left out of the food pyramid is water, yet water is a vital component of everyone's body. To keep their bodies refreshed and replenished, people should have at least six eight-ounce glasses of water a day. Most people drink far less.

A soccer player, running around and playing under the hot sun, needs a whole lot more than that, because she's losing water by the gallon as she sweats. All that water needs to be replaced. Lots of water at half time and after the game should be provided.

Players should even drink water before the game to make sure they aren't starting with a body that's already slightly water-deficient. They shouldn't drink so much that they can't move because of the lake sloshing around in their stomach.

It's not just a matter of avoiding thirst, heat exhaustion, and heat stroke, although these are certainly things to be avoided. Lack of water can hurt a soccer player's performance because fatigue is the first sign of dehydration, even before thirst.

Many players opt for sports drinks such as Gatorade over water. These aren't terrible substitutes, but water is still the best way to rehydrate your body. The electrolytes that the sports drinks offer usually aren't needed unless you've really extended your body with excessive running under unbearably hot conditions.

Heads Up

You shouldn't wait until you're thirsty to start drinking that water. A sense of thirst is your body's way of telling you it's already dehydrated. Drink water constantly, so your body never reaches that point.

Head's Up

Even if you're not an athlete, if you find yourself perpetually tired or needing a nap, your problem might be simple dehydration. Try drinking more water. That might be all you need.

A Soccer Player's Special Needs

Young people are especially in need of a balanced diet because their bodies are still growing, and young people who are racing around on the soccer field have even more needs to be met.

A soccer player needs energy. Carbohydrates, found in grains, fruits, vegetables, and legumes, provide energy. Most kids don't need to be encouraged to "carbo-load" but they do need to realize that grains aren't the only way to get their carbohydrates. Grains provide only simple carbohydrates, which turn into sugar. Fruits, vegetables, and legumes (beans and nuts) are made up of complex carbohydrates that are actually better for you and a longer-lasting source of energy.

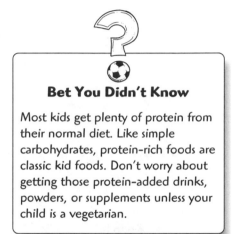

Bet You Didn't Know

Most kids get plenty of protein from their normal diet. Like simple carbohydrates, protein-rich foods are classic kid foods. Don't worry about getting those protein-added drinks, powders, or supplements unless your child is a vegetarian.

A soccer player also needs a lot of protein. Protein can be found in meats, dairy, cheese, and those ever-popular legumes. A body needs protein for bone growth and to repair damaged muscle. Muscles get damaged every time you play; that's why your muscles feel sore.

Make sure your soccer player eats before a game to be sure he isn't going to get dizzy out on the field. Two to three hours before the game is the best time to eat. Any closer to game time and his body will be distracted by the digestion process and not perform at maximum capacity.

Avoid fats when you're planning your pregame meal. They take a long time to digest and are just going to be a heavy, distracting lump in the stomach. And stay away from candy bars and other sugary items, too, because the sugar is only good for a quick energy boost, which will be over long before the game ends. The best pregame meals involve something such as fruit, a sandwich, or a small amount of pancakes or spaghetti.

As you can imagine, when left to themselves, kids will not always choose the best items. It may take some juggling and some sacrifice of some precious time, but try to guide their food choices by having at least some of your meals with them.

School Daze

And if you think finding time for family meals is tough, try juggling sports and schoolwork. Ask anyone from "scholar athletes" to "dumb jocks" and you'll hear the same story. There's pressure from coaches, pressure from teachers, and pressure from parents and peers. Your poor little soccer player is going to be pulled in so many directions, it's going to be hard for her to figure out which path is the right one to take.

Of course, in the early years, your child won't feel this conflict. The games are on the weekends, and the practices usually are, too, and for a child those days are just long empty hours to be filled. But when he makes the more competitive traveling teams or the interscholastic teams that practice daily, it's a whole new ball game, and school-work is sometimes the first thing to go.

Never Enough Time

The main problem is time. Let's say your child gets up at 6:30 a.m. to shower, get dressed, and eat breakfast before catching the bus at 7:15. School starts at 8:00 and goes to 2:30 p.m. Soccer kicks in at 3:00, or even later if there's a game. By the time practice is over, and your child is back home, it's close to 6:00 p.m. To get a good eight hours of sleep, bedtime is 10 or 10:30 p.m., which leaves just about four hours to eat dinner, say a quick hello to the family, and get homework done.

Heads Up

For a student attending a challenging prep school or taking advanced placement and honors courses, dinner may have to be a snack at the desk, because four hours of homework is frequently the norm.

Where's the down time? When can your child read a book for fun, watch a sitcom on television, chat with her friends on the phone, or play a game with the family? Is this something you want for your child? Is there any alternative? What's the answer?

The best solution, of course, would be to add at least 12 more hours to every day, something I've long been pushing. But because that's a near impossibility, something else has to give. Here are the six sufferers:

1. Sleep

My husband chose to give up sleep when he was a student athlete. He'd take a quick nap when he got home, then watch TV, talk with friends and his family and start homework around 11:00. At 2:00 a.m. he'd crawl into bed for four or five hours of sleep and the cycle would begin again the next day.

2. Supper

The supper option seems to work best for many families. The hour-long family dinner is now a quaint old-fashioned custom, not suited for today's busy lifestyles. By getting rid of family time at the table, the student has a little more time to get work done. Unfortunately, study after study has come out showing how important that group meal is for communicating, psychological health, and familial closeness.

3. Schoolwork

Academics are frequently the first to go. A player doesn't bother to do homework, does a halfhearted job when he does squeeze some in, and generally chooses easier courses which don't have so many out of school requirements. This is somewhat shortsighted because except for the exceptional few, soccer will end with graduation, yet your academic record will haunt you every time you try to find a job.

4. Soccer

For players who are not at the top of the game, cutting back on soccer might be the best alternative. Instead of playing in both spring and fall soccer, how about just one season? Even if this hurts your child's chances of making the high school team, maybe she could be satisfied with playing in the town's rec league or intramurals at school.

5. Social life

Bus rides, lunch hours, study halls, and sports do give a teenager plenty of time to socialize, although few would agree that it's enough. A fifteen-year-old has no trouble talking to his friends all day long and then hopping on the phone with them for another hour at night. But phone privileges are a luxury in the time-tight atmosphere of the scholar-athlete, and it's one thing that can easily go.

6. Sitcoms

It's hard to be a teenager and not be up on *South Parks'* newest way to kill Kenny or the latest tragedy in Bailey's life on *Party of Five,* but maybe you could limit TV watching to one or two hours a week, with extra hours on the weekend. That way your child won't be a total dork, but will still keep those balls in the air.

Finally, you could manage to do some juggling just by taking a little bit of each away. Maybe on TV nights, there's no phone talking. Perhaps seven hours of sleep is enough. And consider having family dinners only four out of the seven nights. And a student doesn't necessarily have to be in the top one percent of his class. Life might be a whole lot more enjoyable if you accept the top 10% as his goal.

Coach's Corner

Having a schedule posted somewhere for everyone to see can help students plan. Favorite TV shows can be blocked off, and if your child has a math test on Thursday, you can plan to do self-serve PB&J for Wednesday night dinner.

The good news is that most athletes actually manage to keep up their grades. Whether it's the discipline they learn from participating in a sport or the fear that they'll lose their spot on the team if they get a bad report card, mixing sports and academics is generally a positive combination.

Holding Back

Academics and athletics clash in another way as well. When bigger and stronger often turns into "better" on the playing field, parents feel the pressure to keep their kids back, either before they even start kindergarten or during the high school years.

If your child is a soccer player, size isn't really an issue. Many excellent soccer players have been rather small, and bulk is certainly not a part of the sport. But many parents make the decision to hold back their children, mostly boys, before they even know which sport their child is going to choose.

The first decision-making moment comes in kindergarten. If your child is on the small side or born in the summer months, he's going be at a disadvantage in many sports for quite some time, until genetics starts to show its stuff.

Take the kindergartner who turns six in October. He could easily be six inches taller than the one who doesn't turn six until the following August, regardless of how tall they'll eventually be. The October baby is going to be bigger and stronger probably all through elementary school, well after the first soccer game in kindergarten. Because of this, some parents feel they're giving their summer-born child a leg up if they hold him back another year.

Heads Up

Some parents also hold summer-born kids back for academic reasons, figuring that their children will be smarter students if they start later. Not at all true. Unless your child is actually behind academically or socially, he should stay with his proper grade level.

The next big school-manipulation moment comes at the start of high school. Some parents have their kids repeat eighth or ninth grade at a new school (by enrolling them in a private school), just to get them an extra year of growth. Because boys can start their growth spurt at any time in high school, the extra year can make a huge difference in their performance and their chances for a college scholarship.

Holding your child back may seem like a good idea as far as sports are concerned, but in general, educators advise against it. Kids who are held back feel out of place if they quickly become much larger than their classmates. They are also frequently bored in class because their academic skills have outstripped the education program in the classroom. Boredom can lead to poor performance and low self-esteem. And besides, wouldn't you feel awful if you held your son back before kindergarten so he could excel on the playing fields when it turns out he wants to spend all his time in the art room?

College Bound

When you're talking academics and sports, the college question immediately comes to mind. Sports help a student get into competitive colleges and occasionally, for the elite few, sports solve the money issue when the athlete earns a full scholarship.

Using sports as a means to outside success can present problems. For instance, how do you balance your needs and your child's? Here are a couple of scenarios that parents and their college bound children have to deal with:

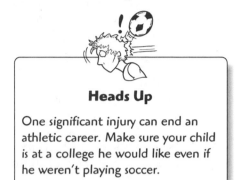

Heads Up

One significant injury can end an athletic career. Make sure your child is at a college he would like even if he weren't playing soccer.

➤ Your child earns a full scholarship to play soccer at Michigan State, but he's dying to head to sunny California. It's his happiness versus your money (and his probable happiness, but he just doesn't know it yet).

➤ Your child is a dabbler. Just when she's getting good at something, she decides she's bored with it and moves on. Your friends with older children tell you that unless she excels at something, she's not going to stand out on college applications, especially at top institutions. Do you try to focus her interests, so she can get into a better college or do you let her personality drift where it may?

➤ Your son gets into Harvard because the soccer coach put in a good word for him. But a good word is all your son gets for his soccer prowess, because they don't offer athletic scholarships. Do you sacrifice an Ivy League education for a free ride somewhere else or do you pony up the $150,000?

➤ After 11 years of driving her to and from soccer games in both the spring and the fall, traveling all over the state to watch her in tournaments, spending a fortune on soccer camps, and sacrificing your weekends so she wouldn't miss anything, your 16-year-old daughter announces she's quitting. She doesn't like the coach at the high school and besides she doesn't have time for her friends. Well, it's her life, you say, but then you remember your chat with the college recruiter who said she was a shoe-in for a scholarship. Is one more year with a bad coach too much to ask?

There are no pat answers when you're dealing with a star athlete, a scholarship, and some hard choices. Each family is going to be different, with varying financial backgrounds, academic expectations, and commitment issues. But it's a good idea to be prepared before you bump into a 16-year-old stone wall.

Family Feuds

And if it weren't enough that you had to juggle your time and your children's time, you're also going to have to juggle your children. Sibling rivalry is a neverending source of dismay for parents. Not only is it annoying to have to play referee all the time, but it's sad to think that your precious little ones don't adore each other as much as you adore them.

In truth, they probably do. But they're frequently put in the position of having to compete for your attention and praise, and disputes and petty jealousies are inevitable. Unfortunately, sports frequently exacerbate the problem.

Too Many Places, Too Little Time

As you already know from the previous chapter, when children are involved in sports, much of the weekend is spent in the car or on the sidelines. But what happens when the kids are all playing at the same time. Who gets dropped off alone? Who is forced to leave something early to accommodate a sibling's more important event? Who gets to have Mom watch the game? And who gets Dad? And what happens if you're a single parent trying to cover all the bases?

Also keep in mind that, it is okay for parent to miss games and often advisable to miss practices. The kids need to be able to express themselves, establish their own identity, and learn to deal with challenges without their parents looking over their shoulder.

Many families have found that a posted schedule works well for ironing out these types of problems. Sunday night the whole family sits down and plots out the week's schedule. If someone has a problem, it can be worked out then rather than in the heat of the moment, minutes before someone else's game starts.

Comparison City

As with all sibling rivalry, comparison is inevitable. If both of your kids are playing soccer, but one is on the traveling team and one is just in the rec league, try to avoid giving more weight to the traveler. Yes, her program is more competitive, probably more fun to watch, and definitely more time-consuming, but your younger one in the rec league program is not going to understand any of that.

Heads Up

You may be inviting comparison unwittingly if you decide to limit your children to one sport a season. Chances are that your older one was able to join as many as he wanted until his siblings joined a team, too. And the little ones may resent the fact that he could and they can't.

On the flip side, don't ignore the older child just because she is old enough to cope without much supervision. Even though she can get to the field herself, she would still love to have you in the bleachers rooting for her.

The biggest difficulty is going to come when one of your kids is a top notch soccer star and the other doesn't have much going for him on the field. Comparisons will abound. No matter how much you try to avoid it, no one else will. And your poor performer will know it, too.

To avoid a major swan dive in his self-esteem, you're going to have to find ways to buck him up. If he still wants to persist in soccer, but can't make the competitive teams, find more casual leagues for him to play in. Don't push him to be just like his big brother. He'll be putting the pressure on himself, believe me.

And if he changes his mind about the sport and wants to quit, let him. Maybe another sport would be more up his alley. Even if he doesn't excel at that, at least the comparison won't be quite as obvious. Or maybe he wants to pursue music or some other hobby significantly removed from athletics. Value every interest that each child has, even if it doesn't match your interests or the image you had of what your children would be like.

The Least You Need to Know

➤ Good nutrition is vital for a healthy athlete, so make sure that your child follows the food pyramid guidelines.

➤ Soccer is going to take away time from schoolwork, so players and their families need to be disciplined and organized.

➤ Planning ahead can minimize sibling rivalry.

➤ Don't compare your children, especially if one is a superstar and the other is a superklutz.

Chapter 21

The Rising Star

In This Chapter

➤ What to do when your child is an exceptional player

➤ The pitfalls of superstardom

➤ Setting goals

➤ Knowing when you've had enough

As your skinny 10-year-old son throws his unpadded body on the ground to make a diving save in front of the net to give his soccer team the win in the local tournament, your eyes mist over with pride. You start to consider the possibilities and plan for the future:

> *The newspapers have voted your son the number one soccer goalie in the state for the past two years. He's gotten a full ride to college and Major League Soccer has already tapped him to be one of the Project 40 players. He'll play for the national team in the 2010 World Cup, the one where the United States is going to win it all. He'll shut out everyone he faces.*

Hello? Wake up! He's only 10. When parents have a child prodigy on their hands, they can get pretty excited. And they should. It's wonderful to have a child with a gift. But there are a lot of pitfalls on the way to the top, and parents have a duty to help their children avoid them.

The Proud Parent

The parents themselves are the first big pothole to avoid. You can be thrilled about your child's success, but you have to step back and take a good look at your role in it.

Are you the one pushing soccer or are they eager too? Whose dream is it, in other words?

You signed your child up for soccer in the first place because you wanted her to have fun. You wanted her to learn teamwork, good sportsmanship, and fair play. Being a physical fitness nut yourself, you felt that aspect was important, too, but that's about the extent of it. If she liked soccer, great. If she didn't, you'd find another sport for her.

But the tide has changed. Your daughter is one of the exceptional few who has real talent. With the right training, coaches and experience, she can go far. Right now there's more at stake than just a fun time and good exercise. Right?

Yes and no. Sports should always be fun. Yes, you're going to want to see where soccer can take her, but only as long as she's still having a good time with it. The minute that it seems to be too much, you have to lay off. Your child's happiness in life is a more important goal than her success on the soccer field.

> **Heads Up**
>
> Leverage is one big reason you want to make sure you're not too caught up in your child's dream. Kids with pushy parents learn early on that threatening to quit can get them a lot. You have to be able to say "go ahead and quit if you want to" or you'll always be at your child's mercy.

Play Time?

If you're quite positive that your child is the one who is excited about pursuing the sport competitively, then you can jump in and help guide him through the rough spots. And there will be some rough spots.

The first effort you have to make is off the field. Sit down with your little superstar and talk about expectations, priorities, and goals. If he wants to become a top-notch player, he has to put in the effort.

Reality Check

Twelve-year-old Ted is riding high as the star of his youth league traveling team. He has visions of international fame every time he steps out on the field. This is great. Don't discourage it, especially if you think he has a chance to succeed at a high level. But you need to give his expectations a reality check if he doesn't seem willing to put the time in.

Ted has achieved considerable success within a 30-mile radius of his town in New Jersey. That's not to be belittled, but it needs to be put into perspective. He needs to understand that there are over a thousand towns just like his in the state, each with its own superstar. There are 50 states in the country, most of them much bigger than New Jersey. There are international players who are much better than the best that his country has to offer. He is small potatoes in the big scheme of things, one in a million. Not great odds at this point.

Your child must have that perspective to have the motivation to work hard toward achieving his goal. Give it to him straight, but then jump in with the positives:

➤ He's already far outstripped his teammates.

➤ He's got his foot in the door.

➤ The potential is there.

➤ If he's serious about playing professionally, he can step up his training a few notches to see how far it will take him.

Right now if your child's training consists of playing on his traveling team in the spring and fall, plus two weeks of soccer camp in summer, it's not going to be enough. If that's all he's willing to put into it, that's fine, but make it clear to him that he's not going to achieve that Major League dream without a little more effort.

Soccer is going to have to become practically an every day, year-round activity. Not all that soccer play has to be organized games or practices, but he's going to have to be organizing pick-up games on the field, kicking against a wall, or working backyard on skills by himself.

Find Out What Counts

Time to play the bad guy again. Your child might be willing to commit to daily practices in theory, thinking what could be better than to play his favorite sport all the time. He may even already be doing that to some extent. But you have to let him know there's more to it than that. He is going to have to make some sacrifices and figure out what his priorities are.

Top athletes frequently make their sport their life, making a lot of necessary sacrifices on their way to the top. Free time is taken up by soccer. There isn't much "hanging out" with friends. Television shows are going to be a thing of the past. Most of the time it's going to be school, soccer, homework, and bed, because your child won't have time for much else and will be too exhausted to play well if he doesn't get enough sleep.

That's not to say that he should become a social outcast in his quest for superstardom. I said priorities, not insanities. He should never practice so much that he loses out on fun times with family and friends. And he may even be able to play another sport in a soccer downtime, such as winter. At the younger ages, coordination is developed along with skill, so playing any sport is going to help him improve that. Of course, when he achieves some success in the second sport, don't be surprised to hear your child say he wants to play lots of sports rather than just focusing on soccer.

Heads Up

A player should never become so one-dimensional that he doesn't have an identity outside of being a soccer player. If his plans were to fall apart or if he were to get injured, he might lose all his feelings of self-worth.

Academics also need to be a priority. Don't assume that your child's soccer ability will be all he needs to get into a college. First of all, he may never get as good you both hope. Second of all, he could get injured, and then where would he be? And finally, what if he wants to quit but has nothing to fall back on. Give him an out.

If you want to go for it, do it. Don't get scared off because you will always regret it. If you find you're not enjoying it, then you can stop, but if you have the chance and don't even try to see where it will take you, you're going to be disappointed in yourself.

Setting Goals

After your child has made the commitment to proceed, you're going to have to help him come up with a plan for reaching his goal. Having the dream is important step, but achieving it is another thing altogether. Setting smaller goals is the best way to do this.

Steady, measured progress not only helps a player know if he's improving but it gives immediate positive feedback to keep him going. With this in mind, help your child set day-to-day goals and season-to-season goals. That's as far ahead as you really need to be looking, with the exception of your long-term plan.

You have to make sure the goals are reasonable, too. They should be things that your child can achieve but also ones that make him put some effort into that achievement. Don't let your goalkeeping child, who is constantly hearing how he's going to be the next Kasey Keller, protecting the goal for the U.S. World Cup team, commit to a goal of a shutout season, for example. It's unrealistic and could backfire. When he gives up two goals in the next game, he might be so devastated by this reality check that he gives up his dream completely.

An example of a more reasonable season-long goal might be to limit the season's goals to 10. For a forward it might be to score 10 goals total against the opponents. Take the previous season as a measure and make sure that the goals your child picks are only a stretch beyond that.

An example of a day-to-day challenge might be to juggle the soccer ball more times in a row each day. If he does it the first time out, great. If it takes him two hours to beat yesterday's record, even better. He's gotten more practice handling the ball.

Just because the goals are limited to the present, doesn't mean you can't plan for the future. Find out what it takes to make an MLS team. Your child first must make his high school team, star on that team, and then perhaps make and star on a college team to even have a chance. Use those checkpoints to see if your dream is a reasonable one.

Coach's Corner

If you're concerned about your child's lack of sportsmanship, you might want to suggest that as a goal as well as the physical goals. Children like accomplishing things. Pretty soon the behavior might become ingrained.

Missteps and Mistakes

Nothing worth having ever comes easily, and pro athletes will tell you this is especially true in sports. Both you and your child are not only going to have to work hard to achieve exceptional success, but you're probably going to make a lot of painful mistakes along the way. Here are some of the most common.

Take It Easy

It's hard to believe but it seems as though your child really wants to make it happen. He's excited, you're excited, and you're both ready to devote your lives to achieving this goal. Whoa! Hold your horses!

You're going to make a few mistakes along the way, but remember the old adage, haste makes waste? If you don't jump in too quickly, you might be able to avoid the whole hassle altogether. The whole gig might sound pretty good up front, but you'll quickly find out if your child has the stomach for the real deal.

First make her take responsibility for her success. It can't be your job to nag her to practice. If you end up doing that, she'll resent you and you'll resent her. If she can't get up enough initiative to get out there on her own, then you'll know she's not committed enough. And that's fine. At least you haven't spent a fortune on special camps or coaches. Just point out the problem to her and you can both do a little dream readjusting.

Setting the Stage

But let's say your little trial period worked out. You child has proven that he can be dedicated, and you're going to step up the commitment. You are now going to team up with your child to make this dream work out.

Your first step should probably be a top soccer camp or team in your area. Ask around for people's recommendations and see if there's one that everyone consistently recommends. Playing for a good team can give both you and your child a sense of just how good he really is. You can also get more information about how to proceed.

Feedback

Chances are that you're going to attend a lot of games and your child is naturally going to expect you to offer him some feedback, and you should. Just keep it upbeat. Almost all of your feedback should be positive, with maybe a tiny tidbit of constructive criticism thrown in, but don't make things up just to be positive. Let the coach give most of the feedback.

The key word here is *constructive*. It's the opposite of destructive, which is exactly what you don't want to be. You might say something like, "You could have had a little more success against that team if you went out to meet the ball instead of waiting for the pass to come to you." That's constructive.

Here's the same information said in a destructive manner. "You're so lazy, you're never going to make it to the pros. Never once did you go meet the ball. I can't believe we thought you had the drive to be great. A person with drive would have been jumping on every ball he saw." That's destructive and probably would put an end to any dreams your child might have. Not to mention any enjoyment he might have.

Even if your child didn't play well, be sure to find something good to say about his performance. "You never gave up." or "You did some hard running and really hustled. You should be proud of that." If you want her to stick with it, she's got to feel good about herself and the game.

But don't make the mistake of giving your child a false compliment, such as "Your defense was terrific" when every single forward on the opponent's team managed to get by him. He's going to know how he did, and your insincere compliment will be worthless to him. It may even cause him to dismiss any other more accurate compliments you may try to give him.

No Special Treatment

Sometimes when a child gains superstar status, he gets a supersize ego along with it. Don't let this happen. Your star soccer player gets no special treatment.

Because the time commitment is so great, your other children might feel a little neglected. You should do your best to make sure they get treated fairly, but you also have to let them know that their sibling has a special situation that requires more of your time. That doesn't mean that the soccer player gets any more privileges, however. He should be treated the same way everyone else in the family is treated.

Let the coach know you feel this way, too, if you sense that your child is becoming obnoxious. No matter how much the coach wants to win, you have to make him understand that benching your child for bad behavior is okay by you and probably a good idea sometimes. If you give the okay, the coach might feel better about it, too.

Your child should also follow the golden rule of sportsmanship, treating others the way he likes to be treated. For some reason, this seems to fly right out the window with some exceptional athletes. When the ego gets too big, it just seems to push out a lot of the decency. Because your little star knows that his skills are superior to others, he feels that he, as a person, is superior to others. You need to let him know that he is not.

He still must shake hands with the opponents, respect the referees, congratulate others on achievements, and accept both losing and winning gracefully without sulking or gloating. If you ever see him act otherwise, you should make the correction of that behavior your top priority.

But to avoid appearing hypocritical, you have to make sure that your behavior is beyond reproach as well. You can't very well tell your daughter to respect the officials when you're yelling at the refs and blaming them or others for your child's disappointing performance. Both you and she need to realize that she is the only one responsible for the way she performs.

Enough Is Enough

Quitting after years of dedicated practice and development can be a difficult choice, but sometimes it's one that has to be made. If your child is miserable, you must convince her to stop. And if she's the one trying to convince you to stop, then you've gone on way too long as it is.

But don't overreact at the first "I quit!" Sometimes this can be an outburst of frustration, something said in the heat of the moment but not really meant. If your child is upset when she's talking about quitting, let her cool off for a week or two before you have The Talk. There's nothing urgent about quitting. If she seems serious about it after an extended period of time, however, then you need to sit down and sort things out.

Heads Up

Be careful you're not constantly complaining about all the hassles you have to endure as the mother of a superstar. Your child might interpret this as a sign that you want him to quit, and he'll start manufacturing reasons to make you happy.

Kids who push themselves in a sport have given up a lot. Sometimes this sacrifice gets to be too much. Sometimes they're burnt out on a sport. It's just not interesting anymore. Maybe your child is still loving the game but not loving the commitment. If any of these seems to be sidetracking your child, let him take a break to see if this is really what he wants. Taking one season off probably won't make or break his soccer career, but it might help him realize how important (or not) the sport actually is to him.

Coach's Corner

Remind your child that excellence in sports doesn't come without hard work. Top athletes are revered in every country for just that reason. If it were easy, it wouldn't be anything special.

You might be the one who has to talk her into quitting. She might be miserable but unable to let go, fearing that if she doesn't do well, she'll never have the opportunity to play again. Set her straight. Playing in the Olympics or the World Cup isn't her only option. There are adult leagues and plenty of college teams on which to play.

Tell her of your concerns about her unhappiness and her apparent disillusionment with the game. But also let her know that ultimately, she is going to have to make the decision to continue or quit. You can't tell her to quit or she'll blame you for life.

Bet You Didn't Know

Some players fear they won't be able to make the college team without being outstanding. Even if she might not make the team at a big-time state school, there are plenty of smaller schools out there with a wide range of academic reputations. Maybe that's a better fit if continuing to play *is* important.

After a season of no soccer, see how your child feels. If she's dying to get back in the game, great. She just needed a little down time. If she's still not sure about it or if she's sure she doesn't want to pursue it at the highest levels, then it's time to stop. Make sure that your child is aware that at this point, there's probably no going back. Missing one season is a slight setback. Taking much more time off than that is probably a career killer. But you never know. It depends on what stage of development and how far along they are.

Once the decision is made, you and your child both are going to go through some difficult times. Your child may be second-guessing himself. Why did he waste all those years practicing for nothing? You may be furious that you've spent all this time and money on a worthless cause.

If this is the case, both of you need to sit down and really focus on the positives that this experience has provided. Your child is still quite skilled at soccer even if he's not going to push himself to become a professional. If he's that good, he'll probably still play in college and he'll have an activity that he can enjoy for years to come, perhaps in a semipro league or as a coach to your grandchildren.

Or perhaps he's so burnt out that he'll drop the sport altogether. It's still not a waste. Any other sport he chooses will be easy for him to pick up because he has taken so much time to develop his coordination for soccer. On top of that, he still has many personal skills that have arisen from his long devotion to the sport:

➤ Persistence

➤ Dedication

➤ Self-discipline

➤ The many other positive qualities people get from playing sports in general (see Chapter 18 if you've forgotten them)

Remember, sports are supposed to be fun, and as a parent you should strive to make your child happy. You had no trouble sacrificing your time to give him a shot at playing soccer professionally, because that made him happy. You also should be willing to sacrifice that particular dream, if once again his happiness is at stake.

The Least You Need to Know

➤ Make sure your child understands the demands that will be placed on her before you embark on your quest for excellence.

➤ Feedback should be mostly positive and always honest.

➤ Don't let your child have special treatment, at home or on the field.

➤ It's okay for your child to change his mind.

Part 6

And Now
They Have You Coaching

They gave you one of the pitch lines:

"We need volunteers desperately. You're our last hope."

"Your child will love it."

"You're athletic. You have a good sense of the game. You'd be a great coach."

"It's so much fun! You'll never regret it."

So you signed on. You said you'd be a rec league coach, and now you're panicking. You don't know the first thing about coaching. But you also didn't know much about soccer until you read the first part of this book. So never fear. The book is here.

Chapter 22 deals with the types of programs you might find, what might be a good fit for you as a coach, and coaching basics that could be applied to any sport. You'll find the stuff you're going want for day-to-day coaching in Chapter 23, which describes a practice from start to finish, and Chapter 24 covers a bunch of excellent drills and games that keep kids learning and loving the game. Finally, Chapter 25 takes coaching a step further and adds some strategy.

And by the way, the people who pitched you weren't lying. Coaching is fun, your child will love having you as a coach, and you won't regret it.

The I's Have It

You thought you'd do the nice thing. You're going to volunteer to coach. No big deal, right? How difficult can it be? You teach the kids some basic skills, you all go out and have fun, you win some, and you lose some. Or not.

There are a number of issues you may want to think about before you sign on. Namely, the three I's:

➤ Ideology

➤ Insurance

➤ Inspiration

And odd mix to be sure, but coaching isn't just an exercise in instruction (a fourth "I" word, by the way). There are a number of intangibles (need I say it?) that also play a part in making your coaching experience a positive one for both you and the players on your team.

Ideology

Youth soccer has become an incredible force in this country, and a majority of the programs are staffed with volunteers. These volunteers are frequently parents, but occasionally they are other members of the community who love soccer and want to help its development where they can.

But programs differ in their philosophies, and if you've been tapped to head up a team, you're going to want to make sure that you've signed on with a program that's going to be in synch with your coaching beliefs. One quick question should take care of the main issue:

Which philosophy is closer to your personality?

> *It doesn't matter whether you win or lose, it's how you play the game.*

Or

> *It doesn't matter whether you win or lose, as long as I win.*

In other words, are you a feel good, "we're all out here for fun" kind of coach? Or is it competition that gives you a high? There are good and bad points to each philosophy, and you need to figure out where you fit before you sign up to be a coach.

Bet You Didn't Know

If you share this no-competition philosophy, there's a group called The New Games Foundation who have put out several books describing their "new games" in detail. These games are teamwork activities, like pushing a giant ball across a field or keeping a ball in the air using a parachute.

Winning Isn't Everything

At some point in the '70s, some feel-good gurus tried to take the competition out of sports. They were probably from California and no doubt were picked last for basketball during that childhood torture known as gym class. The movement had its followers, and still does, but competition remains ingrained in the American psyche. (And it's not unheard of in Canada.)

Nonetheless, the movement had an impact by focusing the spotlight on the negative aspects of competition, and America, where a passion for competition is almost a requirement for citizenship, got a wake up call. What starts out as "my lunch is better than yours" can eventually lead to "my [pick one of these]

➤ religion

➤ political beliefs

➤ heritage

➤ country

is better than yours" with a few bombings, riots, and even wars thrown in. And because youth sports are most people's first competitive training ground, it seems like a good place to begin the reform.

Aside from reducing competition in general in this country, eliminating the competitive aspect of youth sports helps less experienced or talented kids enjoy a fun game and a physical activity.

A coach who is concerned about winning is less likely to play his least coordinated players any longer than he has to or put his slowest player in the goal, even if that player desperately wants his chance to try it. Yet a coach who's in a noncompetitive program will probably give everyone a fair chance to play equal amounts at all positions.

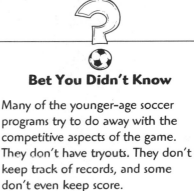

Bet You Didn't Know

Many of the younger-age soccer programs try to do away with the competitive aspects of the game. They don't have tryouts. They don't keep track of records, and some don't even keep score.

Most of these noncompetitive programs take anyone who signs up (or at least turn players away only because the program is full, not because their ability isn't up to speed). They also usually require that each player play at least half a game.

A noncompetitive environment is especially good when players are just learning how to play. It's impossible to tell who is going to be the next Ronaldo at this age. If you're playing competitive soccer, you may keep a less skilled player from playing as much, which could in turn discourage him from pursuing the sport.

Your first grade bench sitter could be a superb athlete who just didn't have an older sibling showing him the ropes in preschool. It might take that player a year to catch up, but if he's given a chance, he could outstrip the less coordinated kid who knew more the first year because he'd played with his older brother and sister.

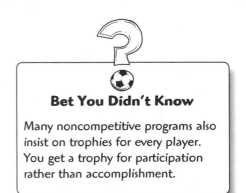

Bet You Didn't Know

Many noncompetitive programs also insist on trophies for every player. You get a trophy for participation rather than accomplishment.

All these are valid arguments, yet they might not suit your personality. If you're the "winning is everything" type of coach, then you have to find a program that suits your coaching style. If not, you're going to be frustrated by the lack of reward for your efforts, and parents who entered their kids

265

in a noncompetitive program are going to be upset when their children don't play an equal amount of time.

Winning Isn't Everything . . . Unless You're Losing

But then there's the flip side of the coin. It's the competition that makes the sport fun. What's the point of working hard when scoring a goal won't matter? Why not let the other team dribble by you? It doesn't mean anything after all.

Heads Up

A recent study just debunked the philosophy that we should build up a kid's self-esteem through frequent compliments, even if the child isn't particularly competent in an area of endeavor. The conflicting messages he hears from adults versus what he hears from kids (who more often describe a more realistic picture) will actually make him more prone to frustration and violence.

By the time kids reach about the third grade, they're desperate for a more competitive environment. After all, they've been competing in every other aspect of their lives, and yet in sports, a natural competitive setting, they've been forced to live with the warm and fuzzy approach.

Most soccer programs recognize this. At slightly older ages, scoring is allowed, records are kept, and there are no more do-overs when you don't execute a throw-in quite right.

There are also even more competitive opportunities for older kids. There are traveling teams and school teams that play against other towns. These teams have tryouts to get the best kids for the team, and there are no rules about how many minutes a player has to be in the game.

A competitive person would thrive in this environment, but if you don't have that edge, steer clear. When you put Slow Simon in at sweeper because you feel sorry for him sitting so patiently on the bench, you set yourself up for some major criticism when he's beaten in a one-on-one breakaway by the other team and it scores.

A small act of kindness could lose the game and ruin the chance to make it into the tournament. Your other players and their parents won't be pleased. (Of course, Simon's parents will be thrilled that he finally got into the game, so you'll have two people fond of you.) Even Simon, himself, may not end up feeling so good about playing if he's aware that he's the main reason for losing.

The Good Fit Test

While the overall philosophy toward competition is probably the most crucial area to get a good match in, there are a few other things you want to consider, too.

Take this quick multiple-choice quiz:

1. What's the extent of your soccer experience?

    a. You know the game has something to do with the feet.

    b. You played for your high school team a long, long time ago.

    c. You wish Project 40 had been in place when you were a college player.

2. Which group personality bugs you the least?

    a. Hyperactivity and inattentiveness

    b. Sass and brass

    c. Apathy and overreaction

3. Which leader are you most like?

    a. Captain Kangaroo (fun and games)

    b. General Patton (take no prisoners)

    c. Larry Bird (knowledge is power)

If you found yourself answering mostly "a" to each question, then go for the little ones. You enjoy being around these little balls of energy, and your lack of knowledge will make higher levels difficult.

Mostly "b" and you're suited to the prepubescent crowd. You're amused rather than frustrated with changing voices, changing bodies, and raging hormones, you have the tough-love personality to not let them get away with everything they try to get away with, and you know enough to teach them something.

And with "c" you're headed for high schoolers. You are knowledgeable and you want to deal with players at a higher level of skill. Their complicated personalities are appealing rather than irritating.

Do your best to make your coaching experience a good fit. It will make it a lot more fun for both you and the kids you coach.

Insurance

You wouldn't think that insurance would have to be an issue in soccer, but isn't it everywhere nowadays? We've become quite the litigious society and even a slight link to some tragedy could be financial ruin. Here are some scary scenarios:

➤ As coach, you decide the team needs to work on corner kicks. You set up an offense and a defense, just like you've done a thousand times before. The ball gets lofted into the middle, and your star forward Wild Bill goes after the ball with a vengeance. He sees an opportunity to score with a diving header and flies through the air toward the ball. Wild Bill was right on target. He gets the ball, he scores a goal, but he sails headfirst into the goal post. He's knocked unconscious, and after a week in the hospital, his parents are told that he'll have some permanent but minor brain damage.

➤ Again, you're at practice. This time, Calamity Jane, who tends to tumble to the ground every chance she gets, gets knocked over as she's trying to score. The play continues on around her. You blow the whistle for the play to stop (because technically she is committing an indirect kick infraction—dangerous play—by lying in the middle of play), but not before Buffalo Bonnie barrels her way through and accidentally kicks Calamity Jane in the head. A trip to the hospital. Diagnosis: brain damage.

Wild Bill's parents and Calamity Jane's parents are understandably upset. The more they think about it, the more they feel you could have prevented the accident. You should have disallowed diving headers. You should have blown the whistle sooner. Friends tell them they should sue. You are the target.

Chances are if they sue, you'll win. Accidents happen, and you weren't doing anything unusual. But can you afford to take that risk, and can you afford to pay for a good lawyer? Insurance is something you may want to think about.

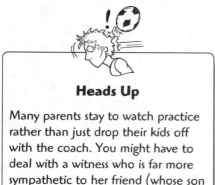

Heads Up

Many parents stay to watch practice rather than just drop their kids off with the coach. You might have to deal with a witness who is far more sympathetic to her friend (whose son just got hurt in your care) than she is to you.

Many soccer programs have a plan to cover their volunteer coaches. Some provide the coverage by having their coaches join a national group that provides insurance, such as the National Youth Sports Coaches Association (NYSCA). The catch with a national group is that they usually require that the coaches undergo some sort of training and testing before they are insured.

And this makes sense. Parents want a trained adult supervising their child, not only in a coaching sense but also in a safety sense. For example, coaches need to know not to move a body that might have a neck or back injury. They need to know to provide plenty of water breaks and be familiar with signs of heat stroke and heat exhaustion. And they need to be familiar with the limitations that a younger age group might have. Everyone benefits from a knowledgeable coach.

You shouldn't be scared away from coaching because there's a chance you might lose your shirt in a lawsuit. The odds are more than slim that anything like this might happen. But insurance is an issue you should bring up with your organization. If they don't already provide any for you, you can suggest that they start.

Inspiration

Okay, you're comfortable with the program you've chosen. It's a good fit for the type of coach you are. Now comes the tough part. You actually have to coach. Teaching your players the right skills is only part of it. Inspiring them to perform well in practice and during the game is a whole new, well, ball game.

There are a few guidelines to help you earn the players' respect and hold their attention.

Coach's Corner

It isn't enough to say "practice makes perfect," you really want to say "perfect practice makes perfect play." If you don't go all out in practice then you're not going to learn anything because you'll be playing a different way in the game.

Do Your Homework

Even the youngest players are going to lose respect for the coach who can't tell them the difference between a direct and an indirect kick. If you've never played soccer yourself, you need to do some homework, like reading this book cover to cover.

Commit the rules to memory. Learn what skills are important to teach. Get some basic strategy. And don't rest on your laurels just because you're already knowledgeable about soccer. You need to do the homework of planning a practice so you don't run out of activities with a half-hour left to go (more on that in Chapter 23).

Time Flies When You're Having Fun

Nothing is worse than looking forward to a good soccer game outside on a beautiful fall day and finding instead that you're standing in line for 10 minutes, waiting for your turn to dribble through the slalom course. Or standing in a group listening to your coach expound on the advantages of the 4–4–2 formation. Or passing back and forth to your partner for half the practice as the coach tries to perfect the form on each player.

A good coach keeps practice interesting. There needs to be variety, movement, and activity. If you want to see how your players perform on a slalom course, set up three or four courses so the lines aren't so long, and make the exercise into a race.

If they are more advanced and you want to instruct them in the finer points of a formation, get them out on the field instead of in front of a chalkboard. Have them make runs without a ball or a defense to challenge them, so they are focusing on the movement rather than being distracted by getting the ball in the goal.

If you need to work on passing skills, design a varied and fun practice that's centered around the theme of passing, but actually uses 10 different exercises to do this. While your focus still remains getting to each player individually, they'll be entertained by the variety of drills.

A player standing around is going to be looking for a clock, eager to get practice over with. A player who's kept busy will be stunned and disappointed that the end has crept up so quickly.

Coach's Corner

There are a number of reasons to end practice with a quick game, but maybe the most important reason is to end on a high note. The players love the game more than any other part of practice, so if you end with it, that's what they'll be thinking of when they go home and someone says, "How was practice?"

Team Bonding

A current TV commercial with a member of the U. S. women's national soccer team asks the player the question, "What do you think you'll remember the most about this experience?" The woman's answer is quick, without hesitation, "The friendships I've made."

Because soccer is a team sport, it is one of the best ways to create close friendships with a group of people who share similar interests. This is not only a personally enriching experience for a player, but it helps a team in incalculable ways.

A close team is going to work harder, enjoy being together more and therefore eager to come to practice, and understand each other better on and off the field. All of this enhances the team's performance, and a coach shouldn't take it lightly. You need to do everything in your power to foster good feelings among your players.

As coach, you need to mix and match your players constantly, not letting little cliques form or having the same people pair off together during practice. And try to put an older player with a younger player or a good player with a weak player, so there's unity across the board rather than just within certain predetermined groups. That's not to say that you can't ever put your best players together—but just make sure this doesn't always happen. Sometimes keeping the better players in a group helps their development.

Coach's Corner

Striking the right balance on the bus can be tricky. Letting the players hang out and talk can be a tremendous source of bonding but it can also turn very cliquish quickly. See if you can enlist the help of your captains, if the team has any, to make team unity a priority.

Some of the best bonding can happen off the field, too, but you still need to initiate it, rather than rely on the players to think of ideas themselves. Here are some fun team bonding ideas at the high school or junior high level:

➤ Team breakfast or team dinner

➤ Fundraisers such as bake sales or car washes

➤ A trip to a MLS game, using money from fundraisers

➤ Dressing up on game days; for example, wearing coats and ties to school

➤ Dressing down on game days by wearing team sweats to school

➤ Guys all get buzz cuts

➤ Girls all paint their nails in school colors

➤ Players team up to decorate lockers in school for game days

Most of these won't work for the youngest kids, but a few can be adapted. There are, however, some other ways to be creative about team bonding, and even at this age, team unity is important. Think about it. How many times have you seen a six-year-old pass only to his friend on the team and no one else. Wouldn't it be better to have him be friends with everyone?

Naming a team is a fun bonding process. If your team is known by its T-shirt color (for example, the blue team), then have a pow-wow session to come up with a team name. It could be the Blue Whales or the Blue Knights or the Blue Bombers, and so on. Write down everyone's suggestions and then have a team vote. Call yourselves by that name as much as possible.

The Thrill of the Drill

Even practice time can be a bonding experience. For example, during warm up, you can have the players link arms and try to jog around the field as a unit without falling.

Rather than having a breakfast or dinner with just you and the team (after all, you've probably had enough babysitting responsibilities just being the coach), have a team picnic with parents and siblings. Make it potluck, and let the kids on the team have a hand in deciding what everyone should bring. Make a list and then have the kids pick out one item of a hat or sign up for the item they'd like to bring. Hold the picnic somewhere where they can kick a ball around and play together.

Playing a fun game outdoors in the sun is a great experience to begin with, but it's often the intangibles that make it memorable. Build a close team, and you won't regret it. ·

Rules Are Rules

There's another intangible that a coach needs to provide, and that's consistency with rules and discipline. It helps players perform at a higher level, because they are aware that Behavior G (for good behavior) is going to elicit Response G and Behavior B (for bad behavior) will elicit Response B.

For instance, if you have no rules about attending practices, you'll probably get about three-quarters of your team at any one particular practice, and it definitely won't always be the same group. Johnny will miss it this week because his cousins are in town. Penelope might miss it next week because Mom and Dad have a mixed-doubles tennis tournament they're in and it's too much hassle to get Penny to the field. Fred has a T-ball game. You can just imagine the excuses.

Coach's Corner

"Anyone who misses a practice does not play for the first 15 minutes of the game?" Fifteen minutes is an arbitrary number, but one that works nicely with rec league teams that require every player to play at least half a game. You can, however, be stricter in other leagues by saying a player won't play for a half or won't play at all.

However, if you come up with a rule, such as "Anyone who misses a practice does not play for the first 15 minutes of the game," you're going to find that attendance is much better. But here's the catch. You have to be consistent. I don't care if your best, or perhaps only, goalie is the player to miss practice. I don't care if it's your sweeper and your center midfielder who miss. Don't put them in until 15 minutes have passed. If the team loses, they won't blame you, and I'd be willing to bet they don't miss practice again.

If you don't enforce the rule, then it's as if you have no rule at all. And worse, if you enforce it generally but make an exception when it's your best player, you will lose the respect of the team and any control you might have had over that one player.

Here are some other rules you may want to think about including in your team by-laws:

Heads Up

This red card and yellow card plan doesn't work quite as well with the youngest players. They think it's a real kick to see you whip the cards out, and because the consequences aren't immediate or too severe (after all, the starting lineup is always rotated at this age), the punishment doesn't really serve as a deterrent.

➤ Don't be late.
➤ No talking when I'm talking.
➤ No back talk.
➤ No goofing off during practice.
➤ Treat teammates with respect.
➤ Good sportsmanship in the game and during practice.

A fun, yet still effective, way to enforce the rules is to carry a yellow card and a red card with you the way the referees do. For the first offense, show them the yellow card. For the second offense, show them the red card. The red card means that they lose the first 15 minutes of the next game.

Depriving players of a chance to play in the game is a valuable tool for a coach, because it is, after all, the reason the players are there in the first place.

The Least You Need to Know

➤ Find a program that fits with your level of competitiveness and your knowledge of the game.

➤ See if your program provides insurance for its volunteer coaches.

➤ Keep kids excited and motivated in practice through constant activity, team bonding, and consistent rules.

Chapter 23

Practice Makes Perfect

In This Chapter

➤ Prep for practice

➤ Learning how to pick up the pace

➤ A sample plan

Practice time. This is where a soccer coach can make her mark. Practice is when you teach them all you know, however little that may be. You can't do it during game time. The kids can barely hear you when they're out on the field, and soccer doesn't get any time outs. You have to do it when the players are your rapt audience for an hour or two.

But how do you get their attention? How can you impart your knowledge in a way that is both instructive and fun. You want the players to have a good time, but you also want them to learn how to play the game. This chapter tells you everything you need to know about running a practice and, just in case that's not enough, it leads you by the nose through a sample practice.

Just an aside to clarify things:

I'm going to assume that you're coaching recreation league soccer, because if you are experienced enough to take on anything more competitive, you wouldn't need this book. I'll also assume that the ages of the kids will be somewhere in the elementary school years, for the same reason. If they're a little older, you don't have to be quite as much of an entertainer. If they're younger, just take the same practice but make it easier and sillier.

Be Prepared

Like a teacher preparing his lesson plans for the classroom, you need to be prepared to go out on the field with a group of 15 or so hyperactive kids. This is not something that you can wing. There are too many of them and too few of you.

If you can, enlist the help of another parent or an older player as assistant coach. Not only will this help if you can't make it to a game or practice, but it's sometimes a lot easier to break down the kids into two smaller groups.

The kid's attention span will kill you, too. These kids love a new activity for about five minutes. At minute six, they'll start being a little sloppy. At minute eight, they'll begin the silly act. At minute ten, the whole drill has fallen apart. Aim for five minutes for an activity, and then if it seems to be working push it to eight. But never go farther than ten minutes on one activity because they'll just be bored, and you really want them to love the sport and love coming to practice. The more enthusiastic they are, the more they're going to learn. Of course, once it's game time they can play forever. Don't forget to make that a big part of practice.

So when you plan your practice session, plan enough to fill up one-and-a-half practice sessions. So if your practice is an hour, think of enough activities to go for an hour and a half. That way, if something falls apart earlier than you expected, you won't have to keep pushing it just to fill up time. Remember you also can just let them play a game. A game itself is often the best teacher.

Coach's Corner

Write down your practice schedule. Don't trust your memory to work when Jimmy asks which team he's on again for the fifth time, Cory wants water, and Olivia has to go to the bathroom. Put times down next to the activities, and then don't forget your watch.

The Theme Scheme

Picking and choosing from all the different drills and skills and activities that you can put in your practice can be daunting. Having a theme to your practice can help narrow it down.

You can do it a couple of ways. If you and your team are just starting out, then the theme of the first practice could just be learning the basics of the game. You want to do this in a fun way, but they're going to have to know the difference between a kickoff and a throw-in and how to execute each one before you throw them into a game.

At the next practice, your theme might be a skill, like dribbling or passing. If you've had a few games, then you can take your cues from that and work on something that's giving them trouble. Here are some possible themes:

Coach's Corner

The basics that you might want to cover in a first practice are: the object of the game, how the game is played, how a throw-in is executed, what the various kicks are, and what responsibilities the players have when you put them in at offense, defense, midfield, and goalie.

- ➤ The basics
- ➤ Dribbling
- ➤ Passing
- ➤ Shooting
- ➤ Goalie work
- ➤ Defense

If your practices are more than an hour, then the theme plan won't work quite as well, because the practice will end up being a little boring. But don't go crazy introducing a whole lot of ideas. If you have one or possibly two skills a practice, then you and the

Learning the Lingo

A *scrimmage* is a game that doesn't count for anything. So a game in the middle of practice is a scrimmage, and so are preseason games with another team.

players can really work on improving in one area rather than dabbling in many. Or you can spend the bulk of your time just playing the game.

So let's review. The players warm up, get a little instruction in the particular skill, play a few related games, and then play a *scrimmage*. Practice over.

Notice that heading is not listed among the popular theme practices. To begin with, heading is not a big part of the game at the younger levels. It seems wasteful to spend an entire practice on something that might be used twice in a season. Secondly, spending an entire practice on heading is going to send a lot kids home begging for Tylenol.

Mounting Pressure

So now you've got your theme. Let's say you're going to run a practice that focuses on passing. Where to begin? Well, the first thing you're going to want to do is instruct the players on the proper form for passing. There's no point in running an entire practice on one subject if they're not going to execute it properly at the start. Manfred Schellscheidt, a Soccer Hall of Famer, always says, "Practice makes permanent." Some players get very good at bad habits by practicing them over and over.

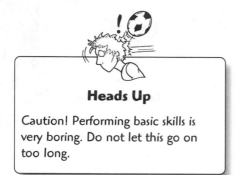

Heads Up

Caution! Performing basic skills is very boring. Do not let this go on too long.

So explain what to do, and then have them get into pairs and pass to one another, while you wander through the ranks to make sure they're doing it right.

Now take it up a notch. Add some movement. Have them pass to each other as they run down the field. Add a shot on the goal at the end. After they seem comfortable doing that, you can add a defender or turn the same run into a relay race.

What you're doing is trying to teach them the skill first and then duplicate the conditions that they're going to find when they play a real game. Most kids can pass the ball to a teammate who's standing still and undefended, but how many times is that going to happen in a game?

There are four ways you can increase pressure on a player to make a skill more challenging and matchlike:

1. Increase speed
2. Increase defense
3. Limit space
4. Limit touches

This mounting-pressure philosophy should be at the crux of any coaching plan. Teach them the skill with no pressure, then gradually increase it to match a game. If the kids don't practice the skill with gamelike pressure, then they're not going to be able perform that skill well in a game.

Speed It Up

The first method of building up the pressure is to add movement. The passing example I just used shows this. There are always three levels of difficulty that you can bring to each drill:

➤ Standing—no pressure

➤ Jogging—limited pressure

➤ Full speed—gamelike pressure

Every skill should be taught with all three of these levels of difficulty. Jumping right into a gamelike situation not only exhausts your players, but it won't help them learn the subtleties of a skill.

A Defender in the Mix

You can also beef up the defense to add pressure. For the passing example, first have two players run down the field passing to each other and then shooting into an empty goal.

Then add a goalie. Now the players have to be a little more careful how close they get to the goal, which of the two of them will be better suited to take the shot, and where exactly the shot should go in the goal to catch the goalie out of position.

Finally, add a defender with the goalie. Now they might have to shoot sooner, make more accurate passes, and take less of a perfect shot.

Here are the three progressions:

➤ No defender—no pressure

➤ Goalie—limited pressure

➤ Defender—gamelike pressure

You can even make it more complicated by adding more passers and more defenders.

Running Out of Space

When you see the youngest players clumped together you have to wonder how they ever get the ball to move at all. Doesn't it just bump into legs? You need to have room to maneuver. This is why limiting the space can be so valuable.

Here is the progression in its more succinct form:

➤ Unlimited space—no pressure

➤ Limited space—limited pressure

➤ Crowded space—gamelike pressure

Going back to the passing example, if the two players have the entire field to run down, passing is easy. If you tell them that they have to make five passes before midfield, that's a little harder. Now throw in all your players on that half of the field. Not only do the pairs have to make good, accurate passes to each other, but they have to avoid all the other good, accurate passes that might be going on nearby.

Don't Touch

Finally, you can limit the number of touches that a player is allowed to use to control the ball. For instance, if you're doing the same passing drill in which the players run down the field passing to one another, you can give them an unlimited number of touches before they have to pass the ball to start. Then when they feel comfortable with that, reduce it to two touches. They may stop the ball, but then they immediately have to send it back. Finally, drop it to one, where they must pass the ball back as soon as they get it, without bringing it under control.

➤ Unlimited touches—no pressure

➤ Two touches—limited pressure

➤ One touch—gamelike pressure

You can also use a combination of these to up the ante even more. Add a goalie, reduce the space, and make it two-touch ball. It's still only limited pressure, but it's more intense than just one of the limitations all by itself.

Small Ball

You can't keep working on the same drill forever, even if you continually make it more difficult. The kids are going to rebel. So now you have to make it a little more fun. You want to still work on the passing, but now you might want to work it into a game.

Play monkey in the middle, with one player trying to get the ball away from two others. Make it a bigger game, say five on two or six on three. If one of the defenders steals the ball, then the player who lost the ball goes in the middle and the defender comes out to pass.

You can also assign certain players to different areas of the field. The ball might not be dribbled out of your area. You have to pass to someone in another area to move the ball down the field. This works especially well if you have a grid field you can work on. Put one player in each box. If the ball goes through another box, the defense may intercept it, but if you're making good passes, you should be able to get it by them. Add two balls to this drill to liven it up after your players get the hang of it.

Another great passing game is The Weave. It's not really a competition, but kids like it because it's fun to try to figure out the movement. This figure shows the progression.

The ball starts in the middle of the field, with two players on either wing. The middle player passes the ball to the side and runs behind his pass. The side player receives the ball and then dribbles to the middle, passing to the remaining player on the other side, again following his pass. The third player dribbles to the middle and so on. The line shoot in the goal at the end of the field.

The Thrill of the Drill

Probably the top passing drill I know of is a game called Passing for Points. In this game, there are no goals. The two teams have to complete five (or three or eight, depending on the level) consecutive passes to get a point. The other team can't touch the ball in between. It really gives the kids a sense of what they should be doing on the field.

The Weave

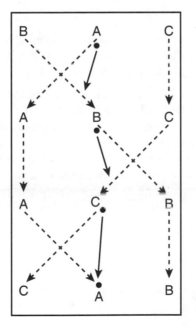

Coach's Corner

It's always good to have your players take a shot on goal at the end of every drill. This keeps the ultimate goal of the game fresh in their minds. If they're used to shooting when they're at that end of the field, then they'll naturally try to do it in the game.

Small games like these can make practice seem like fun rather than an exercise in skill improvement. After you've played a few games like these, you should also play a few small-sided games, say three-on-three or four-on-four. If you're with the youngest players this may be as big as your regular match, so you wouldn't want to do this until the end of the practice time.

Match Play

Which brings us the last part of practice. This is where the players get to experience the real deal. This is nearly everyone's favorite part of practice, and that's as it should be. The game is, after all, the reason why kids are playing and practicing soccer.

Some coaches feel that they don't want to waste valuable practice time with a game, but there are two reasons why they shouldn't look at it this way. To start, it's fun. The kids are out there to have fun, and they deserve this treat at the end. But on top of that, this is the chance to teach a little strategy, compliment players on a good pass or a good run, and fix some tactical errors that might not come up in practice. For example, players might not realize that they're not supposed to kick a goal kick in front of their own goal. If it happens in a game, it will probably end up as a goal for the other team. If it happens in practice, you can blow the whistle and start the kick over again. No harm done.

Sample the Goods

So now you have a basic sense of the progression of a practice. It's time to see the whole thing put together. First, figure out what you want to work on. You decide dribbling. Next write your practice plan:

4:00   Warm up

4:10   Demonstrate dribbling skills. Players practice this.

4:15	Demonstrate how to protect your dribble. Add a defender.
4:20	Add the goal.
4:25	Dribbling relay races
4:35	Bulls in the Ring
4:40	Red Rover
4:45	Game time
5:00	Practice is over.

You probably won't have time to do all of these, but it's nice to have them written down, so that you have some plans if one of your other activities doesn't take as long. You don't want to be scrambling to come up with something at the last minute, and end up with something that is either boring or doesn't focus on the skill you're working on.

If this practice still sounds overwhelming to you, read on. I'll break it down in greater detail.

Warm Up

If 10 minutes sounds a bit excessive for warm-up, don't worry. It won't take the full time. The reason you allot 10 minutes to warm up is because your players are going to take their time arriving. You probably won't have a full team until 4:05.

While you're waiting for the other players, give the ones who are already there an activity. Have them pass to one another, play follow the leader dribbling the ball, or try to juggle the ball. You don't want them just sitting there. You also want to keep them from doing something like taking shots on goal, which they really shouldn't do until they've stretched. Just give them an easy exercise.

Coach's Corner

If you can, include the ball in everything you do, so while you're warming up, add the ball. The more familiar players are with how the ball feels on their feet, the better players they will become.

When everyone's there, have them take a lap around the field dribbling the ball. This gets their muscles warm and still ties in with the dribbling theme.

Next it's stretch time. Read Chapter 14 again, so you know what to do, then bring your players into a circle, and get those muscles loose. Don't worry too much if the kids don't really work at stretching. At their age, they're already plenty loose, but it's good to get them into the habit.

With the youngest kids, it's best if you lead the stretches, but with older kids you can go around the circle and have everyone add a stretch for the group to do. This is a good time to tell the team what you're working on or ask questions about things they should know.

Show Time

Now it's dribbling time. Show them how to use all parts of the foot and how to go in all directions. Let them dribble for a while. Then you play policeman and point in different directions to see if they can look up and dribble at the same time.

When they look as if they're getting bored with this, stop and show them how to defend their dribble if they have a defender on their backs. Ask them to pair up, with one ball for every pair. One player is the defender and one is the dribbler. After a minute or so, switch positions.

Finally, have them stay in their pairs but line up at one end of the field. The dribblers start on the six, and the defenders start on the end line. The dribblers have to get their ball down to the other end of the field and take a shot on goal. The defenders try to stop them. Blow the whistle, and they're off.

Notice how the progression has gone from no pressure, for learning the skill, to high pressure, trying to score with a defender first on your back and eventually in front of you.

May the Best Team Win

This is where the fun really starts. It's time for the relay races and other competitions. Do your best to divide the group into two or three fairly equal teams. If you have more than four or five in a line, you should divide into more teams, so that players aren't standing around too much.

You can set up any number of relay races, and it's probably good to have two or three different ones, all related to dribbling. Have them dribble up to one cone, around it, and then back. Then have them dribble through a slalom course of cones. If they seem to be having fun, then have them dribble to the other end of the field, take a shot, retrieve their ball, and dribble back.

Coach's Corner

Adding a shot to a relay race has an extra bonus. The kids are careful to get the ball into the net, because if they miss, they're chasing the ball and hurting the relay.

Take your cues from the kids. If they seem to be having a good time, do all three. If one team is discouraged because they lost both races by a lot, don't make them suffer through a third loss.

Bulls in the Ring

Bulls in the Ring is a really fun dribbling drill. Each player has a ball inside the penalty box. (The players are the bulls and the box is the ring, for those of you who didn't catch the metaphor.) At the starting whistle, each player dribbles around the box, trying to protect his ball from the other players. At the same time, he is trying to kick other players' balls out of the ring.

When players get their ball kicked out of the ring, they must leave as well. It's a good idea to have them do toe touches on the ball or juggle it or something so they're not just standing there. Once all the other players have been eliminated, the last player who still has his ball is the winner.

The only flaw with this drill is that you're bound to have at least one player who has figured out he can win by dribbling around the edges, out of the fray, not going for anyone else's ball, so he doesn't have to risk his own.

The Thrill of the Drill

Another variation of Bulls in the Ring pits three teams against one another. Two teams have balls, and the other team doesn't. The team without the balls tries to kick away the balls from the other two teams. Again, if a player has his ball kicked out, he leaves the ring. Time how long it takes a team to do this. Let the other two teams have their chances and see which one did it the fastest.

Red Rover

You probably are not going to have any time to squeeze in this last game, because the other drills will run overtime. It's always good to have an extra game or an extra relay in your back pocket, however, just in case drills are running shorter than you thought.

Coach's Corner

You can cut anything short but the game time. Don't try to squeeze Red Rover in at the expense of the game. If you have 17 minutes left, play a 17-minute game rather than Red Rover and a 13-minute game.

For those of you who don't remember Red Rover, a quick overview, with a few modifications for soccer practice. One or two people are out in the middle of the field. They yell, "Red Rover, Red Rover, let [a color] come over." If the person in the center yells "Blue" for instance, then everyone with blue on runs to the other side, dribbling a ball. The people in the middle who called for them try to steal the balls away. Go through the whole line of players on the end line and then change the middle people. Try to give everyone a turn in the middle.

Then it's game time and practice is over. Hallelujah! You sailed through with flying colors.

The Least You Need to Know

➤ Always be prepared with a plan for practice.

➤ Work around a theme rather than trying to introduce too many skills at once.

➤ Increase the pressure for each skill to challenge the players the way they'd be challenged in a game.

➤ Plan extra activities for practice just in case an exercise doesn't take as long as you thought.

➤ Always leave time for a scrimmage at the end.

Chapter 24

The Dirty Dozen Drill List

In This Chapter

➤ Honing those skills

➤ Fun games to play

➤ A fun time for the littlest ones

You can't run a practice without drills, and while you've been getting a taste of a few good ones throughout the book (and especially in the previous chapter), there are some excellent exercises that have yet to be included. This chapter is their moment in the sun.

Many of these drills are good because they focus on a specific skill and really enable you to zero in on developing that skill. Others are great because they're just plain fun to do, so players learn while having a great time. I've tried to include one more drill for each major skill, and then a bunch of games that incorporate several skills, some for older kids and some for the young ones.

Skill Drills

The skill drills aren't always as much fun as the games because they don't involve much competition, but the ones listed here are excellent for working on technique under pressure. The drills cover six basic skills:

1. Passing (Middle Man)
2. Receiving (Corners)

3. Dribbling (Through the Legs)
4. Shooting (Serve It Up)
5. Goalkeeping (Rapid Fire)
6. Juggling (Hunter)

There's one drill for each skill, but each drill works on other skills as well. Middle Man and Corners, for instance, work on both passing and receiving because you really can't have one without the other, while Rapid Fire works on shooting as well as goalkeeping for the same reason.

Middle Man

Middle Man is one of the all time great drills. It forces the players to make good accurate passes when they're exhausted, which is exactly the situation they're going to find themselves in during a game.

This drill uses three players. Two stand about 20 yards apart and the third one is, you guessed it, the man in the middle. There are two balls for the three of them, one for each of the end players. You can see this rather simple setup in this figure.

Middle Man

At the start of the coach's whistle, a player on one end passes the ball to the middle man. He receives it and passes it back. Then he turns to face the player behind him who should already have passed the ball. Therefore, just as he's turning, he's receiving the ball. The key is not to let this middle person rest. Do this drill for two minutes and then switch change the middle man.

Coach's Corner

This drill Middle Man can also be adapted to work on either heading or trapping out of the air. Instead of passing the ball with their feet, the two end players toss it to the person in the middle.

For more novice players, you might want to allow the middle man two touches, but as players get more skilled, move up to one touch and see if they can still maintain accuracy.

Corners

Corners is a perfect receiving drill, because it teaches players how to move to the open spaces. It's an excellent teaching drill, although when you boil it down to the basics, it's really just Monkey in the Middle.

You need four players and a square marked off by cones at the corners. Three of the players take a stand at three of the four cones. The fourth player is the monkey in the middle, otherwise known as the defender. Take a look at this figure for the drill set up.

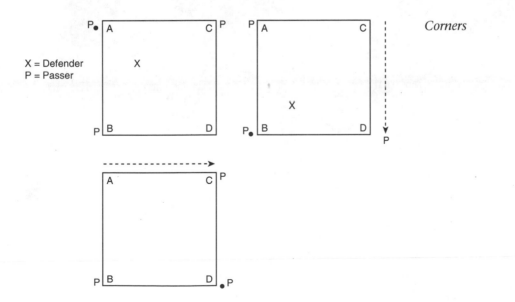

Corners

Players may only run along the sides of the square. They cannot run across the middle. The ball also can only travel along the sides and not through the middle. Because of these restrictions, players must give the player with the ball two passing options or the defender can get the ball. When there's an open corner next to the player with the ball, then someone is going to have to fill it.

To get a visual picture, go back to the figure. Basically, if the ball is in corner A, then corners B and C must be filled by other players. If the ball is in corner B, then corners A and D must be filled. If the ball is in corner D, then corners B and C must be filled, and I'll let you figure out the last scenario on your own. Remember, players can only run along the sides of the square, so the player who is next to the open corner is the one who makes the run to fill the corner.

Through the Legs

This drill uses four players. Two start the drill about 20 yards apart. They are considered the goals and stand with their legs spread. Look at this figure for the big picture.

Through the Legs

The other two players begin in the middle with the ball and, through a little one-on-one game, each tries to get it through the opposite goal. In other words, through the player's legs.

Play should go on for two minutes and then the two on the inside get to rest as they switch with the two on the outside.

Serve It Up

This game works best with seven or eight players plus one goalie. One player begins as the designated shooter. She stands at about the penalty mark. The other players each have a ball and form a semicircle around her, as you can see in this figure.

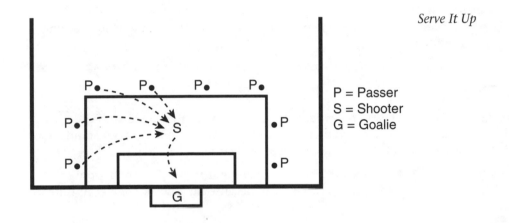

Serve It Up

P = Passer
S = Shooter
G = Goalie

One by one, the servers pass the ball to the shooter. She either gets the ball under control and then shoots, or she one-touches it into the goal. The minute the shooter's foot is on the ball, the next server should be passing her the next ball. After all the balls have been served up, the shooter switches places with a server.

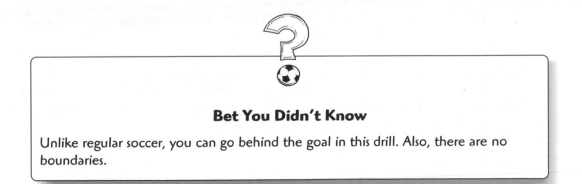

Bet You Didn't Know

Unlike regular soccer, you can go behind the goal in this drill. Also, there are no boundaries.

This is really an excellent drill for attackers because they can't take a lot of time setting up their shot because there's another ball coming in. The reason they're under the gun is different, but the pressure to move quickly is the same as during a game.

Coach's Corner

You can make this drill more difficult by having the servers toss the ball to the shooter rather than passing it to her feet. You can also turn this into a head shot only drill or add a defender.

Rapid Fire

Rapid Fire is an easier version of Serve It Up. Unless you're the goalie, and then it's a killer. Players each take a ball and place it across the 18. The players then stand a few feet behind the balls and one by one move in to take a shot on goal.

The goalie does his best to block the balls from going into the goal by slapping them out of the way. He shouldn't try to catch them because he'll never recover in time to get the next one.

Each player should start to move just as the ball in front is reaching the goalie. Any faster wouldn't be fair. Any slower and the goalie won't be working hard enough. Do this drill twice, the first time aiming for the goalkeeper, to warm him up, and the second time aiming away from him to challenge both the goalie and the shooters.

Hunter

Hunter is a juggling drill. This is a good drill to use at the beginning of a practice while you're waiting for everyone to show up. It's also good to use after you've given your team a good workout and they need a little down time.

All but one of the players have a ball and they begin juggling them. The player without the ball moves among the jugglers waiting for a ball to drop. If it does, she goes for it and tries to gain possession. If she does, she begins juggling and the other player starts hunting. The hunter has three rules to follow:

1. She may not interfere with a juggler.
2. She must always keep moving rather than hovering near a weak juggler.
3. She may not take the ball away from the person who took it from her.

This drill is best for players who are fairly proficient at juggling. It becomes absurdly easy otherwise.

Game Time

Now let's have some fun. It's game time! But just because these games are fun, it doesn't mean that all learning stops. Quite the contrary. These games enable a player to develop soccer smarts by creating a competition. Not to mention the fact that a few skills also get honed.

Three on Three on Three

This game is really more of a conditioning exercise than anything else. You can play with nine or eleven players, depending on whether you want to use goalies.

Coach's Corner

Use goalies if you have enough players, because it's more gamelike. If you can't, then reduce the goal size to at least make it harder to score.

Divide the players into three teams of three. Let's call them Teams A, B, and C. Team A lines up in front of one goal, Team B goes to the center line, and Team C is in front of the other goal. Step 1 in this figure shows the lineup.

Three on Three on Three

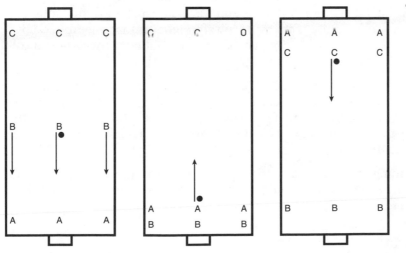

Team B starts with the ball. It heads toward Team A (or C for that matter) and tries to score while Team A tries to prevent it from scoring. If Team B scores, it gets a point. If Team A gets the ball (either by stealing it away or after it gives up a goal), it heads down the field toward Team C, but this time it is on the attack. Team B stays at the other end and awaits the return of the ball from Team C. And so on and so on and so on. Take one more peek at the figure, looking at all the steps this time. The team with the most goals at the end is the winner.

Steal the Bacon

The more the merrier as far as Steal the Bacon is concerned, although you could probably have a decent game with as few as eight players. The coach divides the players into two equal teams, and the players count off on each team. In other words, if there are four players on each team, then each team has players numbered one through four.

The game is played in the penalty box. One team lines up on the 18 and the other team lines up on the end line. The setup is shown in this figure.

Steal the Bacon

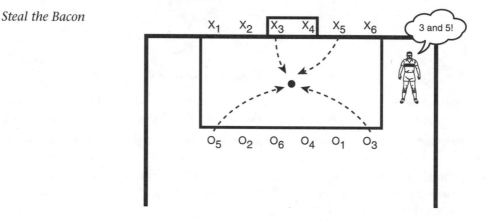

The coach then calls out one or more numbers and throws the ball into the center of the field. The players whose numbers are called out (it might be only one from each team, two from each team, the entire team, and so on) race out onto the field and try to be the first to retrieve the ball. Look at the previous figure again.

After a player gets the ball, she then tries to kick it across the other team's line. If she succeeds, her team scores a point. Obviously, whoever doesn't get the ball is going to try to prevent this from happening and if she gains control, she'll try to get it over the other line. It becomes a mini one-on-one (or if there are more players out there, a mini three-on-three for example).

The players left standing on the line are allowed to defend their line, but they may not move off the line. The coach may also suddenly call out extra players to help out if nothing is getting resolved.

Once a point is scored, players return to their lines and the game starts over again.

Foosball

Have you ever played Foosball? It's that great pub game where several lines of wooden soccer players are attached to metal rods over a table. You drop the ball in the center and then try to spin the rods to make your players "kick" the ball into the other team's goal. Well, there's a fun drill that's just like this game, and guess what it's called? A+ for you. Yes, it's Foosball.

With Foosball, you're going to need at least ten to twelve players and a field that is marked with soccer lines (therefore not a good drill for those of you who have to find practice space where you can grab it, and spend most of your time in the outfield of a baseball diamond).

Divide the two players into two teams, and then divide those teams in half again. Put half of each team between the 18 and the end line. Put the other half of each team on the opposite side of the field, between the 18 and the center line. Looking at the setup in this figure will make it a little clearer.

Learning the Lingo

The name *Steal the Bacon* might come from the fact that this game originated as a totally un-soccer-related kids' game, where the kids try to grab an object in the middle rather than play a mini-soccer match.

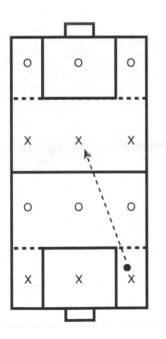

Foosball

Players on a team now try to pass the ball back and forth to their teammates in the other part of the field without letting it get intercepted by the opposing team, no lofting allowed (anything below the head counts). Every time a team manages to do this, they get one point. Players may also get a point if they can turn, catch the defense off guard, and pop the ball into the goal.

Coach's Corner

Here's a hint to get the most out of Foosball: Mix up the players on the outside of the field and the inside, because the middle players see more action.

Players in the same zone should pass between each other to catch the other team out of position and players in the receiving zone should also be moving to create a good angle for the pass.

Kiddie Play

Little kids are a different breed. It's hard enough to find drills that their undeveloped muscles, short legs, and minimal coordination can handle, but then you have to worry about comprehension as well. You might as well be trying to explain the tax code to them. Your team might as well be called the Blue Zombies with the amount of blank stares you face as you try to teach them how to play Corners.

So you need to have some simpler games. Ones that are already familiar to them, such as Red Light, Green Light or Red Rover work pretty well, and here are a few others that seem to fit the bill as well.

Sink the Subs

If you need a time killer, this game could go on forever. Get at least eight cones and set them up randomly around a fairly small area. Tell the kids that these are enemy submarines, and it's their job to put them out of commission.

All but two players should have a ball. At your whistle, the players with the balls start dribbling around the cones and shooting at them, trying to knock the cones over (sinking the subs).

The other two players are the enemy. They try to "repair" the subs, by standing them back up, as fast as the other players are sinking them. Play ends when the sinkers have gotten all the subs. If you find that this isn't happening, then play in a larger area, so that it takes the enemy longer to get to the cones. Or if you have six or fewer players, then you probably should only have one enemy rather than two.

After all the subs have been sunk, change enemies and repeat. Kids love this game, and they all want a turn to be the enemy, so it takes quite a long time to get through the drill. Of course, you're not just out there to kill time. This also helps with dribbling, passing, and shooting skills, and it gives your designated enemy players a good workout.

Spud

Few people escape childhood without playing Spud. However, I am aware that there are a few of you out there with failing memories, so I'll do a quick recap of the rules. Besides, it's a little more complicated when you try to relate it to soccer.

Before the game begins, the coach secretly whispers a number to each of the players, giving out one more number than there are players. In other words, if there are eight players, then the coach assigns numbers one through nine, leaving one number out.

All players gather around in a group. The coach hands one player the ball, and he throws the ball up and yells out a number. The player whose number is called must trap the ball out of the air, put his foot on top of the ball and yell "Spud!"

When the other players hear "Spud," they must freeze in their tracks. The player with his foot on the ball then takes three steps, dribbling the ball along with him, toward the nearest player. Then he kicks the ball at that player. The kick must be a pass along the ground—no lofted shots!

If the ball hits its mark, then the targeted player gets an "S" (or a "P" or a "U" or a "D" depending on how many times he's been hit). If the ball misses the target, then the shooting player gets the "S." Whoever gets the letter throws the ball up in the air. The only other way to get a letter is to call the number that wasn't assigned to anyone.

Coach's Corner

Because it's not productive to have players standing out, you might want to eliminate the letters from the game and just play for a certain amount of time.

After a player has spelled out Spud, then he is eliminated. He should get a ball and juggle along the side. Now players have to remember that his number is taken out, too. The final player left is the winner.

Soccer Golf

How sweet it is when you can combine two sports into a new fun game. Set up holes (called cones at any other time) around the playing area. Don't restrict this drill to just the soccer field if you have the option. Fun holes are part of the game.

Learning the Lingo

In *match play* you get one point for winning the hole and no points if you lose it. That way, on an 18-hole course, the highest score you could possibly get is 18. With regular scoring you keep track of every stroke, so scores could be up over 100.

Tee off at the first hole by kicking the ball toward the first cone. The cone should be far enough away so that the first pass, at least, is a long, hard drive. After that, the passes are short and accurate "putts."

Count how many kicks it takes to hit the cone. That's a player's score. After all players have reached the cone, then the player who made it there with the least amount of kicks gets to pick which cone is hole two.

Obviously, with little kids they're not going to be able to keep track of their score for all the holes, even if you try to do it match play.

If you have more than four or five kids playing this game, start them all off at different holes in groups of two, three, or four. Bumping into each other's passes are just one of the hazards of the Soccer Golf course.

The Least You Need to Know

➤ Hone your skills through drills.

➤ Using small-sided games can create matchlike pressure in a smaller setting.

➤ Young kids need extra entertainment to help them use their skills.

Chapter 25

Fitting the Pieces Together

In This Chapter

➤ Surviving tryouts

➤ Putting players in the right places

➤ Winning combinations

➤ Coach's Code of Ethics

Coach Winston was a riot. The kids adored him and loved going to practice. He was always coming up with inventive games, keeping things moving in practice, and generally being silly. Like the time he told them they could all be forwards and they really surprised the other team with a blitz.

But as the kids aged, they needed a little bit more than Coach Winston could offer. His antics frustrated the kids because they weren't learning as much as they needed to, and they certainly weren't winning any games. They wanted someone who was more concerned with strategy than fun. Enter Coach Otis.

Coach Otis knew the game. He could quickly assess a player and make the most of his skills. The team was whipped into shape, and the group began a slow, hard trek toward a winning season.

At some point, players are going to stop looking at the sport as a fun diversion (everyone plays, it doesn't matter if you win or lose, we're all here to have fun, and so

Heads Up

Don't start thinking Coach Otis is the ideal coach. If the positions were reversed and Coach Otis had the little ones, it would have been just as much of a bad fit as Coach Winston with the big ones.

on) and they're going to want to start taking the game seriously. If you're a Coach Winston, you're going to have to step aside or transform yourself into a Coach Otis. This chapter gives you a start in the right direction.

Athlete Analysis

When you're at the higher levels of the game, teams are no longer picked by lottery. The group of coaches drafts players or kids try out for a town or school team. Either way, a coach has to know what she's looking for when she's confronted with a group of 50 kids that she's going to have to narrow down to 16 or 17.

Personality Profile

It may sound odd, but the first thing you should do is look for kids you would like to coach. This is obviously not the only criteria, but it's one that can frequently determine your satisfaction as coach, and that in turn can translate into enthusiasm for the team, and that can become a winning attitude, and now you've gotten the ball rolling so to speak.

Seriously, you need to find players you can work with and enjoy being around. That's not to say that you cut a self-centered and unpleasant superstar from the team or take an out-of-shape, uncoordinated comedian just because he keeps you laughing. It just means that you should consider personality when you're looking at team criteria. Here are some qualities to look for:

➤ **Enthusiasm**—Enthusiasm translates into a good mood, fun times, and more energy. I mean, really, who would you rather have on your soccer team—Tigger or Eeyore?

➤ **Good listener**—You're the coach, so it's your job to teach. As you can imagine, it's pretty tough to teach someone who isn't paying attention. Make your job easier. Find players who are receptive and coachable.

➤ **Team player**—An egocentric wonder child might work well as the pitcher on a baseball team or a quarterback on a football team, but there's no room for him in soccer. One person can't do it alone and can actually hurt the team if he tries.

➤ **Commitment**—Good Time Gary and Chatty Cathy might be fun to have around, but if they're not willing to buckle down and get the job done, then they're not much use to you. You want to look for enthusiastic players, but don't misinterpret raw energy for enthusiasm and end up with the team clown. Look for players who can stay focused and get the job done when called on.

➤ **Energy**—This is also called hustle, and not everyone has it. Whether they're out of shape or just plain lazy people, there are going to be a few players who cut corners at every opportunity. They're always dead last on the warm-up jog, they don't take their sprints all the way to the line during practice and at game time, they slowly jog into position rather than sprinting to get back and mark their man. They may have the skills, but they're going to have a tough time getting the ball to show them off.

Maybe not all of these traits are important to you. Maybe some other ones are. Desire to win, eager to please, thick-skinned (not literally), or something else might be on your list. But make that list, and put a mark in that column next to each person that fits the mold. Then when you're reviewing who to keep, you'll know who has the intangibles.

The Running Game

Now you know who has the right personality, but next you have to see who has the right body. Not everyone can handle the physical demands of soccer. More for the checklist:

➤ Endurance

➤ Speed

➤ Strength

Before you do anything else, take the players on a two- or three-mile run. Can everyone make it? They're going to have to do at least that in the game, so you have an easy cut if you find some players walking.

Then see who can run a mile in under eight minutes. Running long distances at fairly high speed is the way the game is played. Or lead the players through sprinting exercises and time them. Then make them do it again with a ball and see if those who were initially the fastest are still out in front. Speed by itself won't do as much good in soccer as speed and agility combined.

And finally, as they go through drills, notice their strength. Can they make the long pass? The hard shot? This might not be a make or break category but it could influence your decision for a player who's on the bubble.

Talent Show

Now let's get to the real deal. It's talent time. You're into the competitive league now, so you're going to be trying to win. It's not an "everyone plays" situation, and you don't have to worry about getting your daughter's best friend on the team. (Okay, maybe you do have to worry about that, but you shouldn't.)

Pull out that checklist again, and under the intangibles write down the basic skills:

➤ Passing

➤ Trapping

➤ Dribbling

➤ Shooting

➤ Heading

➤ Goalkeeping

Then, as you go through each drill in tryout, make a notation as to how they perform. You can use any sort of mark you feel is necessary, from letter grades like used school, to a simple +/– system. I recommend the +/– system, because it's easier. You're going to be making a truckload of decisions during tryouts and you don't need to be grappling with whether it was a B or a C performance. And you can still write ++ if someone is extra good at something.

After basic skills, you might want to grade the players on more advanced skills:

➤ Moving to open spaces

➤ Meeting the ball

➤ Man-to-man marking

➤ Recovering quickly after losing the ball

➤ Creating opportunities

➤ Defensive skills

➤ Finishing skills

Put them all together into the type of chart you see in the figure.

Coach's Corner

Even if you don't have an assistant coach, try to get one or even two to help out for tryouts. Not only do you want to have someone else to bounce gut feelings off of, but you're also going to need help with crowd

	Enthusiasm	Listening	Teamwork	Commitment	Energy	Endurance	Speed	Strength	Passing	Trapping	Dribbling	Shooting	Heading	Goal Keeping	Move to Open Spaces	Meets Ball	Marks Up	Good Recovery	Creates Opportunities	Defensive Skills	Finishing Skills
1. Jay																					
2. Cori																					
3. Teddy																					
4. Alex																					
5. Hannah																					
6. William																					
7. Courtney																					
8. Amanda																					
9. Lindsey																					
10. Megan																					
11. Jasper																					
12. Evan																					
13. Michael																					
14. Spencer																					
15. Natalie																					
16. Ian																					
17. Katie																					
18. Pete																					
19. Ryan																					
20. Allison																					

Tryout chart

It's a good idea if you can get the names of the kids ahead of time. If you can study the list, it will be easier to remember their names if you don't know them all (something that would be rather remarkable if you did). If you have a large group, you might want to preassign numbers to everyone, having the numbers ready to put on their backs so you don't get the surprise of your life when your star forward Sally Duncan turns out to be the lazy girl with the bad attitude rather than the enthusiastic top-notch shooter you thought you were getting.

The other trick for dealing with a large group is to weed out the ones who are obviously not going to make it. This is sort of a last resort option, however, that you should avoid if you can help it. A couple of reasons.

1. Psychologically it's rough, both on the ones who get cut and the ones who make the cut. The ones that get cut are basically being told that they're so bad, they don't even get a full tryout, and the ones that make the first cut have to go through the anxiety of waiting for the list twice. And believe me, for a kid who really wants to make a team, waiting for the list can be torture.

2. You might blow it. Say you plan to spend two days with the whole group and then one or two more days with the smaller group. In only two days, you might very well undervalue a talented player who is either stuck with much better players, making him look worse than he really is, or stuck with terrible players who make everyone with them look bad. Or he might just be having an off day.

If you have three or four days to make the cuts, it's best if you can keep the players altogether and really get a good feel for what you have. If you need to break them down into groups, you can have one group do a conditioning circuit on their own while you look at the other group and then switch. The players who eventually make the team even benefit from that.

Player A into Slot B

But don't think your job is over after you've picked your team. Now you have to decide who plays where and who are your top 11 choices for the starting slots on the field.

First go back to your tryout chart. Everyone with a ++ on the defensive skill line gets to be a defender. The top shooters go on the forward line. The players with good hustle who know how to pass go into the midfield. And anyone who's willing to take the job gets put in the goalie slot. So now you have a rough idea of where you might put everyone.

Now you do the big tease. You ask them what they think they'd be good at or what they might want to play. Write this down too. Pray that some are good matches and that you don't end up with a team of forwards.

Finally, it's time to do your salesman routine. "Marcy, I know you've got a lot of speed and would probably be quite valuable on the forward line, but the team could use you even more if we put you back at fullback. You have a real sense of how the defense works, and you're one of the toughest players I have. I can't waste you up on the wing."

Coach's Corner

Be open-minded. If a player thinks he can play a certain position, even *if* you think it's a mismatch, you owe it to him to give him the chance to prove himself.

Sometimes it works. Sometimes it turns into, "I'm sorry you don't agree, but I'm still going to have to play you there, because I'm the coach and I'm going to do what I think is best for the team." If that's the case, be sure you lay the praise on thick and give Marcy that extra attention so she'll feel like playing fullback was the right decision.

Finding a Formation

You've done the tryouts, you've had preseason practice, and you've taught this fairly talented bunch of kids everything you know. Now it's game time. Gear up for the hardest part of all: reality check. Face it, your team is going to get out on the field and be a jumbled mess, or so it will seem. You've watched the World Cup, you've checked out a few MLS games. This is not what it's supposed to look like.

Heads Up

You can't expect 12-year-olds, for example, to put on a World Cup caliber performance, no matter how good they may be for their age. Be careful that you're not asking them to do more than they're capable of.

Unless you're coaching at the top high school or college level and above (and if you're using this book at those levels, you're way out of your league), you're not going to going to get a seamless performance.

Coaching at this level is actually quite tricky. You're going to have to figure out the team's strengths and emphasize them, and then figure out the weaknesses and cover them up. Easy for you to say, you say. Well, the first place to do this is with choosing the proper formation.

While there are quite a few formations to use, you can make it easier on yourself by first narrowing whether your team is going to be better in a balanced formation (the

4–3–3 and the 3–4–3) or in a more fluid formation (the 4–4–2 or the 3–5–2). There are a number of factors that can help you do this.

Playing with the Numbers

The first thing you might want to do is take a look at your 10 best players (outside of the goalie). Are they varied enough position-wise so that you have your formation ready-made? In other words, are there four defenders, three midfielders, and three forwards in the top 10 list? Or perhaps your players fit more into the 3–5–2 mold.

If they don't fit into any known formation, then you can either pull a Steve Sampson (the U.S. national team coach who created the 3–6–1) and make up your own, inform your best players of their new positions, or bring in some other players who might be weaker overall but strong in the area you need them.

Running Circles

Has conditioning training been a big part of your preseason workout? If it has, then your players will be in shape enough to run a more fluid formation. Get them running around the field. If you give your players a formation that allows them to overlap a lot, then you'll run circles around the other team. It will make your opponents question whether you have an extra player on the field.

On the flip side, if your players are not in great shape, then you want to stick with the balanced formations, because if you have less conditioned players making long runs, they cannot recover quickly.

Coach's Corner

If you have a running team, you can push the opponents with more than just your formation. The fullbacks should be pushing way up and the forwards should be dropping way back.

Smarts

We learn from experience, or so a common cliché would have us believe. So by the transitive property, the less experienced your team is, the less knowledge they are going to have. This is a roundabout way of saying don't confuse the little ones. The younger they are, the easier the formation should be. Make it a balanced one.

If you're dealing with older players, then you have a little more leeway, but again, make sure they can handle it. Even if the rest of the pieces fit for a 3–5–2, if the players aren't advanced enough (or smart enough) to grasp the concept, it's going to be a disaster on the field.

Coach's Corner

If you have more advanced players, it's a good idea to train them to use a couple of formations, one that has three defensive players for opponents that use a two forward formation and one that has four defensive players for the opponents with three forwards.

Get in the Game

One of the reasons players like soccer so much is that it's different every time. There are no set plays to run. The coach does her stuff in practice and then it's up to the players to adapt what they've learned to what they encounter on the field. They have to use their heads.

This might seem like a disaster to a coach who feels the preseason has been much too short. The basics were taught, but that's about it and here it is game time already. But just because the games have started, it doesn't mean that learning has to end. There are many more practices to be had, and the game itself instructs your players at every turn.

Tactical Advantage

It's a beautiful thing when you start to see your players developing a head for the game. If you have a smart team, you can really make soccer tactics work for you. But be careful. You don't want to overload your players with too many advanced concepts. Start with one concept and if they use it in the first game, then move on to another for the next game.

Here are some tactical things you might want to impart, going from extremely basic to some that are more advanced.

➤ Pass to an open player if a defender is approaching. (This sounds simple but you have to tell them this or they're going to try to drive to the goal by themselves.)

➤ Get the ball out to the sideline on your goal end and in the middle on their goal end.

307

➤ Spread out.

➤ Don't commit too quickly on defense. Contain the player.

➤ Switch fields.

➤ Execute the offside trap.

➤ Overlap

➤ Use the Wall pass.

Coach's Corner

If you're dealing with younger kids, put two friends on the same side of the field to increase the passing frequency. Kids love to pass to their best buddy.

These are some of the most basic tactics, but there are lots more. Reviewing the strategy chapters in Part 3 of this book to help you figure out what to teach your players.

A smart team can beat a more physically skilled but less smart team almost every time. Try to squeeze some tactical lessons into your practice. In truth, however, when it comes to learning strategy, the best teacher is the game.

Playing with a Superstar

You can also tailor your game around your best players. Put them in the middle and let them work both sides of the field to maximize their influence. You can give them extra strategy tips that might not be as clear for less experienced players.

For instance, teach your center midfielder to switch fields. He's going to be in a position to do this more than anyone else, so make sure that this is one concept he grasps. If you have an excellent shooter up front, show her how to make some off-the-ball runs so that she can get free to receive the ball. Otherwise what good are her talents? Take your best defender off man-to-man duty and put him at sweeper where he can be all things to all people.

Another way to use your stars to the utmost is to take advantage of their excellence by allowing the rest of the strong players to go elsewhere while you fill in the nearby spots with weaker players. Unless of course, you have 10 strong players, which in that case, lucky you.

To explain this in more tangible terms, if your best player is your sweeper, then you can move all your other top players into more offensive positions, creating a sort of blitz attack plan. You have so much confidence in your sweeper that even if the ball gets back to her, you know she can handle it. (That doesn't mean that you put her back there alone—even superstar sweeper need a little backup from their wing full-backs now and then—just don't waste your talent by putting other top players back there with her.)

Code of Conduct

Just as the NYSCA has a code of ethics for parents and players, it also has one for coaches. While you might not be an NYSCA coach, most of these principles are worth following. It's just a reminder of what you signed on for when you volunteered:

➤ I hereby pledge to live up to my certification as a NYSCA Coach by following the NYSCA Coaches' Code of Ethics.

➤ I will place the emotional and physical well-being of my players ahead of a personal desire to win.

➤ I will treat each player as an individual, remembering the large range of emotional and physical development for the same age group.

➤ I will do my best to provide a safe playing situation for my players.

➤ I will promise to review and practice the basic first aid principles needed to treat injuries of my players.

➤ I will do my best to organize practices that are fun and challenging for all my players.

➤ I will provide a sports environment for my team that is free of drugs, tobacco, and alcohol, and I will refrain from their use at all youth sports events.

➤ I will be knowledgeable in the rules of each sport that I coach, and I will teach these rules to my players.

➤ I will use those coaching techniques appropriate for each of the skills that I teach.

➤ I will remember that I am a youth sports coach, and that the game is for children and not adults.

And I'd like to add one more. Enjoy yourself. If you're having fun out on the field, then the kids probably are, too.

> ## The Least You Need to Know
>
> ➤ Look for a combination of personality, conditioning strength, and physical ability when choosing a player for your team.
>
> ➤ Listen to what position players feel suits them and give them a shot at it, still relying on your own judgement if it doesn't seem to be working.
>
> ➤ Choose a formation that fits your team.
>
> ➤ Coach with ethics.

Glossary

advantage   If a referee decides that a fouled team would benefit more from not having the whistle blown, then he can opt not to blow it.

back pass   A pass away from the goal.

bicycle kick   A kick backward made when a player has leapt into the air and his body is parallel to the ground.

box   See *penalty box*.

cap   To play for your national team during international competition.

caution   A yellow card warning given to a player by a referee.

center line   The line dividing the field in half.

clear   Getting the ball out away from the goal.

creator   A player whose main goal on the team is to create opportunities.

corner kick   The free kick given to the attacking team when the defending team has knocked the ball over the end line.

cross   A ball that is sent from the sideline across the field in front of the goal.

direct kick   A free kick awarded to a team that was fouled. A goal may be scored directly from this kick.

dribble   Moving the ball by repeated taps with the foot.

drop kick   A restart where the referee drops the ball between both teams and they try to kick it as soon as it touches the ground.

FIFA Stands for Federation Internationale de Football Association. The governing body of soccer.

finisher A player who scores.

forward A player who is part of the front line of attack on a team.

friendly A match played that is not part of the World Cup qualifying matches.

fullback Also called a defensive back. Considered the last line of players before the goalie.

goal area The area within the six-yard-line box.

goalkeeper The one player on a team who is allowed to use his hands.

goal kick The free kick awarded to the defensive team when the attacking team kicks the ball over the end line.

half volley A kick where the foot connects with the ball the instant after the ball touches the ground.

handball Touching the ball with the hand.

hat trick Three goals in one game.

head ball The ball and your head making contact. Also called a header.

indirect kick A free kick awarded when the other team fouls. The ball must be touched by at least two players before it can go into the goal.

juggling Keeping the ball off the ground through a series of touches, using any legal part of the body.

kickoff The manner in which the play begins at the beginning of each half, each overtime, and after a goal.

mark up To guard one player closely and exclusively.

midfielders The players who cover the center area between the forwards and the defenders. Must play both offense and defense.

nutmeg Putting a ball through an opposing player's legs. Also shortened to a meg.

offside The rule that requires an offensive player to have either the ball or two defenders between him and the goal.

own goal When a defender scores in his goal accidentally.

overlap When a player in a position behind another player makes a run forward to end up in front.

passing The act of sending the ball from one player to another.

penalty box The area within the 18-yard marking, where the goalie can use his hands. No direct foul may be committed in the penalty box without a penalty kick being awarded.

penalty kick   A free kick awarded to a team that has been fouled within the penalty box. The team chooses one kicker to face the goalie.

playmaker   See *creator.*

Project 40   The efforts by Major League Soccer and U.S. Soccer to get younger talent into the professional system earlier.

red card   A signal given by the referee for egregious offenses, which means that the signaled player is ejected from the game.

restart   Putting the ball back in play.

save   Preventing the ball from going into the goal.

shooting   Kicking the ball in the direction of the goal.

sideline   The line marking the outer limits of the field.

slide tackle   A method of stealing the ball which involves coming from behind, sliding on the ground, and hooking your foot onto the ball without touching the opposing player.

square pass   A pass to the side that has no forward progression.

stopper   The defensive back who marks up the striker.

striker   The forward in the center.

sweeper   The defensive back who is not required to mark up on anyone but instead is free to roam to support the other defenders and take care of loose balls.

tackle   To steal the ball from an attacker.

through pass   A pass that is made through a gap between two defensive players.

throw-in   The method of inbounding the ball when it has gone over the sideline.

touchline   See *sideline.*

trap   Controlling the ball so that it drops directly in front of you.

volley   A kick out of the air.

wall   A defensive tactic, where human bodies line up shoulder to shoulder to block a portion of the net.

wall pass   Also called a give-and-go. One player passes the ball to another and then races forward to receive it back.

wing   The player on the front line who plays out by the sideline.

yellow card   The signal given by the referee to warn a player that he has done something inappropriate.

Soccer Sources

Organizations

American Youth Soccer Organization
5403 West 138th Street
Hawthorne, CA 90250
Phone: (310) 643–6455
Fax: (310) 643–5310

U.S. Youth Soccer Association
899 Presidential Drive, Suite 117
Richardson, TX 75081
Phone: (972) 235–4499
Fax: (972) 235–4480

U.S. Soccer Association
1801–1811 S. Prairie Ave.
Chicago, IL 60616
Phone: (312) 808–1300
Fax: (312) 808–9566

United System of Independent Soccer Leagues
14497 North Dale Mabry Highway, Suite 211
Tampa, FL 33618–2047
Phone: (813) 963–3909
Fax: (813) 963–3807

U.S. Amateur Soccer Association
7800 River Rd.
North Bergen, NJ 07047
Phone: (201) 861–6221
Fax: (201) 861–6341

Canadian Soccer Association
237 Metcalfe St.
Ottawa, Ontario K2P 1RS
Phone: (613) 237–7678
Fax: (613) 237–1516

Major League Soccer
110 East 42nd St., 10th floor
New York, NY 10017
Phone: (212) 450–1200
Fax: (212) 450–1300

Soccer on the Printed Page

1998 Major League Soccer Media Guide and Register. New York: Major League Soccer, 1998.

Parenting Your Superstar by Dr. Bob Rotella and Dr. Linda K. Bunker. Chicago: Triumph Books, 1998.

Soccer on the Web

Organizations

United States Youth Soccer Association
www.usysa.org

U.S. Soccer Association/American Youth Soccer Organization
www.us-soccer.com

Canadian Soccer Association
www.canoe.ca/SoccerCanada/home.html

FIFA
www.fifa.com

Major League Soccer (with links to individual team sites)
www.mlsnet.com

Soccer Association for Youth, USA
www.saysoccer.org

National Soccer Coaches Association of America
www.nscaa.com

Internet Soccer Clinics (information for coaches)
www.soccerclinics.com/coaches.htm

National Soccer Hall of Fame
www.wpe.com/~nshof/

Online Magazines

Soccer America
www.socceramerica.com

Soccer Times
www.soccertimes.com

Canada Kicks
www.canadakicks.com

Planet Soccer
www.planet-soccer.com

The Soccer Spot
www.soccerspot.com

Women's Soccer World
www.womensoccer.com

Major League Soccer Team Addresses

The Columbus Crew
77 East Nationwide Blvd.
Columbus, OH 43215
(614) 221–2739

D.C. United
13832 Redskin Drive
Herndon, VA 22071
(703) 478–6600

MetroStars
One Harmon Plaza, 8th floor
Secaucus, NJ 07094
(201) 583–7000

Miami Fusion
2200 Commercial Blvd.
Fort Lauderdale, FL 33309
(954) 717–2200

New England Revolution
Foxboro Stadium
60 Washington St.-Rte. 1
Foxboro, MA 02035
(508) 543–0350

Tampa Bay Mutiny
1408 N. Westshore Blvd, Suite 1004
Tampa, FL 33607
(813)288–0096

Chicago Fire
311 W. Superior
Suite 444
Chicago, IL 60610
(312) 705–7393

Colorado Rapids
555 17th St., Suite 3350
Denver, CO 80202
(303) 299–1570

Dallas Burn
2602 McKinney, Suite 200
Dallas, TX 75204
(214) 979–0303

Kansas City Wizards
706 Broadway St., Suite 100
Kansas City, MO 64105-2300
(816) 472–4625

Los Angeles Galaxy
1640 So. Sepulveda Blvd., Suite 114
Los Angeles, CA 90025
(310) 445–1260

San Jose Clash
1265 El Camino Real
Second Floor
Santa Clara, CA 95050
(408) 260–6300

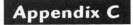

The World Cup Team

Jeff Agoos

Marcelo Balboa

Mike Burns

Chad Deering

Thomas Dooley

Brad Friedel

Frankie Hejduk

Cobi Jones

Kasey Keller

Alexi Lalas

Brian Maisonneuve

Brian McBride

Joe-Max Moore

Eddie Pope

Preki

Tab Ramos

David Regis

Claudio Reyna

Juergen Sommer

Ernie Stewart

Roy Wegerle

Eric Wynalda

These team rosters are current for the 1998 soccer season.

The MLS Teams' Top Players
The Columbus Crew

Jeurgen Sommer (goalkeeper)

Thomas Dooley (defender)

Brian McBride (forward)

Mike Lapper (defender)

D.C. United

Jaime Moreno (forward)

Marco Etcheverry (midfielder)

John Harkes (midfielder)

Eddie Pope (defender)

Roy Lassiter (forward)

319

MetroStars

Tony Meola (goalkeeper)

Giovanni Savarese (forward)

Tab Ramos (midfielder)

Alexi Lalas (defender)

Eduardo Hurtado (forward)

Miami Fusion

Carlos Valderrama (midfielder)

Diego Serna (midfielder, forward)

Cle Kooiman (defender)

New England Revolution

Raul Diaz Arce (forward)

Joe-Max Moore (forward)

Mike Burns (defender)

Ted Chronopoulos (defender)

Tampa Bay Mutiny

Thomas Ravelli (goalkeeper)

Steve Ralston (midfielder)

Frank Yallop (defender)

Chicago Fire

Peter Nowak (midfielder)

Jorge Campos (goalkeeper)

Chris Armas (midfielder)

Frank Klopas (midfielder/forward)

Colorado Rapids

Chris Henderson (midfielder)

Marcelo Balboa (defender)

Paul Bravo (forward)

Adrian Paz (midfielder)

David Vaudreuil (defender)

Dallas Burn

Damian (forward)

Leonel Alvarez (midfielder)

Alain Sutter (midfielder)

Mark Dodd (goalkeeper)

Kansas City Wizards

Preki (midfielder)

Mark Chung (midfielder)

Mike Ammann (goalkeeper)

Matt McKeon (defender)

Los Angeles Galaxy

Mauricio Cienfuegos (midfielder)

Welton (forward)

Dan Calichman (defender)

San Jose Clash

Eric Wynalda (forward)

Ronald Cerritos (forward)

Martin Vasquez (midfielder)

Richard Gough (defender)

Index

W-X

Y-Z